Divine Footprints

Divine Footprints

Understanding God's Plan in Scripture and History

WILLIAM P. PAYNE

Foreword by W. Joseph Stallings

WIPF & STOCK · Eugene, Oregon

DIVINE FOOTPRINTS
Understanding God's Plan in Scripture and History

Copyright © 2025 William P. Payne. All rights reserved. Except for brief quotations in critical publications or reviews, no part of this book may be reproduced in any manner without prior written permission from the publisher. Write: Permissions, Wipf and Stock Publishers, 199 W. 8th Ave., Suite 3, Eugene, OR 97401.

Wipf & Stock
An Imprint of Wipf and Stock Publishers
199 W. 8th Ave., Suite 3
Eugene, OR 97401

www.wipfandstock.com

PAPERBACK ISBN: 979-8-3852-3003-7
HARDCOVER ISBN: 979-8-3852-3004-4
EBOOK ISBN: 979-8-3852-3005-1

03/10/25

Unless otherwise stated, Scripture quotations are taken from the Holy Bible, New International Version®, NIV®. Copyright © 1973, 1978, 1984, 2011 by Biblica, Inc.™ Used by permission of Zondervan. All rights reserved worldwide. www.zondervan.com The "NIV" and "New International Version" are trademarks registered in the United States Patent and Trademark Office by Biblica, Inc.™

Scriptures quotations from the Revised Standard Version of the Bible, copyright 1952 [2nd edition, 1971] by the Division of Christian Education of the National Council of the Churches of Christ in the United States of America. Used by permission. All rights reserved.

I owe Ashland Theological Seminary profound gratitude for granting me a study leave to write this book. Particularly, I want to thank my dean, Yvonne Glass. I also want to acknowledge all the students who challenged me to focus and distill my thinking on this topic. This book is for you. Additionally, I want to thank Kevin Tasker for helping me clarify my writing. I dedicate this book to my wife, Ann Payne.

Contents

Foreword by W. Joseph Stallings | ix

Introduction: Presenting the Missional Hermeneutic | xiii

1. What Is a Hermeneutic? | 1
2. Approaches to Biblical Interpretation | 11
3. What Is a Metanarrative? | 23
4. Interpreting Scripture with the Missional Hermeneutic | 28
5. Applying the Missional Hermeneutic to Acts | 40
6. Analyzing the Current Immigration Debate in the US with the Missional Hermeneutic | 99
7. The Divine Preparation for the Gospel | 122
8. Applying the Missional Hermeneutic to History | 139

Bibliography | 159

Subject Index | 171

Scripture Index | 191

Foreword

LET CHRIST THE LORD be praised.

God is going somewhere with all of the time, space, matter, and energy of his created universe. He has a plan and his ultimate plan will finally come to fruition. This is the Divine Metanarrative and it is this that the Bible in its entirety does definitively proclaim.

Years ago, the late Rev. Dr. Gerald Harris, my former theology professor at Atlantic Christian College (now Barton College), used to tell us often, "God reveals himself through history." He meant that the Living God of all history works continuously in and through his active will and for his purpose. He never stops. God has a relentless mission. It will not be thwarted. Not by the anger and pure evil of the devil and his fallen angels. Not by the allure of the flesh or the world. Not by the power of sin and death or the gates of hell. Not by the disobedience or cynicism of his creatures. Not even by the faithlessness or inefficacy of Israel and the church. In spite of any and all malefaction, God's mission will be victoriously and completely accomplished throughout his creation in accordance with his perfect will. In fact, God-in-Christ Incarnate proclaimed from the cross of Calvary, "It is finished." Thus, at the passion event, Christ had already won the final victory of God that became confirmed to us by his resurrection from the dead. Indeed, in the eternal mind of God, that work was as good as done even before the foundation of the world. We are just now awaiting its visible and conclusive eschatological manifestation. In the meantime, as we wait, it is our portion to desire and to seek our alignment with Jesus Christ, the Lord of all.

As professing Christians who hopefully hold a very high view of the holy Scriptures, which are the canon of Christ's holy church, this should never even be a point of doubt or contention. The Apostle Paul writes in the second strophe of his "Christ-Is" pericope, "He is the beginning, the first-born from the dead, that in everything he might be preeminent. For in him all the fulness of God was pleased to dwell, and through him to reconcile to himself all things, whether on earth or in heaven, making peace by the blood of his cross" (Col 1:18b–20; full pericope: 1:15–20). It is here that the mission of God, i.e., the *missio Dei*, is clearly and concisely stated. The preeminent One, Christ the Lord, will decisively and irrevocably reconcile *all* things (Greek *pas*, lit. "all" or "all things") to himself. Though in this Colossian text Paul does not emphatically add the word *ktisis* to *pas* (i.e., Greek *pas ktisis*, lit. "whole creation") as he does in Romans, it is clearly his Hebraic-minded intention to refer to the entire created order—the greater cosmos, both earth and heaven. The full tenor of the text is gloriously resplendent. In the final rendition of reality, all things (all creation, including all *creatures*) will be reconciled to Christ—some through redemption, some through perdition—but all reconciled in accordance with the absoluteness of God's holy perfection and holy love. By the work of Christ, all defiance and chaos will be abolished and there will be a final and endless harmony and reign of peace inherent to God's renewed creation. The Divine Metanarrative is moving toward this holy *telos*.

It is from just such a backdrop that this present treatise is conceived. The Rev. Dr. Bill Payne is a man grounded by faith and love for King Jesus, trust in God's holy Bible, and fueled by his corresponding heart for Christian mission and evangelism. And he truly practices what he preaches: he serves as a Methodist pastor, as a professor of world missions and evangelism, as a domestic and foreign missioner, and as a teacher and practitioner of spiritual warfare. Like John and Charles Wesley before him, his unquenchable passion is that the full *evangel* of life cannot be contained and must be shared and lived. Since God is on a mission—actually, as he says very early on in this book, "God is a missionary God"—Dr. Payne believes without question that the Bible should be read, studied, and interpreted missionally. With proper focus, this scriptural mission is seen plainly through the immense celestial lens of God's all-encompassing salvific mission in Christ Jesus, viz., again—his *missio Dei* (think, the divine-supernatural wideness of the Colossian text above and, as the church, our granted co-participation with Christ, the Head of the church, in his work to bring about the holy reconciliation of the *universe* to himself). Everything is about the mission of God. The mission is theocentric and Christocentric—not anthropocentric; God-in-Christ is the Supreme Missioner. By the grace of God, the mission does involve us as both a target and a co-participant, but it is far more majestic than us. God and his mission are cosmic and eternal and he is even now making "all things new" (Rev 21:5). There is coming a new heaven and a new earth and this present order of darkness shall by his power pass away. The holy Scriptures should always be read, interpreted, and taught in this far more splendid light.

Dr. Payne calls this clearly biblical concept *the missional hermeneutic* and demonstrates its practical application throughout his writing. Mind you, the mission is not fundamentally our mission; rather it is God's mission to which we are adjured to discover, adhere, and participate. Dr. Payne invites the reader to consider how God is working his mission throughout all of supernatural, natural, and human history and without any exception. From creation to the fall to the eschaton, from Joseph to Israel to the church, from the highest mountains of revivals and reformations to the lowest valleys of spiritual struggle and depravity, from the workings of the natural order to the subjugation of the evil supernatural, from Jesus' teaching about the good Samaritan two millennia ago to the love of Christ for immigrants in our present day, from God seeking out the tares from among the wheat to his many miracles of freeing up souls enslaved by false religions, Dr. Payne's book reminds us that God's vast mission advances onward—sometimes up, sometimes down; sometimes slow, sometimes fast; sometimes two steps forward and one step back (at least it can seem that way to us)—but always in his time and way and in every jot and tittle of all that is. Dr. Payne's missional fervor comes from knowing that the gospel mission, properly interpreted, is full-scale and has both individual and universal salvific ramifications. God's mission is not merely about reconciling the social order or even the crown of his creation, but certainly the very comprehensive totality of creation itself. All things. The Bible begs to be understood in this expansive way. After all, it is the written Word of the Great I AM. Any lesser understanding diminishes Christ Jesus as Lord.

This volume seeks to deal powerfully with this very matter: how to authentically see the grand salvific metanarrative of Almighty God (from Genesis through Revelation) and then how to faithfully exegete, interpret, proclaim, and live the entirety of the holy Scriptures in a way that this salvation comes alive in those who have ears to hear and hearts to receive. I believe that this work has been on the end of Dr. Payne's quill for years, being incrementally realized in the form of multiple and periodic academic papers, but never until now put down comprehensively in the form of a single major text. I, for one, as one of his former students, am very glad that his work in this area is now compiled into one accessible volume. This book helps to fill a significant academic hole in the evangelical niche of theological literature.

In this recent period of Postmodernity, often called Post-Christian, the very idea of metanarrative has become unpopular in many circles. This is one of the main reasons why the Judeo-Christian Scriptures often become interpretively abused by a rampant subjective-individualism. When God's "Big Picture" is neglected or not seen at all, then the Bible is easily misread by the masses as a haphazard human-centered collective of spiritualistic, partisan, political, therapeutic, and moralistic gobbledygook. However, when understood as the missionary God's revealed story of all reality—from Alpha to Omega—the whole text of the Bible (think, God's Word-in-text) conclusively falls into place and we of the creaturely realm become enabled to view ourselves precisely in our God-ordained position within his salvific program. Dr. Payne wants to teach us how to clearly see and understand this reality as it abounds across all the pages of Scripture. I aver that he does a very good job at achieving this end. He presents the subject from a broad bandwidth, includes many diverse perspectives, and then proceeds to show why those other non-evangelical dogs don't hunt. He makes his evaluative and honorable presentation through a flowing narrative that includes bite-size chunks of explanatory precepts as it moves along. The offering is easy to read and easy to follow. It is well explained and very systematic. Dr. Payne's work will serve well as a course textbook for the vocational theologue, but also as a scholarly resource for those deeper thinkers in the local church. As such, I highly recommend this book to every diligently truth-seeking practitioner of the Christian faith. This book needs to be read.

Let Christ the Lord be praised.

W. Joseph Stallings, DPhil, DMin
Methodist Pastor & Christian Apologist
Wilson, North Carolina
Pentecost 2024

Introduction: Presenting the Missional Hermeneutic

IMAGINE YOU ARE TOURING a large mansion. Upon entering, a labyrinth of opulent corridors greets you. As the tour guide leads you through the halls, you notice that each room is painted a different color, has a unique design, and is furnished in a particular way. To get a better feel for the floor plan, you walk around the perimeter. As you stroll, you notice large walls, yard decorations, a solid foundation, and gorgeous landscaping. You note that the building is not rectangular because the walls do not connect at ninety-degree angles. Because of all the turns, you cannot visualize the full layout of the mansion. Finally, you go up in a hot air balloon and look down upon the mansion. From this vantage point, you can see the external design.

In this metaphor, the mansion is the Bible. The rooms are the books of the Bible. The outside walls are the main groupings of Scripture. The foundation is the eternal truth that the Bible reveals. The landscaping is the sociocultural context that influenced the Bible writers. The corridors are varying themes that hold the books together. The tour guide is the history of interpretation. And the roof is the grand design that overshadows the Bible.[1] The hot air balloon is the hermeneutic that allows you to see the grand design.

The missio Dei (God's mission) is the grand design of the Bible and the missional hermeneutic allows one to see it.[2] In this sense, the missio Dei is the hermeneutical key that unlocks the Bible's unified message—the

---

1. Payne, "How the Missional Hermeneutic," part 1.
2. Hoedemaker provides an excellent overview and critique of missio Dei in "People of God," 162–66. See also Sarisky, "Meaning of the Missio Dei," 258–69; Arthur, "Missio Dei," 1–7; and Tennent, *Invitation to World Mission*, 487–89.

Introduction: Presenting the Missional Hermeneutic

all-inclusive story that the Bible tells.³ Michael Goheen calls it the "one unfolding story of redemption against the backdrop of creation and humanity's fall into sin."⁴ In its simplest form, the missio Dei says that God is a missionary God; the Bible from Genesis to Revelation tells God's missional story; and the church is God's missional agent in this age. The missio Dei begins with God, runs through the church, and ends when God fulfills his purposes on earth and in the heavenly realms (Eph 1:19–20).⁵ When the end comes, every knee in heaven, on the Earth, and below the Earth will bow before the glorious name of Jesus (Phil 2:10–11). Until that time, God continues to pursue his mission.⁶

Mission is the mother of theology because it is the theological hub around which all other biblical themes revolve.⁷ The Bible declares God's mission. God's action in history shows his mission. Prophecy proclaims the direction of God's mission. Jesus incarnates God's mission. The Holy Spirit enables God's mission.⁸ The church serves God's mission. God's mission is his purpose and his will. God's missional character and his missional work are fully intertwined. To know God is to be caught up in God's mission.

David Bosch avers that the missio Dei is "God's self-revelation as the One who loves the world."⁹ God's love is demonstrated through his involvement with the world. For instance, God created humans because he loves them and wants to live in a relationship with them. When they inhaled

---

3. Sanou, "Missio Dei as the Hermeneutical Key," 301.

4. Goheen, "Continuing Steps," 61.

5. In Ephesians, the "heavenly realms" (*epouranios*) refers to the place where God is (Eph 1:3, 20; 2:6) and the place where the powers and principalities reign (Eph 3:10 and 6:20). As a general term, it means, the spiritual realm.

6. In theology, "salvation history" describes how God works through the recorded history of the Jews and the New Testament to save his people and the world. The salvation history hermeneutic is similar to the missional hermeneutic. Only, it focuses exclusively on the Plan of Redemption. This book affirms that salvation history is a subset of the missio Dei. Scholars also refer to the history of redemption or a theology of history. See Hughes, "Salvation-History as Hermeneutic," 81.

7. Kahler, *Schriften zur Christologie und Mission*, 190.

8. Newbigin connects the mission of the Spirit to the mission of the church when he says, "It is the Spirit who will give them [the disciples who are sent out in Jesus' name to do his work] power and the Spirit who will bear witness. It is not that they must speak and act, asking the help of the Spirit to do so. It is rather that in their faithfulness to Jesus they become the place where the Spirit speaks and acts" (*Gospel in a Pluralistic Society*, 117–18).

9. Bosch, *Transforming Mission*, 10.

Introduction: Presenting the Missional Hermeneutic

his Spirit and became sapient beings (Gen 2:7), God gave them rulership and invited them to serve with him (Gen 2:16 and Ps 8:5–6). They were to be God's representatives on this Earth. When they rebelled against God's design, he did not abandon them to sin, death, and Satan. Rather, he said that he would save them. The sacrificial system points to God's redemptive plan (Lev 16).

In the New Testament, the missio Dei announces the good news that God is in Christ reconciling the world to himself (2 Cor 5:19). Jesus is the Lamb of God who takes away the sin of the world and brings people into a right relationship with the Father (John 1:29 and 36). In this age, Jesus is undoing the catastrophe of the fall. His ministry, death, resurrection, and exaltation destroy the power of Satan and give people the hope of full restoration into the image of God. Those who receive Christ and live under God's rule are called the children of God (1 John 3:2–3). They are restored to their rightful place as members of God's family (John 1:12–13).

The church is apostolic because God sends it into the world to announce his mission and do his work (John 20:21). The church does not have its own mission. Rather, it manifests and extends God's mission.[10] Leslie Newbigin captures this when he says, "Mission is God's, not ours. But God chooses men and women for the service of his mission."[11] As the living body of Christ, the church is the face of God's mission in the world.

Theologians who make an exaggerated distinction between the mission of God and the mission of the church fail to realize that the church is dynamically and intimately connected to God's mission. In the same way that God worked through Moses to defeat the gods of Egypt and set the Israelites free, God works through his church to accomplish his mission today. This does not mean that God cannot work through a donkey, a Persian king, magi, angels, a traitor, or an earthquake. Rather, it means that the apostolic church is so tightly tied to God's mission in this world that it is defined by it.[12] The church has no reason to exist if it is not accomplishing God's mission.[13]

The missio Dei affirms four central points. First, God is a missionary God who is overcoming the fall and reconciling all things to himself. In this

---

10. Bosch, *Transforming Mission*, 391.
11. Newbigin, *Open Secret*, 19.
12. Emile Brunner says that "the Church exists by mission just as fire exists by burning" (*Word and the World*, 108).
13. Bekele, "Biblical Narrative of the Missio Dei," 154.

sense, God's mission is salvific. Scripture indicates that God desires that all should be saved (2 Pet 3:9). That is why he sent the Son into the world (John 3:16). However, his mission portends judgment for those who reject his Son, spurn his love, and rebel against his will (John 3:18). To be reconciled to God, one must believe in Christ, turn from one's sins, and live as a disciple in the fellowship of God's church. Jesus invites people to enter the kingdom of God by following him (Matt 19:16–26). At its core, salvation means living in a right relationship with God through Christ.

Second, the Scriptures reveal God's missional heart. In particular, the names of God describe aspects of God's benevolent character. He is our righteousness, a merciful God, the One who saves, the One who heals, the One who sees me, the Father, the One who gives life, the Lord of the Harvest, and the shepherd. God is love (1 John 4:16). Love is the primary attribute of God. Like the father in the parable of the prodigal son, God seeks to save wayward people because he is madly in love with humankind. God is always calling lost humanity back to himself. In accordance with his benevolent character and determined will, God is destroying the works of the devil (1 John 3:9) as he restores all things to himself (Col 1:20). This implies that spiritual warfare is intricately attached to God's salvific mission.[14]

Third, God covenants with others as he accomplishes his mission. For instance, God called Noah so that he could purify the earth and save a righteous seed (Gen 6:11–21). If God had not purified the earth, the seed of the serpent would have corrupted God's missional purposes. Yet, for God's missional purposes to go forward, Noah had to believe God's word (there will be a flood) and obey God (build an ark and enter it). Otherwise, Noah would have perished in the flood (Gen 6:22). The same is true for Abraham (Gen 12), Moses (Exod 3), and David when he killed the giant (1 Sam 17). In each case, God advanced his missional plan with the help of human partners.

Henry Blackaby illustrates point three when he says that God is always working to accomplish his purposes so that his name is glorified, his kingdom is established on earth, and the world is reconciled to him with and through human partners. When God reveals himself to a partner, he also announces his will. When he discloses his will, he invites the person to join him in his mission. Normally, people do not know what God is doing until

---

14. Payne, *Satan Exposed*, 151–53.

Introduction: Presenting the Missional Hermeneutic

God reveals it to them. If the person agrees, God empowers and enables the partner to do God's work.[15]

Fourth, God's mission is moving toward an end goal (telos or eschaton) that will be realized in history. Scripture points to the eschatological horizon. Furthermore, the eschatological framework of mission presupposes a purposive view of history or a goal toward which God's plan of salvation is moving.[16] Despite the present darkness and the ongoing struggle with evil, Scripture declares that God will create a new heaven and new Earth (Rev 21). When that happens, evil will be fully vanquished, and humankind will be saved. Salvation is larger than being delivered from evil. It means being freed from one's sinful nature, restored into the image of God, and perfectly aligned with God's will. For those who know Christ, the end is the blessed hope that enables them to endure suffering because it keeps them focused on the future God is preparing for them (Titus 2:13 and Heb 12:1–2).

---

15. Blackaby and King, *Experiencing God*, 49–64.
16. Carriker, "Missiological Hermeneutic," 51.

1

What Is a Hermeneutic?

ONE NEEDS A BASIC understanding of hermeneutics to see the big picture of Scripture. Hermeneutics deals with the theory and methodology of interpretation. Some refer to hermeneutics as a science and others as an art.[1] In short, a hermeneutic is a means, tool, rule, or approach by which one interprets and gives meaning to a text. Biblical hermeneutics focuses on the interpretation of Scripture and associated texts.[2]

A person's hermeneutical approach determines how one interprets the Bible and applies the text to ministry. For instance, those who emphasize literal interpretation stress the plain meaning rule, i.e., interpret the Bible literally unless something within the text requires that you interpret it in another way. John Wesley endorsed this rule when he stated that one should not depart from the plain, literal sense of a Scripture text unless the interpretation leads to an absurdity.[3] The "absurdity idea" causes most literalists to interpret the Song of Solomon allegorically because few imagine that the Bible would contain a graphic love story. Also, when Jesus says that his followers are the light of the world (Matt 5:14), he does not mean that they shine like Jesus shined in the transfiguration. Rather, they reflect God's

---

1. Exegesis is a science because it utilizes a critical approach. It is an art because one needs skill to do it well (Ramm, *Protestant Biblical Interpretation*, 1).

2. Those interested in biblical hermeneutics should review Porter, *Biblical Hermeneutics*.

3. "It is a stated rule in interpreting Scripture, never to depart from the plain, literal sense, unless it implies an absurdity" (Wesley, "Of the Church," 395). For a fuller understanding, see Edward, "John Wesley's Non-Literal Literalism."

light when they follow him and do his works so people can see God's truth and be converted, i.e., they bear the fruit of light and are the children of light (Eph 5:8–9 and 1 Thess 5:5–11). Likewise, even though there are wise and foolish virgins, the parable of the ten virgins is about people who are prepared and not prepared for the return of Jesus (Matt 25:1–13). Finally, even though Jesus' parables use plausible imagery to communicate sacred truth, they are not literal.[4]

There are three basic steps to biblical interpretation. Exegesis: What does the text say? Interpretation: What does it mean? Application: How does it inform the reader or enable the practitioner to use the text for ministry?[5] When discussing the three lenses of interpretation, Michael Barram and John Franke argue that understanding the reader's "location" should be the third lens because one's personal experiences, life context, and biases greatly influence how a person interprets the Bible.[6] Regardless of one's location, practical application must not be minimized. Too often, application is the stepchild of exegesis. Likewise, application without competent exegesis leads to compromised ministry practices.

Even though exegesis is not a hermeneutic, it is intimately connected to biblical interpretation. For this reason, some incorrectly interchange "biblical hermeneutics" and "exegesis." In common parlance, exegesis is associated with a "deep reading" of a biblical text. In academia, exegesis is a historical, grammatical, and critical method of interpretation that focuses on the processes by which one uncovers the original meaning of a biblical text. To understand the meaning of the text, one must study the context, language, culture of the author, and the community to which it was written. For this reason, exegetes examine original languages, archeology, ethnohistory, and ancient manuscripts. Most utilize specialized Bible software. All biblical scholars sing the same mantra, "Context, context, context."[7]

---

4. Besides parables, other types of biblical genres are a prophetic call story, prophecy, an epistle, a historical narrative, apocalyptic writing, a sermon, poetry, and a proverb.

5. McMickle, *Living Water for Thirsty Souls* is an excellent example of this step. For more on these points, see McMickle, "Tuesday Lecture Series."

6. Barram and Franke, *Liberating Scripture*, 26–31.

7. Similarly, the historical approach to the study of religion says one cannot understand a religion until one uncovers its origins. Since the essence of a religion is found in its sacred writings, one must understand the lived context and the original meaning of its scriptures to discover its core essence.

What Is a Hermeneutic?

INTERPRETING THE CONSTITUTION ILLUSTRATES PRINCIPLES OF EXEGESIS

Examining how courts interpret America's Constitution will help one understand the intricacies and nuances of biblical exegesis since the courts must say what the Constitution means before applying it to American life. There are two main schools of interpretation. One says the Constitution is a living document that needs to be interpreted in line with the evolving values and practices of the ever-changing culture. Accordingly, what the document says is less important than how it is interpreted. Progressives favor this approach. The other approach argues that the courts should conduct judicial review (legal decisions that interpret and apply the Constitution) by discerning and adhering to the original meaning. Traditionalists favor this position because it protects the people from judges who minimize or ignore the original meaning to achieve ideological or political goals.

Since the Constitution is a contract between the people and their government, how the courts interpret the document has immense importance. The living document approach untethers the courts from a strict reliance on the inherent wording of the Constitution. This allows the courts to create new precedents by interpreting and applying the Constitution in novel ways that do not connect to the original meaning. On the other hand, if the courts followed the doctrine of originalism (adherence to the literal sense of the Constitution), justices of varying political ideologies could come to similar conclusions about any aspect of judicial review to the extent that they agreed on the original meaning of the text (authorial intent). Sadly, this is not a straightforward process.

Interpreting the First Amendment illustrates the problem. It states: "Congress shall make no law respecting an establishment of religion or prohibiting the free exercise thereof." What is an establishment of religion? The literal meaning of this statement is vague. Since the phrase grew out of the debate surrounding Thomas Jefferson's religious freedom bill in Virginia, one should refer to that statute when defining the establishment of religion.[8] The Virginia context included a state church (Anglicanism), the

---

8. "Be it enacted by the General Assembly [of Virginia], that no man shall be compelled to frequent or support any religious worship, place, or ministry whatsoever, nor shall be enforced, restrained, molested, or burthened in his body or goods, nor shall otherwise suffer on account of his religious opinions or belief; but that all men shall be free to profess, and by argument to maintain, their opinion in matters of religion, and that the same shall in no wise diminish, enlarge, or affect their civil capacities" (Jefferson,

war with England, the Crown manipulating America via the state church, resentment against religious taxation, the doctrine of natural rights, religious competition, and a burgeoning Deism that successfully questioned the place of religion in society.

Regarding religion, Jefferson stressed three points. One, the government should not interfere with a person's religion or conscience to the extent that the person's practice does not hurt others, i.e., he advocated minimum government interference and maximum tolerance of religion. Two, religion is a basic right that pertains to the people, not the government. Three, in matters of religion, the government should not have a preference, show favoritism, or affirm a religious doctrine. The separation of church and state flows from these points. In Jefferson's original context, Virginia would not have a state church, and the Anglican Church would not be favored above other religious organizations.

This seems very clear until you try to apply it. Does the religious clause in the First Amendment mean the federal government cannot have a state religion like England or the Roman Catholic countries in Latin America? If so, does the prohibition also apply to the individual states?[9] Or does it mean that the federal government must build a wall of separation between the state and organized religion so that the state is not "infected" by religion, since the commingling of state and religion threatens personal liberty and caused problems in Europe? The Deistic ideology of Jefferson would point to the latter. Nonetheless, other founders who assented to the First Amendment did not share Jefferson's grievance or antipathy toward evangelical faith.

In the history of American jurisprudence, the answer and its application have depended on a judge's ideological bent. Harold Leventhal refers to the practice of reading one's biases into one's rulings as "looking over the heads of the crowd [the historical context] and picking out your friends [that part of the historical record that favors your bias]."[10] It is a selective reading of history that allows an ideological interpretation of the Constitution. In theory, originalism would restrain this.

"An Act for Establishing Religious Freedom," 2).

9. Considering that Massachusetts did not abolish its state church (Congregationalism) and religious tax until 1833, one can argue that the founders and courts were not of one opinion on this point.

10. Samah, "Looking Over a Crowd," 556.

What Is a Hermeneutic?

Today, tolerance-affirming Americans embrace secularism. While rejecting atheistic totalitarianism (communism), Islamic law (sharia), and the establishment of Christianity (theocracy) they, like Jefferson, agree that the United States should not have an official state religion. However, political parties do not agree on the definition of religion, the meaning of religious freedom, what constitutes an established religion, and how the state should enable (not prohibit) the free exercise of religion in the public arena. For example, evangelicalism has argued that the combined beliefs of atheism, naturalism, and humanism have become the established religion of the liberal state. Furthermore, they claim that liberal courts have weakened the place and public influence of Christianity in American society because of religious bias. Additionally, they assert that secularism is not a value-neutral ideology free of religious bias. Rather, in every Western country it requires the establishment of humanism. Based on this critique, they contend that the American courts have diminished Christianity to establish humanism as the state religion. In making this claim, they point to the example of a post-Christian Europe that is hostile to public manifestations of evangelical faith and thought. In response, humanists say that secularism ensures religious freedom, and atheism is not a religion because religion requires a belief in God.

Things came to a head in 2016 when the Obama administration attempted to define religious freedom as the right to worship. In response, the chair of the U.S. Commission on International Religious Freedom stated that freedom of religion includes freedom of worship and "the right of believers to evangelize, change their religion, have schools and charitable institutions, and participate in the public square."[11] In the aftermath, the Obama administration said that it wanted to narrow the definition of religious freedom "to protect religious minorities."[12] In a highly polarized nation in which a coalition of evangelicals attempted to influence government via political activism, the administration suggested that religious freedom meant protecting religious minorities from the religious majority (Christians)—not enabling all people to practice their faith without government interference or discrimination. The religious activism of Muslims, Black churches, and mainline Christians who aligned with the values of the Obama administration was exempted from the larger critique. As such, Obama's approach created a governmental disadvantage for traditional

---

11. Reese, "'Freedom to Worship.'"
12. Reese, "'Freedom to Worship.'"

Christianity while bolstering liberal Christianity and minority faiths that aligned with liberal ideology. It also helped the administration minimize the public influence of Christians who supported the Republican vision for America.

Before the Obama administration tied the freedom of religion to the protection of religious minorities, did courts use the doctrine of separation of church and state to minimize the public influence of religion?[13] To answer this, consider the following questions. Can one pray in school? Can a student in a public school argue against the theory of evolution by arguing for creationism? Can public school teachers lecture on creationism while critiquing the theory of evolution? Can cities create zoning rules to restrict home Bible studies? Can government scholarships be given to those who attend religious schools? What happens when one's religious convictions collide with government civil rights policies? If society believes that life begins at conception, could states ban elective abortions? Should the government fund abortions? Can a teacher have a Bible on her desk or wear a cross at school? Do memorials on public land have to remove Christian symbols to protect state neutrality? Can a church employee (minister) who is fired for immoral conduct or wrong theology sue the employer for wrongful termination? Can a military officer be reprimanded for sharing his faith on a personal social media platform?

Past decisions show that the courts ruled in ways that minimized the cultural and political influence of traditional Christianity. Since 1962, many judicial rulings have been hostile to religious symbols, religiously informed values, religious speech, religious practice in public spaces, and the influence of religion on culture. A cultural influence is not the establishment of religion; it is the way a society lives out its values. When the government built a wall between itself and cultural Christianity, it adopted practical atheism as the state religion. Like Christianity, atheism is a way of life that is influenced by what people believe about God and ultimate reality.

Today, traditional Christians argue that the First Amendment should protect them from the biased interpretations of judges who favor practical atheism, humanism, and liberal politics. Hence, they favor originalism and want the Supreme Court to mandate that approach. On the other hand, liberals believe that judicial review should reflect the values of the progressive

---

13. The courts applied the Lemon Test to determine if the separation of church and state was properly followed. This rule discriminated against religious America and disproportionately hurt religious people. In 2022, the Supreme Court invalidated the Lemon test.

society and that the courts must be free to reinterpret the Constitution so it can speak to their concerns.

DISCERNING BIAS (CRITICAL THINKING)

Similarly, the social location, worldview, academic training, and theological beliefs of Bible scholars greatly influence how they utilize the exegetical method to interpret and apply the Bible. David Bosch, a South African theologian, says that everyone reads the Bible from a particular vantage point which colors their interpretation.[14] Michael Barram and John Franke say, "Despite what early biblical scholarship may have assumed, there is no such thing as entirely 'disinterested'—that is, completely 'objective,' bias-free interpretation. All forms of interpretation are perspectival and contextual, and thus inherently 'interested.'"[15] Girma Bekele, an Ethiopian Bible scholar, writes, "Our attempt to understand the self-definition of the biblical authors and their first readers is [tainted] by our own socio-political, cultural, and economic context. . . . One cannot read the text of the Bible passively, nor approach it as a neutral reader and objectively claim to know the mind of the authors."[16] Instead of uncovering the original meaning of a text, Bekele says scholars discover their understanding of the text when doing exegesis. Admittedly, that sounds a bit harsh. However, Bekele writes as an African who has routinely objected to exegetical conclusions that reflect Western worldview assumptions.

Michael Barram makes a broad conclusion:

> Every interpretation [of a biblical text] comes from a "place" to the extent that no interpreter can fully avoid the influences of personal history, gender, ethnicity, race, nationality, place of residence, education, occupation, political perspective, economic status, religious views or commitments. . . . What we see, hear, and value is inevitably colored by our own situations, experiences, characteristics, and presuppositions.[17]

While discussing exegesis, Kam Weng Ng, a research fellow at Oxford and Princeton, says that all Bible interpretation is theory-laden because

---

14. Bosch, *Theology of Missions*, 24.
15. Barram and Franke, *Liberating Scripture*, 28.
16. Bekele, "Biblical Narrative," 154.
17. Barram, "Bible, Mission, and Social Location," 44.

researchers operate with assumed models, procedures, and beliefs. The Bible scholar's worldview and operating belief system (theology) always influence how the exegete approaches and interprets the text.[18] For example, a biblical scholar who approaches the Bible with a scientifically informed mindset often demythologizes the Scriptures by making the supernatural content of the Bible align with a naturalistic worldview that rejects supernatural interpretations. This subjugates the supernatural worldview of the Bible to methodological atheism and the scientific mindset of the researcher.

Furthermore, exegesis employs a "critical" method of inquiry connected to modern presuppositions about objectivity, science, and reality. Expert practitioners believe that truth must be objectively discovered and the researcher should be objective. In this regard, the historical-critical method objectifies truth and its corresponding meaning. Modernism and the Enlightenment have greatly influenced this notion.[19] Following this train of thought, exegetes have advocated for "methodological atheism"—the scientific practice of assuming naturalism or ignoring supernatural explanations when using a critical method of inquiry.[20] This is largely assumed when doing research in a state university. Theologian Peter Berger states, "Every inquiry into religious matters that limits itself to the empirical must necessarily be based on a 'methodological atheism.'"[21] Nancey Murphy describes methodological atheism as "the principle that scientific explanations are to be in terms of natural [not supernatural] entities and processes.... Christians and atheists alike must pursue scientific questions in our era without invoking a creator."[22]

Since he was a committed Deist, Thomas Jefferson provides a good example. Between 1803 and 1820, he produced a demythologized Bible by cutting out Jesus' miracles and passages that portray Jesus as divine.[23] Like most Deists of his time, he believed that Jesus was a moral figure who should be an example for others. He rejected the supernatural Jesus of Scripture and tradition. In this way, his Bible reflected his naturalistic worldview—the worldview most associated with humanism.

18. Ng, "Scope and Limits of Science."
19. Bekele, "Biblical Narrative," 154.
20. Cantrell, "Must a Scholar of Religion," 373–75.
21. Berger, *Sacred Canopy*, 100.
22. Murphy, "Phillip Johnson on Trial," 33–34.
23. Jefferson, *Jefferson Bible*.

What Is a Hermeneutic?

Likewise, Rudolf Bultmann, a highly influential biblical scholar, argued against the existence of miracles based on his commitment to modern science.[24] He said, "The resurrection of Jesus cannot be accepted, for it involves an impossible nature-miracle,"[25] and "we cannot use electric lights and radios and, in the event of illness, avail ourselves of modern medical and clinical means and at the same time believe in the spirit and wonder world of the New Testament."[26]

In contrast, through painstaking research, Craig Keener, an eminent New Testament scholar, incontrovertibly demonstrates that the same miracles that the New Testament reports have happened in history and are happening in the modern world.[27] As such, he argues that the anti-supernatural worldview biases behind the movement to demythologize the Scriptures should not be accepted. Keener is not saying that every miracle story in the Bible must be interpreted as a literal event. For example, the story of Jonah could be a literary device by which the nation of Israel reconsidered its mission to the nations while in Babylonian captivity. Regardless, the exegete must accept that the New Testament authors believed in supernatural intervention and thought that the miracles they reported in the New Testament were historical facts.

In *The Historical Jesus of the Gospels and Acts: An Exegetical Commentary*, Craig Keener effectively uses exegesis without employing naturalism. Like Keener, people of deep evangelical faith can employ textual criticism and the exegetical method to address critical issues surrounding the Bible's surviving manuscripts, canon, variant readings, and original meaning without compromising their faith. In other words, one does not have to discard the supernatural worldview of the Bible writers to do good exegesis or employ a deep reading of the text.[28]

---

24. Bultmann believed that the prevailing mythologies of the first century influenced how the New Testament communicated the gospel story. He argued that the mythological worldview of the New Testament church was not compatible with the scientific worldview of modern society. Pointedly, he contended that the concept of miracle is no longer credible in the modern era (Wildman, "Rudolf Bultmann").

25. Bultmann, *New Testament and Mythology*, 107

26. Bultmann, *New Testament and Mythology*, 4.

27. Keener, *Miracles*.

28. Some Christian scholars who affirm God and the supernatural practice methodological naturalism when interpreting the Bible for professional reasons (Geisler, "Naturalism," 521).

In summary, when doing exegesis, there is always an interaction between the author of the text, the community in which he lived, previously written literature, and the exegete. Notice that I did not mention the Holy Spirit. An exegete does not have to affirm that all Scripture must be spiritually discerned to be properly understood (1 Cor 2:13–14). Furthermore, one does not have to believe that the biblical text is God-breathed to employ the historical-critical method of exegesis (cf. 2 Tim 3:16–17). Moreover, most biblical scholars believe that an overemphasis on divine inspiration may obstruct the process of good exegesis. In fact, regardless of one's faith, if two Bible scholars properly employ the exegetical method and the tools associated with it without imposing methodological or ideological bias, they should arrive at similar conclusions about the original meaning of a given text because exegesis is a science whose outcomes can be tested and replicated. The belief that an exegete can discover the correct meaning of a text is called "assured results of scholarship."[29] Science implies objectivity. Objectivity requires a critical analysis of the text. Having said this, the believer who employs exegesis should be careful not to embrace the naturalistic assumptions embedded in the scientific method.

---

29. Barram and Franke, *Liberating Scripture*, 30.

2

Approaches to Biblical Interpretation

BIBLE INTERPRETATION EXISTS ON three levels. First, what does the text say and how did the original hearer understand its meaning? That is exegesis. Second, how does it connect to the great truths of the church? That is theology. Third, how should the meaning of the text be communicated to people of a different language? That is translation.

CONTEXTUALIZATION

Timothy Gabrielson says that traditional hermeneutics is a linear process that moves from the original text to the modern context. The linear process emphasizes the meaning of the original text. Often, this leads to formal correspondence translation interpretations that do not intersect well with the people in the receiving culture. Gabrielson argues that hermeneutics should be a spiral process that constantly moves between the text and the modern context without misconstruing the meaning of the original hearers or minimizing their context. He believes that readers should ask a basic question of the text: What does it mean today? Or how is God using this text to communicate to us as we read it and contemplate it?[1]

Following that lead, missiologists favor dynamic equivalent translation.[2] Some refer to this as culture-specific interpretation. Since a

---

1. Gabrielson, "Along the Grain," 71–73.

2. Nida is the father of dynamic (functional) equivalent translation. His research greatly influenced the American Bible Society. His theory is detailed in "Nature of

significant cultural gap separates the Bible authors from modern readers, contemporary audiences should understand the meaning of the original text in a way that connects with their own culture and experience. For example, when translating Ps 23 for inner-city youth, instead of saying that the Lord is my shepherd (formal correspondence), one could say that the Lord is my coach, my teacher, or my grandparent (dynamic equivalence), as few urban youths have an innate understanding of sheep and shepherds. Dynamic equivalence does not change the meaning of the text. Instead, it communicates the original meaning in ways that are familiar to the modern reader. There is no conflict between the plain meaning rule and dynamic equivalent translation.

Contextualization builds on the model of the incarnation.[3] When God became human, he entered the world as a Jew. His life and teachings were specific to the Jews of his time and place. He spoke their language and used their culture as a medium to teach spiritual truths. When translating the gospel from the original context for people in a new culture, one must reincarnate it so the receptors do not have to learn the Jewish culture to understand the original message. If contextualization is done well, the Jewish Jesus becomes Mexican, Sri Lankan, or any other culture provided the people fully own the faith.[4]

Historically, theological education in the Global South has worked against the goals of contextualization. Since the seminary is a product of late Christendom, it propagates Western approaches to theology. Africans who graduate from traditional seminaries download the ideals and values of the Western church to include worldview assumptions. This prevents them from doing "African theology." In this sense, they become

---

Equivalence in Translating." Robert Thomas argues that dynamic equivalence is a hermeneutical system because it utilizes exegesis to impose the translator's meaning on the text ("Dynamic Equivalence," 150–51).

3. "In the same way that God became a Jew in order to reveal the Divine Self and communicate God's will to a people who were embedded within a cultural context, the church is called to 'incarnate' the gospel into every culture so that the members of every society (people group) can have a culture-specific encounter with God and God's revelation so that they can receive Christ and enter into God's reign" (Payne, "Contextualization," para. 15).

4. Payne, "Jesus Is Every Race." Because of rampant antisemitism, one must acknowledge that the historical Jesus is the Jewish Messiah. Depending on one's theology, one can say that Jesus is a Jew. According to the prophetic tradition, when Jesus returns, he will rule the world from Jerusalem. For these reasons, an appeal to contextualization must never deny or minimize the Jewish connection to the historical Jesus.

ideological apprentices to the socialization process that Western education perpetuates.[5]

In *African Hermeneutics*, Elizabeth Mburu, a professor of New Testament and Greek in Nairobi, Kenya, notes that the dominant models for biblical interpretation come from the West and assume a Western worldview orientation. She contends that the ensuing cultural gap between the Africans and biblical interpretation leads to theological syncretism in Africa. Since African societies connect with the biblical worldview in terms of culture and practice, it should be easier for them to understand the biblical context. For this reason, she believes that Africans must interpret the Bible from the perspective of their worldviews using African tools to understand it so they can properly apply it to their varied contexts. Mburu says African hermeneutics moves "directly from theories, methods, and categories that are familiar in our [African] world into the more unfamiliar world of the Bible, without taking a detour through any foreign methods. It recognizes parallels between biblical cultures and the worldviews of African cultures."[6]

READER-RESPONSE

The reader-response approach is hypercontextual and individualistic. It does not embrace originalism or assume that the meaning of the text is self-evident. Instead, it focuses on the reader and how she experiences the text. It argues that a text does not contain its own meaning. Rather, interpreters bring meaning to the text based on their commitments, experiences, and social location.[7]

Robert Fowler, a religion professor at Baldwin Wallace University, captures this when he says that the biblical text does not contain a meaning waiting to be discovered by exegesis because meaning is not the property of the text but a function of the experience of the person who reads the text. Furthermore, meaning is not static and does not precede the reading of the text. Rather, it is the property of the reader. Instead of asking

---

5. Hendriks, "Contextualising Theological Education in Africa," 3.

6. Mburu, *African Hermeneutics*, 6–7.

7. Barram and John Franke reach a similar point when they emphasize that all theology is biased. "It is important to recognize that located readings of texts are no more 'biased' than interpretations done from either of the other two lenses. Again, all interpretation reflects located biases" (*Liberating Scripture*, 34). This leads to a theological free-for-all in which there is no orthodoxy and everyone gets to say what a text means even if the interpretation is not supported by sound exegesis.

"What determines the meaning of the text?" reader-response asks "Who determines the meaning of the text?"[8] Since a literary text does not have an independent or self-evident meaning, the author's intent is subordinated to the reader's experience and interpretation of the text. The reader could be a group with a common sense of belonging or an individual.

Using reader-response, how should one interpret Robert Frost's "The Road Not Taken"?[9]

> Two roads diverged in a yellow wood,
> And sorry I could not travel both
> And be one traveler, long I stood
> And looked down one as far as I could
> To where it bent in the undergrowth;
>
> Then took the other, as just as fair,
> And having perhaps the better claim,
> Because it was grassy and wanted wear;
> Though as for that the passing there
> Had worn them really about the same,
>
> And both that morning equally lay
> In leaves no step had trodden black.
> Oh, I kept the first for another day!
> Yet knowing how way leads on to way,
>
> I shall be telling this with a sigh
> Somewhere ages and ages hence:
> Two roads diverged in a wood, and I—
> I took the one less traveled by,
> And that has made all the difference.

If one applied the exegetical process of literary interpretation to this poem, one would study the life of Robert Frost, read his other writings, examine the events that influenced his time, and so forth. What prompted him to write the poem? To whom was he writing it? The researcher would carefully unpack his vocabulary, dissect his sentence structure, and identify the genre. The work of other poets might be considered. Finally, if one could divine the meaning Frost intended (if indeed he intended a single meaning), one would understand the poem and could explain it to others.

---

8. Fowler, "Reader-Response Criticism," 52–53.
9. Frost, "Road Not Taken."

Approaches to Biblical Interpretation

However, the meaning of a poem exists on many levels. Truly, a poem has as many meanings as it has readers. When I read Frost's poem, I imagine Gandalf and Frodo sitting before dark tunnels deep in the mines of Moria as they try to discern the correct path. In the aftermath, Frodo is greatly grieved that he chose to go through Moria because a fiery beast killed Gandalf before they emerged.[10] Since few of us have the option of undoing the paths we have chosen or discerning what would have happened if we had taken a different way, most feel regret at some point or another. To be happy, one should accept the choices one made, walk the path with faith, and be content with the life one has.

The exegete will explain the original meaning. In reader-response, the person will say what the text means to them. Those who espouse the reader-response approach will argue that all literature is living and that the original intent is irrelevant. Reader-response advocates contend that those who impose authoritative interpretations speak for the dominant voice. It is an act of power that disenfranchises other voices. In the case of dogmatic or moral interpretation, some would say that the dominant voice has intentionally excluded marginalized groups. Furthermore, such interpretations keep minority populations from reading the Bible in light of their own shared experience of oppression. This critique connects to liberation theology and goes to the heart of postcolonial biblical criticism.[11]

Reader-response does not affirm plenary inspiration. If the Bible is God's message to humanity, reveals God's will, and is essential for salvation, one must discern God's intended meaning. To misrepresent God's intended meaning is to misrepresent God.[12] The reader-response approach argues that God did not have an intended meaning when the Scriptures were produced because the Scriptures are cultural artifacts from a bygone era. At best, they tell the story of a people's search for God. If God intended a universal meaning, it was obfuscated by those who wrote the Scriptures and those who have imposed meaning on them. Furthermore, the process by which the powerful have divined God's meaning has excluded those who do not align with the majority opinion. This approach aligns with the postmodern understanding of truth.

---

10. Tolkien, *Fellowship of the Ring*, 295–320.
11. See Rukundwa, "Postcolonial Theory," 339–51.
12. Paul tells the Corinthians not to use deception or distort the word of God. Rather, they are to set it forth plainly knowing that God sees what they do (2 Cor 4:1).

DECONSTRUCTION AND CRITICAL THEORY

Postcolonial biblical criticism addresses the inequity of power between colonizers and the colonized or between the majority and the minority.[13] In America, postcolonial criticism gives a voice to the indigenous peoples. It maintains that white, Christian America used religion as a tool of exploitation by fomenting or maintaining official narratives that legitimized the oppression of native peoples. For example, manifest destiny was a religio-political idea that justified Western expansion and the removal of Native populations.

Critical theory connects with postcolonial approaches. It deals with knowledge: how one acquires knowledge, what knowledge is considered important, what perspectives are considered, what is ignored, and who benefits from it. It asserts that religious knowledge and those who control it are not neutral or innocent. This includes biblical interpretation and the processes by which it is done. According to Christopher Partridge, "By examining race, gender, sexuality, and economic wealth, one can see how ideas about religion often support those in power, usually the ruling educated elite of white, Western men. Thinking and writing about ideas from the position of the exploited radically changes the subject and the writing of history."[14] When one begins with critical theory, all other approaches to history, religion, economics, and politics are minimized and considered suspect. This is referred to as a hermeneutic of suspicion.

How do methodological biases influence the way critical theory approaches Scripture?[15] First, the critical theory of religion was greatly influenced by people who had a negative view of traditional Christianity, e.g., Marx, Nietzsche, and Freud. Second, critical theory greatly influences communistic interpretations of religion. In communist societies, this leads to the persecution of Christians and the denial of biblical truth. In practice, communist ideology is hostile to a biblical faith that affirms that the Bible is

---

13. Nelus Niemandt, an Afrikaner who teaches at the University of Pretoria, refers to the decolonization of African theology as emancipation. "Decolonialality" responds "to the relationship of direct, political, social and cultural domination established by Europeans.... The postcolonial discourse and decolonial turn represent an important critique of and corrective to the colonial framework and approach" ("Missional Hermeneutic," 3–4).

14. Partridge, *Introduction to World Religions*, 31.

15. Which voices among the exploited are considered and which voices are not heard? Furthermore, can the utilization of a social theory justify the assigning of groups of people into prejudicial social categories based on corporate guilt?

Approaches to Biblical Interpretation

the revealed word of God and the notion that people must submit to what it reveals. Submission to Holy Writ (when properly interpreted and rightly applied) is submission to God. Third, those who apply critical theory to Bible interpretation may not affirm Christian orthodoxy, including its theology of Scripture.

One should ask if critical theory is antithetical to a biblically informed faith that emphasizes Jesus' teaching in the Sermon on the Mount (Matt 5–7) and the vice/virtue lists in the New Testament.[16] Do critical theory approaches to biblical interpretation look at the Bible in terms of its categories or do they impose critical theory ideology onto the Bible? To what extent can an orthodox Christian apply critical theory of religion to the Bible and still affirm that the Bible is the authoritative word of God?

On the other hand, is critical theory merely a justice hermeneutic that contextualizes the Bible and the Christian faith to the growing awareness of injustice and the need for social reform? If the Bible is a living document that must be read in line with contemporary society, shouldn't issues surrounding race, inequality, homophobia, poverty, and white nationalism be read into the Scriptures? Most importantly, doesn't the prophetic tradition of the Bible clearly endorse the justice metanarrative?

In literary criticism, deconstruction connects to the postcolonial approach and the critical theory critique. William Deresiewicz, a former literature professor at Yale, summarizes the postcolonial approach:

> The whole concept of literature—still more, of art—has been discredited. Novels, poems, stories, plays [and Holy Writ]: these are "texts," no different in kind from other texts. The purpose of studying them is not to appreciate or understand them; it is to "interrogate" them for their ideological investments in patriarchy, in white supremacy, in Western imperialism and ethnocentrism, and then to unmask and debunk them, to drain them of their poisonous persuasive power.[17]

In postcolonial interpretation, after deconstructing the Bible and the oppressive narratives attached to its interpretation, the oppressed construct a new narrative of liberation that galvanizes the victims and subverts the power of the oppressors. The Bible is then reread in light of the new narrative. The emerging orthodoxy reads the Bible through a carefully constructed lens that emphasizes one's political commitments more than the

---

16. Charles, "Vice and Virtue Lists."
17. Deresiewicz, "Why I Left Academia."

affirmations of classical orthodoxy.[18] Of course, when discussing Christian orthodoxy or the sufficiency of Scripture, erasing two thousand years of accepted interpretation to realize sociopolitical goals carries risk. After all, orthodoxy erects theological boundaries to ensure that one does not slip into heterodoxy, heresy, or faulty interpretation. Since an orthodox reading of the Bible is essential for knowing God's will and obtaining salvation, the consequences of deconstruction may have serious second-order implications.

CANONICAL CRITICISM

Those who advocate for canonical criticism claim that the church is the Bible's caretaker. Furthermore, because the church wrote the New Testament, they contend that the church has authorial standing to say what it means.[19] Why is this important? In the face of daunting theological controversies, the early church ironed out orthodoxy by saying what the Bible meant. Creedal statements about biblical interpretation became orthodoxy. When people interpret the Bible in ways that contravene orthodoxy, the church says that their interpretation is wrong. At one point in history, the church had the power to enforce its decrees. In canonical criticism, the Bible is not the final authority for determining right faith and right practice. The church is. Approaches that deconstruct the Bible or challenge the authority of the church to interpret it are deemed problematic.

Who speaks for the church? Is it the Roman Catholic Magisterium, the writings of Protestant reformers, African Independent churches, or one of the breakaway churches that claim they are the correct interpreters of Scripture? Also, how does this approach negotiate biblical ambiguity? For example, do the creedal statements about the Trinity and the dual nature of Christ perfectly capture all that the Bible says about God; or did the great councils divine a right meaning to achieve a religiopolitical goal that aligned the church with the Roman Empire and gave power to those who stood for orthodoxy? How much latitude does the Bible allow when

18. Castells, a Spanish sociologist, says that identity formation is a social construction that happens in the context of power relationships. Every society assigns identity to people. When the assigned identity devalues or oppresses a person or a group of people, they may resist the identity and the powers that assigned it. As they seek to establish their preferred identity, they deconstruct the society and create a new one that aligns with their experience and ideology (*Information Age*, 7–8).

19. See Childs, *Introduction to the Old Testament* and Noble, *Canonical Approach*.

debating theological controversies? Based on a "right" interpretation of the Bible, should the church have excommunicated the Nestorians, rejected the Arians, and split from the Eastern Orthodox Church? What about biblical literalists who argue for Jesus'-name baptism based on the examples in Acts? Furthermore, when the church falls into error, how does one correct it? For instance, does the Bible affirm everything that later church teaching said about the Virgin Mary, the saints, purgatory, and salvation? Clearly, the universal community of Jesus believers, now and in the past, has lacked consensus on many important issues. What are the essentials on which all must agree? Is canonical criticism tenable?

RELATIONAL ORTHODOXY AND CENTER-SET THEOLOGY

In response, left-leaning evangelical leaders have proposed a center-set theology that emphasizes the direction one is heading rather than cold confessional boundaries.[20] Brian McLaren calls the relational approach "a generous orthodoxy."[21] This approach defines orthodoxy as a wide road in which people drive in different lanes and at different speeds toward a common goal. In this scenario, curbs keep people from leaving the road and crashing. The curbs are the essentials of the faith as contained in the Apostles' Creed, the Nicene Creed, and the Athanasian Creed. The lanes represent orthodox traditions within the faith. If one is heading toward Christ, one is in the set. If one moves away from Christ or jumps the curb, one has left the set. All who stay in the set remain in a right relationship with Christ and each other because they are moving toward the same goal. Ultimately, the name of the church is less important than the direction one is heading.

The approach champions hospitality and inclusivity. It corrects "bully orthodoxy" without compromising the essentials of the faith. Of course, different orthodox faith communities have different lists of essentials. Often, disagreement swirls around right practice more than right faith. For example, how should the Bible inform one's sexual ethic, one's understanding

---

20. For more information on center-set theology, see Hiebert, *Anthropological Reflections*, 107–136.

21. See McLaren, *A Generous Orthodoxy*. In this book, McLaren does not establish the limits of orthodoxy. Instead, he endorses a relational faith that focuses on Christ. Postmodern theologians often appeal to the ideal of hospitality because they do not like boundaries or confessional communities as they want to make room for everyone. Their relational ethos allows theological ambiguity for the sake of inclusion.

of marriage, and the ordination of women? At a more basic level, what do evangelicals mean when they say the Bible is divine revelation and the primary authority for determining right faith and right practice since application requires interpretation? The affirmation that the Bible is the final authority, and the church is the right interpreter go together. This points back to canonical criticism.

LECTIO DIVINA

Sects that emphasize mystical approaches to the Divine, e.g., Jewish kabbalah, Islamic Sufism, Christian mysticism, and Hindu bhakti, believe that arguments about orthodoxy should not obscure the journey to God. After all, knowing God and being in union with God is the great goal of faith. Inordinate emphasis on right faith and right practice can turn faith into a dead religion of rules and numb rituals. In the *Idea of the Holy*, Rudolf Otto refers to the encounter with the Divine as the *mysterium tremendum et fascinans*. Simultaneously, the seeker is afraid of God and is drawn to God. Once a person encounters God, he will create rituals or religious practices that enable him to return to God. Moses at the burning bush (Exod 3:1–17), Isaiah before the throne of God (Isa 6:1–3), and the disciples on the Mount of Transfiguration (Matt 17:1–8) are examples of *mysterium tremendum et fascinans*.[22]

Michael Goheen says that one should "listen to the biblical text" to hear what God is saying. Hearing what God says while reading the text, i.e., being fully present in the text and mindful of the Spirit's voice, is a primary function of biblical interpretation and core to the missional hermeneutic.[23] Lectio Divina reaches for this. It is an existential approach to biblical interpretation that emphasizes an encounter with God. According to Eugene Peterson, it "is a way of reading the Scriptures that is congruent with the way the Scriptures serve the Christian community as a witness to God's revelation of himself to us."[24] In Lectio Divina, a person reads the text, meditates upon it, prays about it, and then contemplates its meaning as they live into the text. The practitioner believes that the living Word of God reveals himself to those who carefully allow the Spirit to speak to them when they contemplate the written word of God. That is, God reveals

---

22. Rudolf Otto referenced in Goheen, "Continuing Steps," 50.
23. Goheen, "Continuing Steps," 49–50.
24. Peterson, *Eat This Book*, 81.

Approaches to Biblical Interpretation

himself when the Bible is read and proclaimed. As such, reading the Bible under the guidance of the Holy Spirit is a means to encounter God and be shaped by God. For this reason, many pastors use Lectio Divina to inform their preaching. It is a way to get a "word" from God when reading the Bible. It moves from "What does the text say?" to "What is God saying to me as I read the text?" It differs from reader-response (egocentric) because God is the one who communicates meaning (theocentric). In other words, it seeks a word from God.

Similarly, Charismatics affirm that anointed preaching creates a spiritual climate in which the living Word works through the spoken word to quicken a person's conscience, awaken a hearer to God, and enable God to do whatever God wants to do in the life of the seeker.[25] Faith comes by hearing and hearing by the word of God (Rom 10:17). Based on this notion, the sacrament of preaching is an act by which the God of Scripture reveals himself through biblical preaching so that the hearers are touched, empowered, and changed by the Spirit. Obviously, Jesus, the apostles, and the early church preached the word with authority before the New Testament was written. The Bible was meant to be preached. Anointed preaching enlivens and empowers the communication of the written word.

When reading and interpreting the Bible, people should seek inspiration. For this reason, many traditions say a prayer of illumination before reading the Bible. For example, one could pray, "Holy God, as a gathered community of believers, we seek to be illuminated by your Spirit. In the name of Jesus, open our hearts and minds as the Scriptures are read and your Word is proclaimed. May we hear the message that you want to say to us. Amen."

Still, inspiration that is not checked by good theology and proper exegesis can lead to error. For example, in the New Testament church, some peddled "doctrines of demons" or false teachings that came from seducing spirits through personal revelation (1 Cor 12:3 and 1 Tim 4:1). When using a spiritual discipline to get a word from God, one must ensure that the word did not come from a deceiving spirit or the person's imagination. That is why the gathered church applied the rule of faith and discerned if a purported revelation was from God.

The appeal to personal revelation or anointed preaching is subjective. Today, evangelicalism affirms that the Bible is the revelation of God. As

---

25. See Norford, *Anointed Preaching*, 33–52. This section explores hermeneutics and the theological basis for anointed preaching.

such, theology must conform to it. At the same time, a theology that rejects personal revelation and revelatory gifts from the Spirit should be rejected (1 Cor 12:10).

In summary, I have defined hermeneutics and given examples to show how Christians interpret or give meaning to biblical texts. Also, I have pointed out the pros and cons of each approach.

3

What Is a Metanarrative?

A METANARRATIVE INTERPRETS A series of interrelated stories or events in view of a grand theme. As a narrative about narratives, it overshadows and holds together a long series of seemingly disparate stories. Bill Jackson says a metanarrative is a story that explains all the other stories by relating them to a larger story. He argues that one must know the biblical metanarrative when doing exegesis to comprehend the larger meaning of a text.[1] Metanarratives answer the "what does it mean" question by connecting a text to a macro-interpretation. More precisely, they see the story that the text tells through the lens of a larger story.

Let me offer a cinematic example. *Doctor Strange* tells the story of a talented neurosurgeon who must check his ego to learn the secrets of a hidden world of mysticism and alternate dimensions.[2] When analyzing the movie, one can describe the characters, use movie quotes to reinforce the main ideas, and compare the motion picture to other films of the same genre. As a stand-alone movie, it is a masterpiece of cinematography, character development, plot sequencing, and special effects. It perfectly encapsulates the sci-fi genre.

Nevertheless, on a deeper level, you will not understand the meaning of *Doctor Strange* if you do not know the storyline that other Marvel movies disclose about Infinity Stones, superheroes, antiheroes, and a pending apocalyptic showdown with an archvillain named Thanos. In truth, *Doctor*

---

1. Jackson, *Biblical Metanarrative*, 6–8.
2. Derrickson, *Doctor Strange*.

Strange is one of many puzzle pieces that fit together to reveal the larger picture of the Marvel Cinematic Universe.

If *Doctor Strange* were a book of the Bible, it would have its own internal context, characters, and plot. You could analyze it as a separate story. However, it would also be a part of a larger corpus of books that tell a fuller story. The larger narrative is called a metanarrative.

SPIRITUAL WARFARE

Theologians have identified many potential metanarratives. For example, in *Satan Exposed: A Biblical Theology of Spiritual Warfare*,[3] I show that spiritual warfare underlies the entire story of Scripture. From the fall, through the flood, the cleansing of Canaan, the problem with nation gods, the temptation to abandon Yahweh, attempts to destroy the holy remnant, the killing of the innocents after Jesus was born, Jesus' temptation in the wilderness, the in-breaking kingdom of God, the entire crucifixion sequence, the resurrection triumph, and much more show the grand theme of spiritual warfare—the ongoing conflict between the seed of the woman and the seed of the serpent. In fact, the theme is continued in Revelation until Satan, Death, and Hades are thrown into the lake of fire (Rev 20:10 and 14). From the fall to the consummation, the Bible tells the story of the ongoing conflict between God, the gods, and those who have rebelled against him. In this sense, spiritual warfare can function as a metanarrative for reading and interpreting the grand story of Scripture.

Gregory Boyd's massive *God at War: The Bible and Spiritual Conflict*[4] uses this hermeneutic to tell the big story of Scripture. Michael Heiser, a popular blogger, YouTuber, biblical scholar, and prolific writer, also appeals to this approach.[5] In fact, the bibliography in *Satan Exposed* lists thirty or more scholars who read the Bible through the lens of spiritual warfare.

The spiritual warfare theme overlaps with the grand theme of the missio Dei and is a subset of it. It points to what is happening in the spiritual realm (heavenlies) and behind the scenes. God is destroying the powers and principalities because they seek to corrupt his purposes and

---

3. Payne, *Satan Exposed*.
4. Boyd, *God at War*.
5. See Heiser, "Deuteronomy 32:8," and *Supernatural*. Heiser's work on Deut 32:8 is so foundational to his metanarrative that he speaks about the "Deuteronomy 32:8 worldview" in his writings and oral presentations.

interfere with his mission (Col 2:15 and 1 Pet 3:22). More will be said about this theme.

SOCIAL JUSTICE

Today, many use social justice as a grand narrative. The theme emphasizes that God is a just God who demands that the nations construct just societies. God is on the side of the oppressed, the weak, and the neglected. God is against the strong and powerful. Typically, this approach builds upon liberation theology, assumes a benign soteriological universalism, is highly ecumenical, emphasizes the prophetic tradition of the Old Testament, and seeks to work in tandem with political systems to advance its cause.

Tangentially, many Christians who hold to the above approach have defined evangelism as spreading the good news of the kingdom. In this construct, kingdom and social justice are sister terms. In some progressive seminaries, the basic evangelism class has been named "God's *Shalom* and the Church's Witness." The course teaches that the work of evangelism brings the peace of God to suffering and marginalized people by fixing their victimization. This is the good news of the kingdom. *Shalom* is tied to a political theology with strong ties to Marxist analysis. *Shalom* seeks to convert the social order because it locates sin in systems that oppress. Salvation happens as people are freed from social oppression. Political intervention plays into this. In fact, it is impossible to achieve the goals of social justice or *shalom* without having political entanglements. The "social" in social justice shows that it focuses on society more than God. In fact, the goals of social justice can be pursued by conscientized people with or without the help of the church.

Often, social justice proponents personify corporate sin by identifying it with specific systems, issues, and races of people. Walter Wink's many books promote this approach.[6] Even though Wink uses the language of spiritual warfare to describe the systemic evil that inhabits cultures, governments, and systems of power, in continuity with the social justice approach, he emphasizes a materialistic (non-spiritual) approach to their eradication. Of note, he does not talk about individual demonization or territorial spirits.

---

6. Wink wrote *The Powers That Be, Naming the Powers, Engaging the Powers*, and *Unmasking the Powers*. Each uses the language of spiritual warfare to discuss the reality of structural sin and identify the corporate face of evil as it is manifested in society.

I agree with Wink when he uses the language of spiritual warfare to describe the problem of systemic sin and corporate evil because I believe that culture and social systems have been corrupted by the fall, can be animated by evil, and may perpetuate entrenched systems of injustice.[7] Since the fall, people and the societies they create have borne the image of sin. Undoubtedly, fallen people enable Satan's work. Conversely, those who have been transformed by the gospel positively influence the societies in which they live. McGavran refers to this as "redemption and lift."[8] In short, if you want the kingdom of God to impact a nation, you need to evangelize the people and grow them into the image of Christ.

I argue that God claimed America during the Second Great Awakening. In the aftermath, God radically altered the culture and faith of the American people. Since then, America has turned from God many times. Each time, God has answered by sending another revival of some sort. Based on past precedent, America is ready for another encounter with God.

The social justice metanarrative concerns me for four reasons. One, it minimizes the work of personal evangelism by deemphasizing the idea that individual sinners need to be personally saved by the grace of Jesus so that they can be transformed by the Spirit (Rom 3:23). Wink, liberation theologians, and those who push postcolonial approaches rarely talk about the need of individuals to be reconciled to God through Christ so they can live in harmony with him. Instead, sinners are turned into victims and identified with a preferential option without having to repent and be transformed into the image of God via a process of intense discipleship.

---

7. Wagner believes territorial spirits, nation gods, and spiritual strongholds may corrupt institutions and cultures (*Territorial Spirits*, 67–74). Under the heading "Territorial Dynasties," Otis has shown that spirits are attached to populations and regions. He emphasizes spiritual mapping to uncover the connections (*Twilight Labyrinth*, 199–229). Cahn theorizes that a society can be possessed by ruling spirits when it rejects God by aligning with one or more of the gods (*Return of the Gods*, 5–10).

8. McGavran acknowledges that "redemption and lift" is a sociological fact. After getting right with God and others, people alter their values and change their behavior. Drunks become resolute fathers and good workers. As the vices are transformed into virtues, the person experiences a social change. He becomes a new person in Christ and a productive human (*Understanding Church Growth*, 209–20). When large masses of people are simultaneously changed by a revival, a revitalization movement, or some other mass phenomenon, the social force transforms the culture. For example, Anthony Wallace classified Wesleyan Methodism as a "revitalization movement" (Wallace, "Revitalization Movements," 265). Elie Halevy argues that the evangelistic success of the Methodist revival in England prevented the nation from undergoing a revolution. For a critical review of Halevy's thesis, see Itzkin, "Halevy Thesis," 47–56.

What Is a Metanarrative?

Two, in the Bible, God is the paragon of justice. He is a just God and justice is a characteristic of God. The Bible models his justice. Ironically, many who advocate for the justice metanarrative have espoused ideas, behaviors, and sins that are difficult to reconcile with the witness of Scripture or the character of God. Does the teaching of the Bible misrepresent the justice or God? Or is there a disconnect between biblical justice and the social justice theme?

Three, it is difficult to distinguish between the politicking and preaching of those who hold to this metanarrative. Because the church and the political system work together for common social outcomes in the social justice approach, they are partners in the same fight (*la lucha*). Consequently, faith in Christ, orthodox theology, and personal holiness are less essential than right ideology and right activism. Additionally, anyone who identifies with the social justice cause can become an evangelist for it even if the person practices another faith or avows atheism. For this reason, it is not distinctively Christian.[9]

Four, Jesus did not try to realize the kingdom of God by fixing the Roman government or overturning the Jewish Sanhedrin. Rather, he sent the Holy Spirit to an empowered church so it would carry the seed of God's kingdom into every sphere of life. In the gospels, Jesus witnesses to the kingdom when he preaches, heals, saves, and delivers individuals. As he does, he leads repentant people into a personal encounter with a loving God. Jesus is the face of God and the bearer of God's kingdom. Regardless of their sociopolitical context, people are saved when they come to him by faith and live in a right relationship with him. In the New Testament, salvation is personal and always connects a person to Jesus. He invites the oppressed and the oppressor to be transformed by his love.

---

9. For a fuller reading, see "Spiritual Warfare Versus Social Justice" in Payne, *Satan Exposed*, 166–76. The chapter opines that the two approaches belong together.

4

Interpreting Scripture with the Missional Hermeneutic

PREVIOUS CHAPTERS EXPLORED VARIOUS approaches to interpreting the Bible. Each approach had merits and each presented cons. Since evangelicals emphasize a high view of Scripture and require their theology to be tightly tethered to a close reading of Scripture, they are uncomfortable with hermeneutical approaches that overemphasize the role of experience, reason, and culture because progressive theologians appeal to these elements when arguing against a normative or correct way to interpret the Bible. For example, James Brownson writes, "The missional hermeneutic I am advocating begins by affirming the reality and inevitability of plurality of interpretation. Because every reading of the Bible is shaped by the individuality and the historical and cultural particularity of the interpreter."[1] Yes, all theology is contextual theology, but all contextual theology is not equally correct. That is why one must affirm the orthodox faith.[2]

Likewise, some evangelicals are suspicious of creeds and a heavy reliance on church tradition, especially the Magisterium. Because of their unbending commitment to the primacy of Scripture, critics have accused evangelicals of bibliolatry—worshiping the book instead of the God behind the book. Suffice it to say, one can hold to a high view of Scripture while avoiding a cold literalism devoid of grace or a personal encounter with

---

1. Brownson, "Speaking the Truth in Love," 233.
2. Bevans, *Models of Contextual Theology*, 3.

God. Broadly, evangelicals affirm that the Bible is inspired, reveals God's character, points to his will, has moral authority, releases the Holy Spirit when read, communicates knowledge for salvation, and helps the church discern what God is doing. It is authoritative because it has a divine pedigree. After reading from the Bible on Sunday morning, some evangelical pastors say, "The word of God is powerful, reveals truth, and gives life to the one who hears it. Thanks be to his word."

Evangelicals who employ the missional hermeneutic affirm the above theology of Scripture. Also, in alignment with what Scripture teaches, the missio Dei asserts that God is moving history toward the telos he has portended in the Bible. Despite the fact some have appealed to the missional hermeneutic when advocating for positions that are not sustained by Scripture, evangelicals should employ the missional hermeneutic because it is compatible with Scripture, reveals the God behind the Scriptures, and uncovers the metanarrative of Scripture.

WHAT IS A HERMENEUTICAL COMMUNITY?

A hermeneutical community is a group of people who read and interpret the Bible with a similar set of assumptions and the same explanatory lens. Paul Hiebert uses the phrase to describe a homogeneous people, e.g., a tribe, village, or community who work together as they receive, interpret, and apply what the missionaries teach about the Christian faith.[3] The hermeneutical community shares the same culture, and its members are socially connected. Thembinkosi Mngad says that the local church in Africa is a hermeneutical community.[4] As a Roman Catholic priest who has experienced the cultural dissonance between his congregation and the European church, he contends that the local church must receive and contextualize the Latinized faith that is handed to them. For Roman Catholics, the faith includes Scripture and established tradition.

A hermeneutical community is a contextualizing community since all peoples must read the Bible in light of a lived condition. As was previously stated, experience and culture greatly influence how one approaches the hermeneutical task. August Tamawiwy shows the relationship between the hermeneutical community and the maintenance of a grand theme when he

---

3. Hiebert, *Anthropological Reflections*, 89–91.
4. Mngadi, "Local Church," 40.

says that the hermeneutical community interprets all narratives in view of a prevailing grand narrative.[5]

The New Testament church was a hermeneutical community that espoused a "fulfillment theology" as it read the Old Testament in light of the Christ event. The Emmaus Road encounter perfectly captures the New Testament's fulfillment hermeneutic. Jesus said, "'O foolish men, and slow of heart to believe all that the prophets have spoken! Was it not necessary that the Christ should suffer these things and enter into his glory?' And beginning with Moses and all the prophets, he interpreted to them in all the Scriptures the things concerning himself" (Luke 24:25–27 RSV). Jesus' sermon at Nazareth makes the same point. After reading Isa 61, Jesus told the people that the prophecy was about him and that he fulfilled it (Luke 4:21). Also, in Mark 12:36, Jesus quoted Ps 110:1 and said that he was the Lord of whom the Lord spoke.[6] In John, Jesus told the religious leaders that they studied the Scriptures but did not realize that the Scriptures testified about him (John 5:39). A few verses later, Jesus said that Moses wrote about him. John's version of the triumphal entry says that the disciples understood that the quoted prophecies were about Jesus (John 12:16). Even Satan applied Ps 91:11–12 to Jesus (Matt 4:6). Acts, the Pauline corpus, and Hebrews constantly say that Jesus fulfilled Old Testament prophecies or that Old Testament texts were about him.

When read from the perspective of the New Testament fulfillment hermeneutic, Zechariah uttered so many "Jesus" prophecies that it is hard to count them all.[7] The same goes for the Psalms and Second Isaiah. In short, New Testament writers were preoccupied with finding Christ in the text.[8] That is why they pull prophecies out of context and in a helter-skelter fashion apply them to Jesus.

The same fulfillment approach extends to John the Baptist. Jesus said he fulfilled what the Scriptures say about the return of Elijah (Mal 3:1, 23; and Matt 11:14). He is the promised messenger who would prepare the

---

5. Tamawiwy, "Foundation for a Culture of Justice," 62. The article argues that "just-peace" should be the all-inclusive narrative.

6. Mark follows the Septuagint by using a form of *kurios* in both parts. The Hebrew uses YHWH and *doni* (a variation of *Adoni*). Jesus implies that both terms refer to God.

7. See Stovall, "Messianic Prophecies."

8. Jews for Jesus published an article about finding Jesus in the pages of the Jewish Scriptures. It examines major prophetic themes that were fulfill by Jesus. It only analyzes fulfilled prophecies. Also, one should review the fifty-one references. See "Messianic Prophecy."

Interpreting Scripture with the Missional Hermeneutic

way for the Messiah (Mark 1:1–3, 7). For his part, John the Baptist said that Jesus fulfilled messianic expectations about the coming day of the Lord.

If Scripture is divinely inspired, one should encounter predictive prophecy because predictive prophecy authenticates Yahweh as the true God. Second Isaiah says, "New things I declare; before they spring into being I announce them to you" (Isa 42:9 NIV) and "I foretold the former things long ago, my mouth announced them and I made them known; then suddenly I acted, and they came to pass (Isa 48:3 NIV). In contrast, the *elohim* are false gods because they cannot predict the future (Isa 41:23). God can inspire predictive prophecy because he will fulfill what he foretells. Certainly, the prophets believed that the prophecies they wrote would be fulfilled. When the New Testament community read those prophecies in view of the Christ event, they contended that Christ was the fulfillment of them. That is, God acted in and through Christ to fulfill what he had predicted in the Old Testament.

G. Beale, a New Testament professor, sees continuity between the Old and New Testaments because his doctrine of interpretation affirms that God worked through Bible writers in the Old and New Testaments to communicate divine truth. He observes that Old Testament prophecies are like seeds that grow with time. Via the doctrine of progressive revelation, later writers apply the prophecies in ways that reflect the ongoing revelatory work of God.[9] For this reason, Beale does not discount the fulfillment hermeneutic. He opines, "I do not follow some postmodern understandings of intertextuality, which, for example, contend that later references to earlier texts interact in such a way that new meanings are produced that are completely unlinked and dislodged from the originally intended meaning of the earlier text."[10] Beale speaks about postmodern understandings because they greatly influence how scholars apply the historical-critical approach. For this reason, the fulfillment approach is mostly rejected by those who teach Old Testament exegesis.[11] Nonetheless, the New Testament shows that a prophecy that was connected to a specific event near the time of its writing can also have a later meaning, e.g., Isa 7:13–16.

The following anecdote demonstrates Beale's point. When I was a seminary student, I took a Second Isaiah course. For the final, I wrote a

---

9. Beale, *New Testament Biblical Theology*, 4.
10. Beale, *New Testament Biblical Theology*, 3.
11. To review current thought on intertextuality and literary criticism, see D'Angelo, "Rhetoric of Intertextuality."

lengthy exegesis paper on Isa 53. My paper included an original translation from Hebrew and used exegetical tools. The conclusion explained how the New Testament community preached Isa 53 and how the passage informed the church's kerygma and Christology. It is the "so what" or application part of biblical interpretation. Every biblical text has a history of interpretation or "afterlife." Biblical scholars refer to this as reception criticism. An exegetical paper is allowed to interact with it.

In the comments section of my paper, the professor scolded me because I referred to the New Testament when reading Jesus back into Isaiah. She said the Hebrew Scriptures did not point to Jesus, and one should not locate Jesus in those texts. She strongly emphasized that Isa 53 is not about Jesus. Because of my theological alignment with the standard teaching of the church, she gave me a low grade.

Theology says what the text means and how it connects to other doctrines. As a Christian, I read Isa 53 in continuity with the New Testament hermeneutical community. Furthermore, my theological convictions about Jesus colored my reading and application of the text. In the professor's mind, I had committed an egregious error by projecting Jesus onto the text. Ironically, her feedback revealed that she also projected her ideology onto the Scriptures.

WHAT IS THE MISSIONAL HERMENEUTIC?

According to J. D. Payne, the missional hermeneutic "is like a 'map,' that does not provide 'every tiny feature of a landscape,' but offers a way to see the entire biblical terrain and how to navigate it."[12] In this sense, the missional hermeneutic is a heuristic device that enables Christ's followers to read the metanarrative of the Bible in light of God's missional intentions, purposes that supremely swirl around Christ and his ongoing work. It affirms that the whole Bible points to the missio Dei and that God's mission is the central theme of the Bible. An excerpt on the back cover of *The Mission of God: Unlocking the Bible's Grand Narrative* expertly captures the notion of the missional hermeneutic when it states,

> Most Christians would agree that the Bible provides a basis for mission. But Christopher Wright boldly maintains that mission is bigger than that—there is in fact a missional basis for the Bible! The entire Bible is generated by and is all about God's mission. In

---

12. Payne, *Theology of Mission*, 1.

order to understand the Bible, we need a missional hermeneutic of the Bible, an interpretive perspective that is in tune with this great missional theme. We need to see the "big picture" of God's mission and how the familiar bits and pieces fit into the grand narrative of Scripture.[13]

When speaking of the missional hermeneutic, Boubakar Sanou says that the entire Bible reveals the various means by which God is seeking to redeem lost humanity.[14] He drives this point when he writes,

> Missional hermeneutics seeks to recover biblical interpretation from a mere creedal and academic reading of the Bible and refocus it on the missio Dei. As both the central interest and the unitive theme of the scriptural narrative. From this perspective, biblical interpreters will see in Scripture, as a whole, a missional thrust rather than having to focus only on the theme of mission in select texts.[15]

Stephen utilized this approach when he recounted the history of the Jews (Acts 7). His interpretation of sacred history shows that he and the leaders of the Jerusalem church read the Hebrew Scriptures from the perspective of the Christ event. I say this because Stephen reiterated what he had learned while studying at the feet of the apostles (Acts 2:42). Also, when Paul preached in Pisidian Antioch, his sermon recounted the salvation story of the Jews (Acts 13:13–41). Accordingly, God was working through the events of the Jews to bring them to a new reality in Christ. Paul concludes his sermon by saying, "And we bring you the good news that what God promised to the fathers, this he has fulfilled to us their children by raising Jesus" (Acts 13:32–33 RSV). From the perspective of the unfolding story, sacred history points to the crucifixion, resurrection, and the new reality that has come into existence through Jesus. In order to continue with God, the Jews must receive Christ and follow in the new way.

A grand narrative should begin with creation. Creation is important because it shows God's original intent and points to a culmination in which God's purposes will be restored. However, the time between the fall and the consummation preoccupies the thinking of those who employ the missional hermeneutic because the approach focuses on God's activity to overcome the fall and renew all things.

---

13. Wright, *Mission of God*, back cover.
14. Sanou, "Missio Dei," 308.
15. Sanou, "Missio Dei," 306.

The New Testament concurs with this line of thinking. It says that there was never a time in which God was not aware of the fall. From the beginning, he had a plan to fix the consequences of the fall. For example, Rev 13:8 declares that Jesus is the lamb of God who was slain before the foundation of the earth. Ephesians 1:4 says that God chose us in Christ before the foundations of the world. First Peter 1:19–20 refers to Jesus as a perfect lamb without blemish who was chosen to die for us before the world's creation.

In truth, God foresaw the inevitability of rebellion and the consequence of free choice. Before humankind rebelled, God had already enacted a plan to save them. That plan required that he enter the creation, become a human, and die a horrific death as the scapegoat in terms of the Day of Atonement typology that presages Jesus as the one who bears the sins of humankind (Lev 16). Isa 53 says the Suffering Servant is a sacrificial lamb, an offering for sin, and the one who bears their iniquities. John identifies Jesus as the suffering servant when he calls him the Lamb of God who takes away the sin of the world (John 1:29). Theologians call this substitutionary atonement.

Hugh Ross, a renowned astrophysicist, concludes that God created and designed this world so that he could have a suitable place to nurture humankind. The probability that Earth would be inhabitable and evolve sapient life without divine intervention is so minuscule that it is mathematically impossible. The scientific data validates this.[16] Furthermore, if life on Earth evolved per theories of natural evolution, one must assume that the entire universe teems with life. Yet, there is zero evidence that sapient life exists on any other planet in the universe. So, why does life exist on Earth? Answer: God created sapient life on Earth because he desired to have a relationship with humans.[17]

In this way, I extend the missio Dei to the earliest part of creation. Countering Deism's clock metaphor, God did not wind up the creation

---

16. See Ross, "Life on Other Planets" and "Evolutionary Probabilities" in *Lights in the Sky*, 33–54, and "Biblical Truth About ALIENS."

17. Allow me to be daring. This earth is not an accident of chance. It is a perfectly constructed biosphere that God created to make and sustain human life. Humans are not an instrumental means to a greater end. They are the purpose of creation. Furthermore, God's love for humankind is eternal. From the beginning of time, before there was a material creation, God saw humans. He also anticipated the decisions that they would make and the conflicts that would relate to the fall. For that reason, the Bible affirms that Jesus is the Lamb of God who was slain before the foundations of the earth.

and let it run on its own so he could see what would happen. He is not a disinterested cosmic designer who sculpted a universe so he could hang it on his wall and watch it develop. Rather, God is a relational Father who created humankind in his image because he wants to relate to people. History shows how the missionary God is working to accomplish his redemptive purposes. At a later point, those purposes will come to fruition.

Since God's love for people is eternal, when Adam and Eve fell, God did not abandon his children or change his purposes. Instead, he resolved to redeem them and their progeny. That is why he killed animals and used their skins as a covering to hide their nakedness (Gen 3:21). The act symbolizes God's desire to atone for their sins. By means of this protosacrifice, God pledged that he would redeem wayward people by becoming a sacrifice for them.

The actual text in Gen 3:21 does not say that the killing of the animals by which God provided the skins which became a covering (*kippur*) for Adam and Eve was a sacrifice. However, when one reads that passage in light of the redemptive work of Jesus on the cross, a Christian can come to that conclusion. This example shows the missional hermeneutic by reading the Old Testament in light of the Christ event and God's plan for salvation. The one Bible tells one major story.

Bluntly stated, when viewed from the perspective of God's missional plans, all the sacrifices of the Old Testament point to the cross and are completed by it (Heb 9:13—10:18). The sacrifice of Isaac by Abraham on Mount Moriah punctuates this idea. When Paul reads that God will provide for himself a lamb for a sacrifice, he automatically applies that to Jesus (Gen 22:8 and Rom 5:10).

In New Testament theology, Jesus is the scapegoat who carries the sins of the people outside the city when he is sacrificed on their behalf (Heb 9:7 and 13:12). Not only is Jesus the scapegoat; he is called the ransom (Mark 10:45, 1 Tim 2:5-6, 1 Pet 1:18-19, and Rev 5:9) and the kinsman redeemer.[18] That is why evangelicals affirm that the cross was not a tragic afterthought. Instead, it represents God's predetermined plan and was how God freed humankind from its bondage to sin, death, and Satan.[19] It is

---

18. Kinsman-redeemer designates a male relative who delivers or rescues a near relative who has been sold into slavery. He does this by paying the debt. A close relative has the right to redeem his kin from slavery. God is the Father of humanity and Jesus is our redeemer (Heb 2:16-18, and 4:14-16). For more information, see Bramer, "Kinsman-Redeemer," 456-57.

19. Payne, *Satan Exposed*, 136-39.

also why one can say that the animal skins that "covered" the nakedness of Adam and Eve were a protosacrifice.

USING THE MISSIONAL HERMENEUTIC

Decisively, the Bible shows how God has worked together in all things for the good of those who love him and those who are called according to his purposes (Rom 8:28). Paul refers to the called as the elect (Rom 8:33). Previously, I argued that the garden encounter between God and the serpent demonstrated that God intended to redeem humankind via the sacrifice of Jesus on the cross. From eternity God planned for Jesus to be the ransom by which he purchased humankind's freedom. In this regard, the cross was the summation of the sacrificial system in that all Jewish sacrifices found their satisfaction through Jesus' supreme sacrifice. He is the Seed of the Woman who crushed the head of the Serpent. The phrase is capitalized because it serves as a title for Christ. In the process, he was wounded.

Additionally, Jesus embodies the holy remnant of Israel and fulfills its missional calling. As was already noted, the metanarrative points to him. However, before the story could culminate in Jesus, God had to create the nation of Israel, and that nation had to remain faithful to God so his purposes could be accomplished through it (Exod 19:3–6). Deuteronomy states, "When the Most High gave to the nations their inheritance, when he separated the sons of men, he fixed the bounds of the peoples according to the number of the sons of God. For the Lord's portion is his people, Jacob his allotted heritage" (Deut 32:8–9 RSV).[20] In this sense, the picking of Israel entailed the temporary laying aside of the other nations.

Theologians call this the scandal of election. God did not pick Israel because Israel was better than the other nations. Rather, God picked Israel because his missional purposes required that he reveal himself to a nation and work through that nation to fulfill his mission. Whenever Israel slipped into sin and abandoned God, the Lord had to gather a holy remnant and reconstitute a faithful people.[21]

In Gen 12:3, God promises to bless the nations through Abraham. As Abraham's progeny, Jesus fulfilled this promise when he became the world's Savior. The promise runs through him. Yet, it cannot be completed while the nations are separated from God by sin and ignorance. According to the

20. See the Table of Nations in Genesis 10.
21. See Wright, *Paul in Fresh Perspective*, 119.

Interpreting Scripture with the Missional Hermeneutic

metanarrative, the promise to Abraham implies the Great Commission—a time when Jesus will send the church to make disciples of all nations (Matt 28:19). Even though Yahweh placed the nations under the stewardship of the *elohim* or nation gods (Deut 32:8–9 and Ps 82:1–4), he always intended to win them back to himself.[22] In some way, the church's evangelistic mission to the nations is how the *elohim* are dethroned. Nevertheless, as the missional plan goes forward, it goes through Israel. As such, the scandal of Israel's election should be evaluated in light of the eternal missio Dei as revealed in the New Testament and culminated in Jesus.

The inevitable conclusion of the missio Dei will be God's complete rule and reign over the nations. Per Tennent, "A 'whole Bible' perspective on the missio Dei reveals that while the final end or telos of the mission of God is fully present in seed form in the Abrahamic Covenant, it will not be fully realized until the eschaton."[23] When God revealed himself to Abraham, he entered into a covenant that was a prophetic foresight into the better covenant that was to be realized in Jesus (Heb 8:6–12). The Israelites advanced God's missional plan by introducing the world to Yahweh and laying the essential framework for the Messiah to be revealed.

USING THE METANARRATIVE TO INTERPRET THE JOSEPH AND MOSES STORIES

At this point, I will demonstrate how to use the missional hermeneutic to interpret the Joseph and Moses narratives.[24] As I look at the missional direction of the story, I must ask a question.[25] Why did God call Joseph and then cause him so much hardship? Answer: Even though Jacob and his family were situated in the promised land, they could not survive in it as a distinct nation dedicated to God because they were a numerically small people. If they had remained in that land, they would have sustained intense social contact with the Canaanite peoples including bride exchanges, joint business endeavors, and participation in cultural events. In time, they would have been assimilated into the existing social lattice. When that

---

22. Heiser, "Deuteronomy 32:8" 70.
23. Tennent, *Invitation to World Mission*, 123.
24. Payne, "How the Missional Hermeneutic," part 2.
25. See the section "The Missional Direction of the Story" in Hunsberger, "Proposals for a Missional Hermeneutic."

happened, they would have ceased to be God's special people (Lev 18:24–30).[26] The story of Esau demonstrates this. He compromised his identity when he married a Canaanite woman and interacted with the local people. Afterward, he and his descendants assimilated into the Canaanite world.

This concern is illustrated when the Jews began to return from Babylonian captivity. While in Babylon, the people intermingled with the nations and married their daughters. This diluted their Jewish identity and threatened to lead them into idolatry. For this reason, Ezra made them put away their foreign wives and rededicate themselves to their Jewish culture. As he read the Torah to them, they wept because they had forgotten it (Ezra 10:1–3).

So too, cultural assimilation threatened to destroy the Jewish witness when the Jews began to adopt the Greek culture in the time of the Maccabees. In particular, Jason the high priest tried to accelerate the process (2 Macc 4:7–22). The miracle-filled Jewish uprising freed the nation, purged Israel of Greek influences, and restored biblical Judaism.

The Bible says that during the time of Moses the Canaanites were wicked people who had defiled the land. They were so bad that the land wanted to vomit them out (Lev 18:24–26). They practiced the worst forms of idolatry. Also, the Jewish spies said that giants lived in Canaan (Josh 14:6–15). The giants point to genetic contamination from the Nephilim (Gen 6:1–4). So, for the Jews to fulfill God's purposes and fully occupy the promised land that God claimed for them (his portion), they had to leave Canaan and return to it once they were able to displace the nations who did not follow God. This was their "manifest destiny."

When God sent Joseph to Egypt via fraternal betrayal to prepare the way for his family and facilitate the move to Egypt, Joseph could not have imagined that God was working out his missional plan. After all, he was abandoned by his brothers, sold into slavery, and wrongly thrown into jail. But after God put Joseph in a position of power, God utilized a great famine to drive his family to the land of Goshen. When Joseph realized what God was doing, he told his brothers that they meant it for evil, but God intended

---

26. "For we have forsaken thy commandments, which thou didst command by thy servants the prophets, saying, 'The land which you are entering, to take possession of it, is a land unclean with the pollutions of the peoples of the lands, with their abominations which have filled it from end to end with their uncleanness. Therefore give not your daughters to their sons, neither take their daughters for your sons, and never seek their peace or prosperity, that you may be strong, and eat the good of the land, and leave it for an inheritance to your children for ever" (Ezra 9:10–12 RSV).

it for good (Gen 50:20). Furthermore, he knew that God would return them to the promised land at a future time. For that reason, he told them to take his bones with them when they returned (Gen 50:24–25).

The Jews were not assimilated in Egypt because they did not have routine social interactions with the Egyptians when they lived in the land of Goshen. Consequently, the land of Goshen became the womb of Israel. While in Goshen, the people grew into a large nation. Hundreds of years later, God was ready to birth the nation. To do that, he needed a deliverer to lead the people through the birth canal, i.e., a narrow opening in the Red Sea, and into the promised land. He picked Moses.

Previously, when Pharaoh was killing the baby boys, God saved baby Moses from the reeds and placed him in Pharaoh's home to prepare Moses for his mission. After Moses fled for his life, God caused him to learn pastoral skills while tending sheep in the wilderness because Moses would need to shepherd God's people. At the right time, God revealed his plan to Moses and worked through him to defeat the gods of Egypt, free the Hebrew people from slavery, and displace the Canaanites from the land of promise.[27] Up until the time that God revealed his purposes, Moses did not know that he was a part of God's master plan.

When viewed as individual stories, the narratives about Joseph and Moses do not fit together. However, when they are seen in light of the missional direction of the grand narrative, it is obvious that they participate in the same movement of God. They are two parts of the same story. The same process can be applied to the entire Bible.

CONCLUSION

This chapter has made a case for the missional hermeneutic. It flows from the missio Dei and is employed by the New Testament writers. It posits that God has a plan and that he is pursuing that plan. Both Scripture and salvation history reveal that plan. The telos has been divinely ordained. In time, God will undo the negative consequences of the fall and reestablish his perfect will. In this era, the church discerns what God is doing and attempts to join God in his work.

---

27. For a fuller understanding, see Blackaby and King, *Experiencing God*, 51.

5

Applying the Missional Hermeneutic to Acts

A PREVIOUS CHAPTER EXAMINED various hermeneutical approaches to Scripture interpretation before presenting the missional hermeneutic. Afterward, an application section applied the missional hermeneutic to the Joseph and Moses narratives. It demonstrated that they were two acts in the same story even though they were separated by hundreds of years. According to the presentation, God sent Joseph to Egypt to prepare the way for his family. When he became well placed through divine providence and dream interpretation, God used a famine to drive the children of Israel into Joseph's waiting arms because God did not want the Israelites to assimilate into the Canaanite populations. In Egypt, God settled the Hebrews in the land of Goshen so they would not have routine social interactions with the Egyptians. After the Israelites became a large people and were being badly persecuted, God raised up Moses to defeat the Egyptians and return the Hebrews to the promised land in accordance with his pledge to Abraham and his long-term purposes for Israel. Without the period of intense persecution, the Hebrews would not have left Egypt. During their forty-year perambulation en route to the promised land, God bonded the Hebrews to himself and taught them how to be his people so his missional purposes could flow through them.

Israel's national narrative can be read as a birth metaphor. God planted Joseph and his family as a seed into the womb of Goshen. After the fetus (the people) grew very large, it was ready to be delivered into the promised land. The Egyptian persecution caused the birth pangs that pushed the Hebrews through the birth canal (the parted sea). Moses was Israel's midwife. The forty years in the wilderness represents Israel's infancy. In this time, the Israelites learned to follow their God as a child follows its parent. For his part, God fed the Israelites, gave them water, preserved their clothing, protected them, guided them, disciplined them, and taught them his ways.[1]

The above history was central to Stephen's sermon before he was stoned (Acts 7:9–36). The Jews who listened to him did not object to his interpretation of Joseph and Moses because it was a standard retelling of the national narrative. Rather, they rejected his contention that they murdered the Messiah—the fulfillment of God's plan for Israel and the climax of their collective story (Acts 7:52). In Stephen's retelling, the history of Israel pointed to Jesus and focused on him. The sermons in Acts also preach a fulfillment theology about Jesus (Acts 3:15, 7:17, 13:33, and 26:7). Jesus is the Root of Jesse, the Messiah, the fulfillment of God's plans, and the Savior of the world. In this way, Jesus is the culmination of the Jewish metanarrative.[2]

Succinctly, the missional hermeneutic says that God has a plan and is always working toward that plan (Ps 33:11). From a single point in time, God's plan may not be clear. Yet, when the larger story is assessed diachronically, God's missional purposes can be seen.

INTRODUCTION TO ACTS

In the same way that a former chapter applied the missional hermeneutic to the Joseph and Moses narratives, this chapter applies the missional hermeneutic to Acts. Internally, the Book of Acts is structured around the church's movement from Jerusalem to the ends of the earth (Acts 1:8).[3] As the church crosses cultural and geographic boundaries, it expands the reach of the gospel. However, crossing the ensuing barriers challenges the theology and identity of the Jewish believers who compose the Jerusalem church. Ultimately, multiethnic mission triggers an internal struggle between Jewish

---

1. Avnery applies the birth metaphor to Joseph, Moses, and the Exodus in "Pesach is Literally the Story."

2. For a scholarly review of Stephen's sermon, see Scobie, "Origins and Development," 391–99.

3. Hertig and Gallagher, "Introduction," 8–9; Keener, *Acts*, 575; and Scobie, "Origins and Development," 390.

believers who hold to their ethnic privilege as the chosen people, the ones to whom the promises of God were made, and Jewish believers who envision one church composed of multiple populations, a church in which faith in Christ makes one an heir of God's promises.

The first group (the Judaizers) insisted that Jewish believers separate themselves from gentile believers (Gal 2:12). The Judaizers are called the "circumcision party," or those who come from James. Furthermore, they demanded that Jewish believers practice Torah as the reconstituted messianic community that is awaiting the return of the Messiah and his literal reign in Jerusalem. Keeping the law was essential to their identity as Jewish believers (Acts 21:21). Before the great persecution pushed the church into global missions, all the believers were observant Jews. Most worshiped at the temple (Acts 8:1).[4]

The controversy that the gentile mission caused precipitated the Jerusalem Council in Acts 15. According to Acts, the circumcised party was teaching the gentile believers that they had to get circumcised to be saved.[5] Paul became so angry with the Jewish believers who insisted on preaching the law to the gentiles that he accused them of preaching a false gospel. He said that they were accursed because they perverted the gospel of Christ (Gal 1:6–9). In fact, he wished that they would mutilate themselves (Gal 5:12).

The council sided with Paul when it ruled that gentile believers did not have to become Jews or keep the law to be disciples because they were saved by faith in Christ. However, they needed to observe a purity code: abstain from food offered to idols, avoid blood, do not eat strangled animals, and reject all forms of sexual immorality (Acts 15:29). It also said that Jews were not saved by keeping the law (Acts 15:11). In the aftermath, Paul styled himself the "apostle to the gentiles" (Gal 2:7–10).

Even though the Judaizers accepted the council's verdict, they rejected Paul's application of it because he did not separate the Jewish believers from the gentile believers in his evangelistic mission. If Paul had preached only to gentiles, the Judaizers would have left him alone in accordance with the

---

4. Lietzmann, *History of the Early Church*, 63.

5. Lietzmann identifies this mindset with Ps 17: "In the reconstituted kingdom, only Israel shall dwell—no heathen, no Greeks, no Samaritans; and this Israel shall not tolerate within itself sinners or half-Greeks. All shall be pure and holy, and live a happy life according to God's will under the righteous and holy Messianic king" (*History of the Early Church*, 28). For this reason, if gentiles want to enter the messianic kingdom they must become Jews.

council's mandate. However, Paul's mission took him to the Hellenistic synagogues. After preaching to Jews, proselytes, and gentile Godfearers, he would form all who believed into one church (Acts 17:1–5). The Jewish members of the new church were not required to keep the law. In fact, the church's fellowship was compromised when some kept the law and others did not.

Pointedly, Paul said that one who comes to Christ in faith is freed from the law and its demands because the law was fulfilled in Jesus (Rom 7:1–6, 25; 8:1–4; 10:4; Gal 5:1). He calls the law a curse (Gal 3:13). Furthermore, no one can be made right with God by keeping the law (Gal 2:15). Because of this, in the postresurrection period, Paul taught that there was no reason to separate Jewish believers who kept the law from gentile believers who did not keep the law. All were saved by grace through faith. No one was saved by keeping the law (Eph 2:8–9).

The implications of Paul's theology are far reaching. According to him, in Christ, the categories of Jew and gentile do not exist. Furthermore, all who believe in Jesus are Abraham's seed and heirs of the same promises (Rom 11:17, Gal 3:28–29, Col 3:11). For this reason, it is a sin against Christ and his body to segregate Jewish believers from gentile believers because Christ has destroyed the wall that separated Jews from gentiles through his death on the cross (Eph 2:11–16).

The leaders of the Jerusalem church disagreed with Paul's theology. "You see, brother, how many thousands there are among the Jews of those who have believed; they are all zealous for the law, and they have been told about you that you teach all the Jews who are among the Gentiles to forsake Moses, telling them not to circumcise their children or observe the customs. What then is to be done?" (Acts 21:20–21 RSV).

The continuing conflict between the Judaizers and those who envisioned a global mission is played out in Acts and the epistles. Despite the conflict, the New Testament church went from Jerusalem to the ends of the earth. Specifically, Acts shows how the New Testament church slowly enlarged its vision as it evangelized ethnic Jews, Hellenistic Jews, Samaritans, Ethiopian Jews, Godfearing gentiles, pagan Greeks, and the heart of the Roman Empire. Whenever the church traversed a socioreligious barrier, God displayed his approbation via miracles, divine intervention, or the giving of the Holy Spirit so Judaizers would not impede God's forward-moving mission.

ACTS 1:1—7:60 — JERUSALEM

During their apprenticeship years with Jesus, the apostles did not comprehend that he had to die on the cross to ransom humankind and atone for their sins per the Day of Atonement symbolism (Lev 16). Since he was the Messiah, they simply imagined that Jesus would claim the throne of David in Jerusalem and judge the world (Ps 2; Isa 11:12; Ezek 37:19–28; Dan 7:13–14; Mic 5:2; Zech 9:9, 12:10; 1 En 46:1–4, 48:2–7, 69:26–29; and 2 Esd 7:28–29, 12:31–34, 13:32).[6] For example, when Jesus told the Jews that he would be lifted up to heaven, they said that the Messiah must remain on earth forever (John 12:34). Peter told Jesus that he could not die after he confessed that Jesus was the Christ, the Son of the living God, because he thought Jesus would reign in Jerusalem (Matt 16:22). As Jesus was entering Jerusalem before Passover, James and John asked Jesus if they could sit at his right and left when he was inaugurated as the Messiah in the soon to be realized kingdom of God (Mark 10:37). Jesus' triumphal entry into Jerusalem showed that the Galilean Jews who had witnessed Jesus' miracles also believed that Jesus would establish his kingdom at that time (Matt 21:11). Previously, they wanted to take him by force and make him king (John 6:15). Like John the Baptist, they expected that Jesus would bring in the day of the Lord, judge the wicked, save the righteous, and inaugurate God's kingdom on earth (Isa 2:10–22; Ezek 13:5–23, 30:3–26; and Matt 11:2–6).[7]

---

6. Jewish expectations about the messiah and the coming messianic kingdom during the time of Jesus were greatly influenced by Second Temple literature that is not included in the Hebrew Scriptures. The Maccabean revolt played into their imagination. In the same way that God raised up the Maccabees to deliver pious Jews from the Greek tyranny, many Jews expected God to raise up a messiah to deliver them from the Roman occupation. The messiah figure would be religious and political. He would have divine characteristics and establish the kingdom of God. The literature from Qumran also saw the messiah as an eschatological figure who engages in spiritual warfare. Some imagined that there would be two messiahs, a political one and a priestly one. See Schiffman, "Concept of the Messiah," 235–46.

7. According to Treven Hatch, first-century BC Jews believed that the messiah would be a premortal divine figure, all people would worship him, he would be a king, he would reestablish the Davidic dynasty, his kingdom would be everlasting, he would have authority over all nations, he would lead Israel, he would judge the wicked, he would overthrow Israel's foreign enemies, and he would establish righteousness ("Messianism and Jewish Messiahs," 51–65). After examining all the "messianic texts" in the Hebrew Scriptures, Robert Jones derived the following characteristics about the messiah: The messiah will come out of Judah. He'll battle with Satan (the serpent). He'll have both priestly and kingly roles. The messiah will be a redeemer and will live on earth. The messiah is God's Son. The messiah is divine. The messiah will suffer at the hands of his

After the crucifixion, the crestfallen disciples who met Jesus on the road to Emmaus were overwhelmed with disappointment because they believed that Jesus was going to redeem Israel (Luke 24:13–35).

When the resurrected Christ met with the apostles in Acts 1, the disciples believed that Jesus would establish the kingdom at that time (Acts 1:6). Now that they were ransomed, their sins were atoned, and Jesus was glorified they wanted to know if Jesus would "finally" restore the kingdom to Israel, reign in Jerusalem, and bring about the literal kingdom of God. In their minds, everything was ready for what John had preached and they expected.

Even though Jesus did not say when he would return, the early Christians believed he would return quickly. Most thought that he would come during their lifetimes. Because of that expectation, dying before Christ returned caused concerns (1 Thess 4:13 and 1 Cor 15).

In Acts 1–7, the apostles did not have a vision for the evangelization of the nations as commanded in Matt 28:19–20 and Acts 1:8 because they were focused on the return of Christ and the reconstitution of the messianic community of Jews in Jerusalem.[8] For these reasons, they remained in Jerusalem and waited for Jesus' return. That is why they felt compelled to replace Judas Iscariot (Acts 1:21). There had to be twelve apostles when Jesus returned because the apostles would sit on twelve thrones judging the twelve tribes of Israel (Matt 19:28).

Preparing for the second coming of Christ and his subsequent reign in Jerusalem became a primary focus of the Jerusalem church. For example, after Peter preached to the gathered crowd of global Jews on the day of Pentecost, three thousand new believers united with the Jerusalem

---

detractors. The priestly authority of the messiah is through the order of Melchizedek, not through the Levites. The messiah will be rejected by some of his own people. The messiah will be the final judge (and thus will be part of the end times). The messiah will bring peace to believers and a sword to nonbelievers. The messiah will usher in a new era of peace and tranquility. The divine messiah will become incarnate via a virgin-birth. He will reign on David's throne forever. He will be preceded by a messenger (Elijah, according to Malachi). He will bring salvation to the gentiles. He will bear the sins of many (and will be severely persecuted for his efforts). He will perform miracles. He existed before becoming incarnate. He will come up out of Egypt (*Messiah*, 14–15).

8. Martin contends that the hermeneutics of the apostles were changed by their encounter with the resurrected Jesus, the gift of the Holy Spirit, the evangelistic mission, and the eschatological nature of Jesus' kingdom ("Introduction to Pentecostal Biblical Hermeneutics," 2). The eschatological nature related to their belief that they were in the end times and they were going to witness the fulfillment of the prophecies about the regathering and salvation of Israel (Acts 2:17).

church (Acts 2:5–11). These Jews were from all the countries where the Lord had driven their ancestors. The apostles believed that their return to Jerusalem and their acceptance of the Messiah was the fulfillment of prophecy that presaged the return of Christ (Isa 11:11–12; Jer 8:3, 28:3–8, 30:10, 31:8, and 32:37).

Joseph Lynch summarizes Peter's Pentecost sermon in Acts 2:

> The final age has begun, ushered in by Jesus' ministry, death, and resurrection, of which the Jewish-Christian preacher Peter gave a brief account, accompanied by references to the Jewish Scriptures to show that all happened through the "foreknowledge of God." . . . Peter said that Jesus would return soon to end the present age in a judgment. In the period of waiting, the Jewish-Christians interpreted their prophecies, visions, and speaking in tongues as signs that Jesus' Holy Spirit was active among them.[9]

In Acts 2–6, while the disciples waited for Jesus' return, they evangelized Jerusalem by teaching, witnessing, doing miracles, and praying in the temple courts (Acts 5:42). Power evangelism was a major way by which the church witnessed to Jesus and made new converts.[10] For example, as the people saw the extraordinary miracles that the apostles performed, larger numbers of Jews turned to Jesus (Acts 5:14). After Peter healed the lame man at the Beautiful Gate, multitudes were filled with wonder and amazement (Acts 3:9). Because of it, about five thousand believed (Acts 4:1). Acts says that the people were filled with awe and wonder because of the signs and miracles that the apostles did in the name of Jesus (Acts 2:42–44, and 5:12–16).

The religious leaders began a campaign of intimidation and persecution to hinder the work of the apostles and keep the people from turning to Jesus (Acts 4:1–22; 5:17–20, 40; and 6:8–15). Amid persecution, the church prayed for God to heal and do more signs and wonders through the disciples. God affirmed their prayer by shaking the place where they were praying. Afterward, the enthused believers went forth and preached the word of God boldly (Acts 4:30–31). In Acts, preaching is an evangelism verb. For example, after an angel released the apostles from jail, he commanded them to enter the temple and preach (Acts 5:17–20).

As growing numbers of Hellenistic Jews accepted Christ, the Jerusalem church experienced explosive growth. To sustain the growing numbers, the

---

9. Lynch, *Early Christianity*, 39.

10. Wimber coined the term "power evangelism" (Wimber and Spring, *Power Evangelism*, 25–29).

new believers sold their property and gave the money to the apostles (Acts 4:34–35). After doing this, they had everything in common and lived as an extended family like the disciples did while itinerating with Jesus (Acts 2:44–46). This is how the church provided for everyone who was waiting in Jerusalem for the return of Christ.

Because of the delayed second coming (*parousia*), the economic system could not sustain the growing demands. By today's standards, it would be called a pyramid scheme. At one point, the Hellenists complained that their widows were not being fed properly. The complaint points to internal concern regarding the church's ability to feed the growing numbers of global Jews who were not working. To deal with the problem, the apostles appointed seven deacons to administer the church's temporal affairs (Acts 6:1–7). All had Greek names. Later, Paul stipulated that people must work to take food from the community (2 Thess 3:10–13). Paul states that anyone who does not provide for the material needs of his relatives has denied the faith (1 Thess 5:4–8).

ACTS 2 — BAPTISM IN THE HOLY SPIRIT

In Acts 1:4–8, Jesus told the disciples that they needed to be baptized with the Holy Spirit. Baptism with the Spirit would enable them to witness to Jesus from Jerusalem to the ends of the earth. In fact, until they received the baptism of the Spirit, Jesus commanded them to remain in Jerusalem. After three years of sitting at Jesus' feet, they knew a lot. Nonetheless, they still needed Spirit baptism to work effectively for God. The baptism would give them a dispensation of grace so they could preach, evangelize, do miracles, prophesy, teach, and administer the church through the power of the Spirit. Previously, they operated in the Spirit through their proximity to Jesus as extensions of Christ. After Jesus ascended, they needed to be anointed by the Spirit in the same way that Jesus was anointed at his baptism.

Being "filled with the Holy Spirit" (Eph 5:18) and the baptism with the Holy Spirit refer to the same thing. Often, Paul reminds the church that the Spirit dwells in them and that they are the temple of God (Rom 8:9; 1 Cor 3:16, 6:19; and Eph 2:22). However, some baptized believers did not receive Spirit baptism when they believed. For example, the Samaritan believers did not receive Spirit baptism until Peter and John came to them (Acts 8:36). Also in Corinth, Paul and Apollos encountered some disciples who had not received the Holy Spirit until Paul laid his hands on them (Acts 19:1–6).

What does baptism in the Spirit mean? In Greek, baptism has two foci. First, baptism symbolizes a rite of passage. For example, before the crucifixion, Jesus asked James and John if they could be baptized with the baptism by which he was about to be baptized (Mark 10:39). Through the crucifixion, Jesus satisfied the Father's work and moved from his human state to his glorified state. In this way, the crucifixion was a rite of passage that shifted Jesus from one standing to another. Also, 1 Cor 10:1–2 says the Israelites were baptized as they entered the cloud, ate the manna, drank water from the rock, and passed through the parted sea even though they never got wet. When they went through the sea, they died to their old life in Egypt and entered a new relationship with God. As they passed between the waters, God covered them with his outstretched arms and claimed them as his own people. The baptism in the wilderness disassociated the Israelites from Egypt by identifying them with God and his servant Moses. The Letter to the Hebrews uses Egypt as a typology for sin (3:14—4:11). Accordingly, when the Israelites left Egypt, they were baptized and died to sin.

Christian baptism is also a rite of passage. Besides being an initiation into the church, it symbolizes the process by which a new believer dies to the old way of life so the person can become a new creature in Christ (2 Cor 5:17). The Didache[11] describes two ways. One is the way of death, which is under the power of the flesh. Sin dominates this way. The other is the way of life, which is under the transforming power of grace. Through baptism, the new believer leaves the way of darkness and enters the way of life.[12]

Around AD 200, baptism clearly emphasized the rite of passage. After forty days of fasting, those being baptized would confess the Christian faith, be anointed with oil, renounce Satan, take off their old clothes, and enter the water. They would be immersed three times. When they emerged on the other side, they were clothed in a new white robe to symbolize their new identity in Christ. Afterward, they celebrated communion for the first time.[13]

---

11. The Didache was a manual for church discipline and theology that dates to AD 70.

12. As early Christianity became Roman, the processes related to the catechism, the baptism ritual, and the sacred meal were influenced by the Greek mystery religions that prospered during the first three centuries AD. See Fai and Olagunju, "Mystery Religions," 89–95.

13. Jensen, *Baptismal Imagery in Early Christianity*, 165–73. For a contrasting view on nude baptism, see Guy, "Naked Baptism in the Early Church," 141. See also Case, "Christianity and the Mystery Religions," 9.

While living in Japan, I evangelized a woman who converted from Zen Buddhism. Her conversion experience was intense and prolonged. She cried as she received the grace of Jesus. On the day of her baptism, she went into the dressing room to put on her white baptism robe. However, when she exited, she was holding her robe. When I asked her why she was not wearing her robe, she told me that she did not want anything to separate her from the baptismal waters because she needed all her sins to be washed away. Even though I did not accommodate her wish, it reflected the early church's thinking and was a natural thought for a Japanese convert who came out of Buddhism.

While pastoring a Cuban refugee camp in Panama from 1994 through 1995, I baptized countless people in a coffin-shaped box constructed from wood. On the day I did baptisms, the church participants would fill it with water one cup at a time. It took hours to fill the baptistry because the water spigot was one hundred yards away. Often, I baptized fifteen people in the same water. When I finished, the water would look very brown because we lived in dirt. Once, I apologized to a group of men at the end of the line because they had to get submerged in the dirty water. I will never forget their response to me: "Don't worry, pastor. The dirty water shows that God is washing away our sins and making us new people." For them, the dirt in the water symbolized the spiritual cleansing of their souls.

According to Paul, baptism symbolizes three things: dying to the flesh and its sinful proclivities, being reborn into Christ, and receiving new life in the Spirit. The image of taking off the old and putting on the new is central to Paul's teaching (Gal 3:26–27, and Eph 4:22–24). In Romans he says that believers are buried with Christ through baptism into death so they may live a new life (6:4). He also says believers are buried with Christ in baptism so they can be raised up with Christ to new life via faith (Col 2:12).[14]

The second meaning of baptism is more literal. It relates to physical cleansing or the ceremonial washing of articles (*netilat yadayim*). In Mark 7:1–5, some Pharisees complained that Jesus' disciples defiled themselves by eating with unwashed hands. In his commentary, Mark says that the Jews do not eat when they come from the marketplace unless they purify (baptize) themselves (Mark 7:4). In the same way that circumcising the heart is more important than circumcising the flesh (Rom 2:25–29), Jesus teaches that the purifying of the heart is more important than the washing of the external body (Mark 7:14–15).

---

14. Lietzmann, *History of the Early Church*, 120–21.

The washing tradition harkens back to Exodus when God told Moses to put a wash basin in the tabernacle so the priests could cleanse their hands and feet before coming near the altar to minister (Exod 30:17–21). It symbolized purification. Later tradition extended this rule to the people before they ate. So in Mark 7:4, baptism refers to washing hands and feet, not immersing the body. That does not mean that ritual immersion (*tevilah*) did not exist. For example, one had to have a ceremonial immersion after encountering certain contaminants, before Yom Kippur, and when converting to Judaism. Naaman is an example. When he wanted to be cleaned from his leprosy, he had to "baptize" himself in the Jordan River seven times (2 Kgs 7:14 LXX).

The baptizing of John connects to the above meaning. As the people came to him, he called them to repent of their sins so they could be ready for the Messiah and enter his kingdom (Matt 3:6). The external washing of the body in the Jordan River was a *tevilah* that represented purification and renunciation of sin. It was the removal of the stained garments so one could enter the wedding banquet (Matt 22:11–13). Without moral purification, people will not be able to enter God's kingdom when the Messiah comes.[15]

On the other hand, even though Jesus was baptized in water like the others, he did not repent and was not cleansed by his *tevilah*. Rather, he was filled with the Holy Spirit, commissioned for his ministry, and presented as the Son of God. The filling also empowered Jesus to do the work for which the Father had called him (Matt 3:13–17). The empowering was necessary because Jesus emptied himself when he was incarnated so he could live like a human (Phil 2:7). Like any person called and commissioned by God, Jesus needed to be filled with the Spirit. Unlike the disciples on the day of Pentecost, Jesus was given the Spirit without limits (John 3:34). In this way, Jesus' baptism connects to the Spirit baptism of the believers on the day of Pentecost.

ACTS 8:1–4 — THE SCATTERING OF THE CHURCH

After the stoning of Stephen, a great persecution arose against the Jerusalem church. Consequently, the believers scattered (Acts 8:1). Presumably, the fleeing believers returned to the places from which they came since they had familial and social connections in those places. Acts 2 says that the first believers were from Iran, Persia, Elam, Mesopotamia, Judea, Cappadocia, Pontus, Asia Minor, Phrygia, Pamphylia, Egypt, Libya, Cyrene, Rome,

---

15. Lietzmann, *History of the Early Church*, 39–44.

Crete, and Arabia. They were Jews who had come to Jerusalem for the feast of Pentecost. When they received Jesus as their Messiah, they joined the Jerusalem church. Between chapters 2 and 6, more Jews joined the Jerusalem church. It is possible that Hellenistic Jews from every part of the world were attached to the Jerusalem church when the persecution started.

As the Jewish believers dispersed, they preached the gospel (Acts 11:19). In essence, the persecution created an impromptu army of missionaries who seeded the world with the gospel. Before the persecution, the church grew by assimilating Jews into the Jerusalem church (centripetal mission). Afterward, the church grew by taking the gospel to the world and planting churches in the places where the people lived (centrifugal mission).[16] The mission to the Gentiles would not have happened if the church would have remained focused on the mission to the Jews in Jerusalem.

From the beginning, Christ told the church to take the gospel to the world.[17] Yet the believers ignored that commission while they remained in Jerusalem waiting for the reconstituting of the Jewish nation, the second coming of Christ, and the establishment of the messianic kingdom in Jerusalem.[18] Why did God allow that to happen? From the perspective of the scattering, the answer is clear.

Between chapters 2 and 6, the believers sat at the apostles' feet, devoted themselves to the apostles' teaching, and watched the apostles do signs and wonders (Acts 2:42–47). During this time, they absorbed the Christian ethos and learned how the local church should function. More importantly, they learned how to share the gospel by watching the apostles preach in the temple courts. Throughout the week, the apostles taught the believers what Jesus had taught them. Through this, the new believers became fully aware of the gospel content and became mature disciples who were equipped to take the church to new places. Without this "boot camp" period of spiritual formation and training, the church would not have been prepared to fulfill Christ's call to evangelize the nations.

---

16. For a scholarly treatise on centripetal and centrifugal mission approaches, see Matacio, "Centripetal and 'Centrifugal' Mission," 31–42.

17. One could argue that the missionary commissions in the Synoptic Gospels came after Acts was written and were placed in the Gospels because of the ensuing gentile mission. If that is the case, the protocommission came in Acts 1:8 when Jesus directed the apostles to be his witnesses to the ends of the earth. In either case, the global mission to the Jews and gentiles was authored and directed by Jesus.

18. Case, "Christianity and the Mystery Religions," 6.

Some might ask if God caused the persecution. This is a fair question. As has already been shown, God drove Jacob and his family to Egypt so he could grow them into a large people. At the right time, he sent them back to Canaan so they could establish themselves as God's covenant people in the promised land. Without the persecution from the taskmasters, the Hebrew people would not have left Egypt. Similarly, God used nations to judge the Israelites. Also, the residents of Judah were taken to Babylon as a punishment for sin. During the long years of exile, much of the Old Testament was written and the people learned how to be God's special people. When the renewed Jews returned to Jerusalem, they were a holy remnant prepared to do God's work. Additionally, the persecution that led to the Maccabean revolt and the reconstituting of a dedicated Jewish people kept the Jews from being assimilated into Greek culture. Biblical Judaism would have disappeared if the great struggle against compromising Jews and the forces of Hellenism had not occurred.

The above examples show that God worked through hardship and persecution to push his mission forward. They do not say that God caused the suffering. Scripture avers that Satan wanted to corrupt or destroy Israel to sabotage God's missional plans. Joseph's theology is helpful. When he was making sense of his misfortune, he told his brothers that they meant it for evil, but God used it for good (Gen 50:20). In other words, God does not cause evil, but he works through it to bring about his good. This approach to theodicy fits with the missional hermeneutic.

In sum, a missional reading of the text shows that God brought the Jews to Jerusalem to make them disciples. When the number of well-trained disciples reached a critical mass, God used the persecution to drive the disciples into the world as his witnesses following his commandment in Acts 1:8. Ultimately, it does not matter if God caused the persecution of the church, or he worked through the persecution to accomplish his will. Rather, Acts 2–8:1 shows that God worked in tangible ways to push forward his mission. This is the big picture that the metanarrative affirms.

ACTS 8:5-25 — THE SAMARITAN MISSION

After the scattering, in accordance with the "Jerusalem, Judah, Samaria, and to the ends of the earth" outline, Acts focuses on Samaria. Samaria was next in line because it was a quasi-Jewish population with strong connections to the ten northern tribes of Israel. Notwithstanding, the intense

Applying the Missional Hermeneutic to Acts

conflict between Jews and Samaritans should have predisposed the fleeing Jewish believers to avoid Samaria. Inexplicably, Phillip went to Samaria. After his ministry in Samaria, Acts states that an angel told him to go down the "desert road" (Acts 8:26). One wonders if God also directed Phillip to go to Samaria. Charles Scobie argues that Phillip went to Samaria because he was associated with that group. Scobie believes that Samaritans had an oversized influence on the early church.[19]

Who were the Samaritans? After King Solomon died, the northern tribes separated from the temple in Jerusalem because Israel split from Judah. To keep the northern Yahweh-worshipers from orienting themselves to Jerusalem, King Jeroboam built altars with golden calf idols in Bethel and Dan so the Israelites in the North would not go to Jerusalem. When King Omri made the city of Samaria his capital, the northern kingdom was called Samaria (1 Kgs 16:23–24). Sadly, apart from Jehu, all the northern kings were evil in the sight of God because they constantly flirted with foreign gods and led the people into sin (2 Kgs 12–17).

Because of Samaria's sins, God said that he would destroy it (Isa 10:11–21, Hos 13:16, and Mic 1:6–7). God used Assyria as his agent of judgment. In 722 BC, Sargon II and Sennacherib decimated the northern kingdom and carried away a small percentage of the population (10 to 20 percent).[20] The common people were mostly ignored. First Chronicles 5:26 says Reuben, Gad, and the half-tribe of Manasseh were carried away. Many Yahweh-worshipers remained in Samaria after the resettlement of the elite. As a testament to their religious heritage, around 450 BC, the Samaritans built a temple on Mount Gerizim and dedicated it to Yahweh. This may have come in response to the building of the Second Temple in Jerusalem.

The Samaritan Yahweh-worshipers continued following the Torah even though they did not worship in Jerusalem or accept the Prophets and Writings in the Jewish Tanak. Unfortunately, the Samaritan priesthood was compromised by Jeroboam after he appointed non-Levites to be priests in the shrines that served his golden calves (1 Kgs 12:31).[21] When the Jews returned from Babylon, the Samaritans attempted to sabotage their efforts to rebuild Jerusalem and the temple (Ezra 4:10 and Neh 4:2). This embittered the Jews to the Samaritans. Most Jews of Jesus' time believed that the Samaritans

---

19. Scobie, "Origins and Development," 400–401.
20. Knoppers, *Jews and Samaritans*, 18–44 and Radner, "'Lost Tribes of Israel,'" 122–23.
21. Montgomery, *Samaritans*, 17–34.

were a genetically compromised people who had abandoned God. Like half-brothers who had betrayed the family, the Jews despised them.

Jesus' disciples shared this prejudice. For example, when the Samaritans would not supply food to Jesus and his followers because they were going to Jerusalem, James and John wanted to call down fire on them. After nicknaming them the Sons of Thunder (Mark 3:17), Jesus rebuked them (Luke 9:50–55). Obviously, the Samaritans equally disdained the Jews.

The evangelization of the Samaritan woman at the well showed that Jesus did not partake in the hostility (John 4:1–42). During her conversation with Jesus, the Samaritan woman referred to "our father Jacob." The inviting comment pointed to a common ancestor and confirmed that she still identified with her "Israel" roots. When the woman tried to take the conversation in a combative direction, Jesus did not debate about Jerusalem and Mount Gerizim. Instead, he said that the location of worship does not matter because true believers worship God in Spirit and truth (John 4:23). This comment indicated that Jesus would accept the Samaritan woman as a true worshiper of God if she met his conditions. The comment also decentralized the temple cult in Jerusalem. Because of her testimony, Jesus evangelized the Samaritan village where she lived. During his time in her village, Jesus intermingled with the Samaritans and treated them like covenant people. His actions showed the Father's heart.

The people in the unnamed Samaritan village to which Phillip went were under the control of Simon the Magician. Acts calls him a magus. He must have been a potent shaman because the Samaritans branded him "the great power of God" (Acts 8:10). Simon amazed them with his magic. All the people were under his spell until Phillip proclaimed Jesus to them. When Phillip preached, great miracles confirmed that he had more power than Simon the Magician. Acts reports that demons shrieked when Phillip commanded them to leave, and disabled people were healed. Upon witnessing Phillip's power ministry, the Samaritans rejoiced. In the aftermath, the people accepted Christ and were baptized. Phillip was so convincing that Simon the Magician even accepted baptism.

The conversion of the Samaritan city exemplifies power encounter.[22] When people are under the rule of a local spirit or god, they cannot be converted by reason, apologetics, or conviction because they fear that the controlling spirit will punish those who challenge it. For animists,

---

22. For more information on power encounter, see Kraft, *Power Encounter in Spiritual Warfare*, 1–14.

religion is not a matter of truth; it is about power. Usually, a shaman or a group of religious specialists represent the ruling spirit. They receive messages from the spirit, invoke curses, bless babies, and perform miracles in the spirit's name. Idols, fetishes, sacred places, and rituals bind the people to the local deities.

In many ways, missionary Heidi Baker is like Phillip the Evangelist or one of the apostles when she does power evangelism. As she salts Mozambique with Jesus' love, she boldly preaches the gospel, does miracles, and runs a massive ministry that has planted hundreds of churches, raised up indigenous leaders, founded schools, and started a large orphanage. Her ministry feeds about fifty-five thousand people each day. When she is not "working," she sits in the dirt with the orphans.

One day, a notorious witch doctor came into a village where Heidi was ministering. He carried three puff adder vipers. He planned to use them to hurt Heidi. He was accompanied by a slave assistant who had an advanced case of leprosy. When Heidi approached him, God gave her a prophetic word. As she spoke the message to the man, she lovingly caressed his assistant even though the woman was covered in sores. When the power of God settled on the shaman, he fell to the ground and his snakes slithered into a fire pit. Afterward, the couple received Jesus, were baptized, and got married. Unbeknownst to Heidi, the witch doctor was bitterly hated by the village people because he used his powers to hurt them. When the local police saw him receive Christ and baptism, they also came for baptism. Three weeks later, the assistant came to Heidi to show her that God healed her from her leprosy.[23] Baker's ministry demonstrates that the God of Acts 8 is still working today.

When missionaries desire to evangelize people under the power of a false god, they must show them that God has more power than the spirit that controls them and the area in which they live (territorial spirit). In so doing, the missionaries must convince the people that God will protect them if they convert. This leads to a confrontation between the ruling god and God. The clash between Moses and the Egyptian magicians (Exod 7–12) and the contest between Elijah and the prophets of Baal (1 Kgs 18) are examples of power encounters. In the first case, the Hebrews had to believe that Yahweh could defeat the gods of Egypt before they would follow Moses. In the second, Elijah had to show the Israelites that Yahweh was stronger than Baal before the people would publicly reject Baal and kill his

---

23. "Witch Doctor."

prophets. Normally, a power encounter will include miracles that validate the power of God. However, a power encounter is more than a miracle. It is an invitation to reject the false god and accept the true God.

Charles Kraft says that power encounter is part of a larger process that includes truth encounter and allegiance encounter.[24] For example, on the day of Pentecost, God sent a mighty wind, poured out his Spirit, and caused the believers to talk in foreign languages (Acts 2:1–3). That was a power encounter. After the crowds witnessed the event, Peter explained what the miracle meant. In so doing, he preached the gospel. That was a truth encounter (Acts 2:14–36). Finally, he invited the people to accept Christ as their Messiah and join the church. That was an allegiance encounter (Acts 2:37–40). Phillip's mission qualifies as a power encounter because he performed great signs, preached to the people, destroyed the power of the ruling spirit, and baptized those who believed.

Interestingly, after being baptized, the Samaritans were not filled with the Spirit until Peter and John came from Jerusalem and laid hands on them (Acts 8:14–17). When seen from the perspective of Paul's ongoing struggle with the Judaizers, the reason is clear. Since the gospel was crossing a major sociopolitical boundary, God did not let the Samaritan believers receive Spirit baptism until the leaders of the Jerusalem church arrived because they had to witness the giving of the Spirit. Later, Peter told the Judaizers that he had to baptize the gentile believers because God poured out his Spirit on them (Acts 10:47). In Acts, the giving of the Spirit was a supernatural sign that God had accepted the new people and incorporated them into his church. Judaizers could not argue with God.

As Peter and John went to Jerusalem after witnessing what God did in Samaria, they followed Phillip's lead by preaching the gospel in other Samaritan villages. This shows that they accepted the Samaritans as potential believers and wanted to incorporate them into the church. Acts does not say how the Judaizers reacted to the Samaritan mission. Unlike the Hellenistic Jews who believed, if the Samaritan believers had identified with the Jerusalem church, they would not have been allowed in the temple. In other words, even if God erased the barrier between Jewish believers and Samaritan believers, the Jews did not.

---

24. Kraft, "Three Encounters in Christian Witness," 445–50.

Applying the Missional Hermeneutic to Acts

ACTS 8:26-40 — THE ETHIOPIAN EUNUCH

After Phillip left Samaria, an angel of the Lord directed him to travel on the desert road that led to Gaza. On his way, he encountered an Ethiopian official who had worshiped in Jerusalem. He was returning to Ethiopia with a Second Isaiah scroll. Most likely, the community of Ethiopian Yahweh worshipers had sent him to fetch the scroll so they could use it in their worship. It is possible that the scroll was not for the Beta Israel community in Ethiopia because the eunuch was unfamiliar with its content.[25] Phillip understood what the eunuch was saying when the eunuch was reading from Isa 53. Also, Phillip could talk to him in the lingua franca because he was a Hellenistic Jew. There is no evidence that the Ethiopian Jews of that time spoke Hebrew. Based on this, one can assume that the scroll was written in Greek (Septuagint).

According to legend, when the Queen of Sheba visited King Solomon, she converted to Yahweh worship (1 Kgs 10:1–13). Before she returned to Ethiopia, she had a son with Solomon. He was named Menelik. The name is derived from Ben-Melek (son of the king). As an adult, Menelik visited Solomon. Afterward, he returned to Ethiopia with the Ark of the Covenant. An unbroken chain of Ethiopian rulers until Haile Selassie claimed descent from Solomon through Menelik.[26]

Some have argued that the Ethiopian Jews are a social myth invented in the modern era or that they emerged out of Ethiopian Christianity.[27] The story of the Ethiopian Yahweh worshiper in Acts argues against this theory. Also, Ps 87:4 and Isa 11:11 refer to God's dispersed ones beyond the rivers of Cush (Ethiopia). Even if the legend about Menelik is not true, the Bible shows that the Beta Israel community lived in Ethiopia at the time of the New Testament.

Steward Weiss offers a compelling history of the Beta Israel community. He argues that they are a lost tribe of Israel and that they are of ancient origin. Like the Samaritans, they kept the Torah but did not have the Talmud. He shows that rabbis throughout history have attested to their legitimacy.[28]

---

25. Ethiopian Jews call themselves Beta Israel. It means house of Israel. Others call them Falasha (strangers).
26. Zegeye, "Light of Origins," 52–53.
27. Omer. "Sudan Connection."
28. Weiss, "Beta Israel."

Abebe Zegeye quotes many medieval rabbis who claimed that Beta Israel was the lost tribe of Dan. The Ethiopian Jews claim this for themselves.[29] Others say that an honor guard of Jews who accompanied Menelik to Ethiopia fathered the Beta Israel community. Some suggest that Beta Israel emerged when Jews who fled deportation to Babylon went to Ethiopia and mingled with the native people while holding on to their religious identity. Afrocentric theories argue that the Hebrew people in Egypt were black, Moses married an Ethiopian, and the Ethiopian Jews are descended from Moses.[30]

In Acts 8, God told Phillip to go to the eunuch's chariot. When he did, he heard the man reading Isa 53:7–8. Immediately, he asked the man if he understood the passage. The eunuch replied that someone needed to interpret it for him. At that point, he invited Phillip to sit next to him.

While seated at the feet of the apostles in Jerusalem, Phillip heard the church's standard interpretation of this passage. Just like Jesus taught the disciples on the road to Emmaus (Luke 24:26–27), they taught the Jewish believers that Jesus was the suffering servant who bore their sins like a sacrificial lamb when he died on the cross. Starting with this message, Phillip evangelized the eunuch. When the eunuch believed in Jesus, he requested to be baptized. When he came up from the water, God transported Phillip to Azotus. Afterward, Phillip continued to preach the gospel in every village as he traveled to Caesarea.

Acts does not say what happened to the eunuch. After his baptism, he went on his way rejoicing. Logic says he seeded the church in Ethiopia by evangelizing many from the Beta Israel community when he returned to his homeland. History, however, teaches that Christianity did not take hold in Ethiopia until Emperor Constantine issued the Edict of Milan in AD 313. The accepted date may be disputed because archeological evidence shows that churches already existed in Ethiopia during that time.[31] Since Jewish evangelists targeted Jewish communities all over the world during the first century, the faith could have made it to the Beta Israel community before the fourth century. Obviously, Luke knew about the Ethiopian Jews. Otherwise, he would not have included the story about the eunuch. If Luke knew about Beta Israel, one should assume that missionary evangelists also knew about them. Furthermore, the text says that the Ethiopian eunuch

---

29. Zegeye, "Construction of the Beta Israel Identity," 590–93.
30. Windsor, *From Babylon to Timbuktu*, 34–36.
31. Lawler, "Church Unearthed in Ethiopia."

went to Jerusalem to worship Yahweh. That implies that the Beta Israel community has a relationship with the Jews of Israel.

ACTS 9:1-31 — SAUL

On the surface, Paul's conversion does not fit the internal structure of Acts. He was a Jewish scholar who fiercely opposed Christians. In fact, he was instrumental in the stoning of Stephen (Acts 7:58—8:1). Technically, Paul was a Hellenistic Jew since he was from Cilicia. However, he was raised in Jerusalem. In terms of credentials, he was a Roman citizen and a strict Pharisee who studied at the feet of Gamaliel (a guiding light in the Sanhedrin and the son of Simeon ben Hillel). In his own words, he was zealous for God (Acts 22:3). Unlike the Christian Pharisees who argued that gentiles had to keep the Torah to be believers, Paul championed salvation through faith by grace and not by keeping the law (Acts 15:5, Eph 2:8–9).

In one way, Paul's conversion crosses a religious boundary since he represents the rabbinical tradition. Of course, other Pharisees converted, but none were like Paul. He is a one-of-a-kind convert. For that reason, his conversion does not represent the crossing of a boundary. If Paul had been the gateway to the evangelization of the Jewish scholars, his conversion would qualify as the crossing of a religious boundary.

Paul was a reluctant convert who was impervious to the apostles' preaching. For that reason, Jesus evangelized Paul while he was on the road to Damascus to persecute Jewish believers. Fittingly, he had a violent conversion. When the light of God shined on him, he fell to the ground and the bright light blinded him.[32] While he was on the ground, Jesus confronted Paul. During the conversation, Jesus sent the befuddled Paul to the house of Judas on Straight Street. After three days, God sent Ananias to Paul. In accordance with Jesus' instructions, Ananias imparted the Holy Spirit to Paul, healed his blindness, and baptized him. Afterward, Paul became a mighty apologist, miracle worker, theologian, and missionary apostle. Acts 9:22 says, "Saul grew more and more powerful and baffled the Jews living in Damascus by proving that Jesus is the Messiah" (NIV). Because of his effective witness, the Jews tried to kill Paul. After his daring escape, he fled to

---

32. Without rejecting the historic event, demythologizers offer many explanations for the bright light that blinded Paul. For example, naturalistic theories suggest a dehydrated Paul looked at the sun and fell to the ground or he saw a fireball that boomed as it raced past him.

Jerusalem. While there, he continued to evangelize the Jews with bravado. At some point, the Hellenistic Jews in Jerusalem tried to kill him. Because his preaching stirred up persecution, the believers sent him back to Tarsus. Basically, Paul was exiled until Barnabas reclaimed him (Acts 11:25). In short, Paul was bold, opinionated, fiercely dedicated to his beliefs, and lacked sensitivity. Because of his demeanor, those who rejected the gospel also hated Paul.

The larger plan of God is revealed when God told Ananias that Paul was his chosen instrument and that he was sending him to the Jews, the gentiles, and kings to move his evangelistic mission forward. Like Moses, before Paul knew his role, God had prepared him for his unique mission. Everything about Paul's previous life played into God's purposes for him. Apart from Jesus, no one in the early church had more long-term influence on Christianity than Paul.

ACTS 9:1—10:18 — CORNELIUS THE GODFEARER

To this point, Acts has chronicled the conversion of Judean Jews, Hellenistic Jews, Jewish proselytes, Samaritans, and an Ethiopian Jew. Each represents a cultural boundary moving from Jerusalem (the center) toward the ends of the earth. The Cornelius narrative has tremendous implications because he was the first gentile convert. Ironically, he was a Roman army official and a part of an evil system that oppressed the Jews. In terms of modern oppressor/victim political theology, he was a morally compromised person of privilege who needed to renounce his status to get right with God. Interestingly, in the New Testament, the soldiers who came to John the Baptist (Luke 3:14–18) and various centurions like Cornelius are portrayed positively. This should cause one to question how political theology assigns people to moral categories.

Cornelius was a Roman centurion from the Italian Regiment. His soldiers were volunteers who were recruited in Italy. He had a solid Roman pedigree. He was stationed in Caesarea, the largest port city in the region and the capital of the Roman province of Judea. He would have known the governor and been familiar with the Jews. He was a righteous, devout, and Godfearing man (*phoboumenos ton theon*) who prayed regularly and gave generously to those in need. His family followed his example.[33]

---

33. For an in-depth study of Godfearers, see Sim, "Gentiles, Godfearers, and Proselytes," 9–27. See also Lynch, *Early Christianity*, 19.

Applying the Missional Hermeneutic to Acts

In Greek, a person who "feared the gods" (*deisidaimonesterous*) was a religiously observant person who lived a moral life (Acts 17:22). The Septuagint refers to Godfearers as "those who fear Yahweh" (Pss 15:4, 25:12, 112:1, 115:13, and 118:4). When Paul preached in a Hellenistic synagogue, he addressed the Jews and those who "feared God" because Godfearers attended the synagogues (Acts 13:16, 26). Godfearing gentiles were drawn to Christianity because it allowed them to embrace the faith without becoming Jewish proselytes. Luke uses Godfearers, Godfearing Greeks, and God-worshipers to describe non-Jewish people who worshiped Yahweh, mingled with Jews, and followed the moral precepts of Judaism without becoming Jewish proselytes. Jewish proselytes converted to Judaism. Godfearers worshiped Yahweh without converting to Judaism. Jewish sympathizers were drawn to monotheism and the moral life of Judaism but did not participate in the synagogue. According to Adolf Harnack, 7 to 10 percent of the Roman world became Jewish proselytes, Godfearers, or Jewish sympathizers before the day of Pentecost.[34]

Luke 7 showcases a Godfearing centurion who was closely connected to the Jewish elders of a nearby synagogue. The elders told Jesus that the centurion merited his help because he loved Israel and built their synagogue (Luke 7:5). In humility, the centurion told Jesus that he was not worthy to have him come to his house since he was a gentile. Jews were not allowed to enter a gentile house (see Acts 10:28 and 11:3). He then entreated Jesus to say the word and his sick servant would be healed (Luke 7:6–7). Based on his position as a Roman centurion who could command others because he spoke on behalf of Rome, he knew that Jesus was God's "general" on earth and that he carried God's authority when he spoke. If Jesus spoke the word, he believed that his servant would be healed (Luke 7:8). Because of this great insight, Jesus said that the centurion had more faith than the Jews (Luke 7:9).

Through a series of divine interventions, God arranged for Peter to preach to Cornelius and his family. First, an angel appeared to Cornelius in a vision during the afternoon prayer time (Acts 10:30). He affirmed that Cornelius was a righteous man and told him to fetch Peter from Joppa. Afterward, Cornelius sent a servant and a devout soldier to locate Peter and bring him back to Caesarea.

Second, Peter went to the roof for noon prayers. While he was praying, he had a vision of unclean animals. He was told to kill and eat. As an observant Jew, Peter refused to eat unkosher food. In response, God told

---

34. Harnack, *Mission and Expansion*, 83–84, and Cohen, "Did Ancient Jews Missionize?"

him not to call anything unclean if he had purified it. The vision repeated itself three times.

Because observant Jews considered the gentiles unclean (Acts 10:28), the vision prepared Peter for the evangelization of Cornelius's household. The gathered gentiles are the unclean animals that God has made clean through faith and the blood of Jesus. There is, however, a deeper meaning. Before the Jewish covenant, God told Noah that he could eat any animal that had the breath of life (Gen 9:2–4). From the beginning, no animal was unclean. From the perspective of the New Testament, the kosher rules were given to the Israelites to erect a social boundary between them and the gentile nations so they would not be assimilated and lose their Jewish identity. After the resurrection of Jesus, God removed the kosher rules and the Jewish social boundaries because they no longer served his purposes. Paul emphasized this point when he contended that the wall that separated Jews from gentiles was torn down in Christ (Eph 2:14).

Third, while Peter was contemplating the vision, the Spirit told him to go down to the three gentile men at the gate. After the men explained the reason for their visit, Peter invited them to come into his house. This broke Jewish rules. The next day, Peter and some believers from Joppa traveled to Cornelius's home. A large crowd of gentiles greeted Peter when he arrived. By this time, Peter understood the vision and what God was doing. After recounting his vision, he told them that the gentiles were not unclean (Acts 10:28).

Fourth, Peter began to preach the gospel to the assembled crowd. He started his sermon by restating that God shows no favoritism and that all can be saved through Christ (Acts 10:34–35). After he gave a summary of salvation history, the Holy Spirit fell on all those who were present. When it did, the gentiles spoke in tongues just like the Jews did on the day of Pentecost. Because of their Spirit baptism, Peter knew that God had accepted them. Afterward, he baptized them.

Fifth, when Peter returned to the Jerusalem church, the Judaizers bitterly criticized him because he socialized with gentiles (see Deut 7:1–6). The self-congratulating Judaizers observed every part of the law and the Jewish traditions. They did not realize that God had accepted the gentiles and canceled the religious and ceremonial aspects of the Torah. After Peter recounted his vision and Cornelius's baptism in the Spirit the Judaizers did not respond. The Jerusalem Council shows that the Judaizers did not like the implications of Peter's revelation and the acceptance of the gentiles because they wanted gentile believers to become Jewish proselytes (Acts 15:5). Later, the influence of the Judaizers caused Peter and Barnabas to pull back from the gentiles and not eat with them. When this happened, Paul confronted them with their hypocrisy and reminded them of God's plan (Gal 2:11–18).

In summary, Cornelius was a gentile Godfearer. Despite internal resistance, Peter evangelized Cornelius and the gathered crowd. God punctuated that he wanted them to be saved by filling the gentiles with the Holy Spirit. Only God can give the Spirit. It is always a sign of his acceptance. Throughout the Cornelius narrative, God is the primary actor. He gives visions, sends angels, and tells Peter what to do. God directed his mission even when the Jews resisted it. This points to the missio Dei and affirms that the missional hermeneutic properly couches the narrative in the larger story of God's global mission.

ACTS 11:19-26 — THE ANTIOCH CHURCH

Even though Acts presents the expansion of the early church as a sequential movement from Jerusalem to the ends of the earth, Acts 11:19–21 shows that the mission to Samaria and Antioch happened simultaneously. When Phillip went to Samaria, others went to Phoenicia, Cyprus, and Antioch preaching Jesus to the Jews. While evangelizing in Antioch, some Hellenistic believers from Cyrus and Cyrene began to preach to the Greeks. One should expect that the Hellenistic believers would be the first to preach to the pagan Greeks because they lived near them and completely understood their culture. Previously, by increments, each group that got evangelized had less contact with Judaism. The Greeks, to whom the Hellenists preached, had no connection to Judaism. They were near neighbors to the Jews, but they were not connected to them.

In response to the evangelization of the Greeks, the Jerusalem church sent Barnabas to assess the situation and bring a report back to them. Previously, Barnabas had vouched for Paul's faith when Paul came to Jerusalem (Acts 9:27). Instead of reporting to the Jerusalem church, Barnabas went to Tarsus to find Paul. In the aftermath, he and Paul shepherded the Antioch church for a year. Under their leadership, great numbers of Jews and Greeks came to Christ.

As a nod to the Greek nature of the church, the Antioch believers called themselves Christians (*Christianous*). The term combines Greek and

Latin. It means "follower of Christ." Christ is the Greek translation of messiah. The Hebraic Jews were people of the Way (Acts 9:2, 22:4, and 24:14), members of the Nazarene sect (Acts 24:5), or Messianic Jews. They did not call themselves Christians. The Antioch Church encouraged the church's global mission because of its bicultural nature. As such, missiologists call it the mother church of missions.[35]

ACTS 13:1—14:28 — THE MISSIONARY JOURNEY OF PAUL AND BARNABAS

According to Acts, the first intentional mission happened when the Antioch church dispatched Barnabas and Paul. During a period of prayer, worship, and fasting, the Holy Spirit told the leaders of the Antioch church to send Paul and Barnabas on a missionary journey. The emphasis on the Holy Spirit points to the missio Dei. That is, the mission on which Barnabas and Paul were sent was God's mission. At every step, God guided the church's work in direct and indirect ways. For example, in Acts 5, God sent an angel to release the apostles from jail. Then he directed them to preach in the temple. In Acts 8:26, God's angel told Phillip to go to the desert road. Then the Spirit told him to preach to the eunuch. Afterward, the Spirit took him away (8:39). In Acts 9, God called Paul to his mission. Then God told Ananias to go to Paul. In Acts 10, God told Cornelius to send for Peter and God told Peter to go with the people who came for him. Throughout Acts, God is the primary actor who guides the church in its mission.

Before the Antiochian leaders sent Barnabas and Paul on their mission, they commissioned and anointed them with prayer and the laying on of hands (Acts 6:6, 8:18, 9:17, and 1 Tim 4:14). Since the Holy Spirit dispatched them via the Antioch church, the missionaries reported to the Antioch church when they completed their mission (Acts 14:26–28). Since the Jerusalem church did not send them, they did not report back to the apostles until the controversy in Acts 15.

Unlike the church in Jerusalem, a team of prophets and teachers headed the Antioch church. Even though they were the prototype for the elder team, they are not titled elders (*presbyteroi*) as they are in Acts 11:30; 15; 20:17; and 21:18. Later, Barnabas and Paul appointed elder teams to lead each of the churches that they planted when they took leave of them (Acts 14:23). The members of the elder team were composed of bivocational

---

35. Thomas, "Church at Antioch," 144–46.

people who jointly pastored the people under their care (1 Thess 5:12). Barnabas and Paul functioned as itinerant evangelists. They were not long-term pastors. As they moved on, they often left one of their protégés behind to set things in order (Acts 17:14).[36] In his writings, Paul mentions many of his helpers: Barnabas, Titus, Timothy, Aquila, Epaphras, Epaphroditus, Luke, Mark, Onesimus, Onesiphorus, Silas (Silvanus), Stephanas, Tychicus, and a large group of women (Prisca, Junia, Chloe, and Phoebe).[37]

As the ministry of appointing elders evolved, the church regularized the process of appointing elders. Via prayer and anointing, the Holy Spirit helped with the process of selecting and preparing elders. Yet in the same way that the apostles stated the qualifications for an apostle before they picked Judas's replacement (Acts 1:21–22), Paul told Timothy what to look for when selecting elders:

> Whoever aspires to be an overseer [*episkopon*] desires a noble task.[38] Now the overseer is to be above reproach, faithful to his wife, temperate, self-controlled, respectable, hospitable, able to teach, not given to drunkenness, not violent but gentle, not quarrelsome, not a lover of money. He must manage his own family well and see that his children obey him, and he must do so in a manner worthy of full respect. (If anyone does not know how to manage his own family, how can he take care of God's church?) He must not be a recent convert, or he may become conceited and fall under the same judgment as the devil. He must also have a good reputation with outsiders, so that he will not fall into disgrace and into the devil's trap. (1 Tim 3:1–7 NIV)

After leaving Antioch, Barnabas and Paul went to Cyprus. Initially, they preached the gospel in the Jewish synagogues (Acts 13:5). They followed this strategy in most places (Acts 13:14; 14:1; 17:2, 10; 18:4, 19; and

---

36. For an overview of Paul's helpers and missionary companions, see Holland, "Companions of Paul," 127–32.

37. Lynch, *Early Christianity*, 37.

38. According to Wesley, the terms overseer and elder were different words (synonyms) to describe the same order of ministry in the New Testament. In the New Testament, the overseer term did not refer to a third order of ministry (bishop) superior to elders. For that reason, Wesley called himself a spiritual *episkopos* even though he was ordained as a priest (Payne, "Discerning John Wesley's Missional Ecclesiology," 27–28). By the end of the first century, however, the church made a distinction between bishops and elders. Ignatius and Polycarp say that the elders should be in submission to the bishop. They believed that a strong episcopacy would ensure unity, stop heresy, and prevent schisms in the church (Cairn, *Christianity Through the Centuries*, 73–75).

19:8). The Hellenistic Jews, proselytes, and Godfearers were easier to evangelize because they knew the Old Testament. In modern terms, they would be called the "low-hanging fruit." While preaching to them, the missionaries could follow the same apologetic script that the Jerusalem church used when evangelizing the Jews. They preached that Jesus was the promised Messiah and that he fulfilled all the prophecies of the Hebrew Scriptures (Acts 13:16–41). The fulfillment theme proved that Jesus was who they said he was. Paul knew this approach well because he proved to the Jews that Jesus was the Messiah after he converted (Acts 9:20 and 22). After preaching in the synagogue, the missionaries would form a church out of those who believed in Jesus.

While evangelizing in Cyprus, Barnabas and Paul encountered a Jewish sorcerer named Bar-Jesus. The sorcerer was a close advisor of the proconsul. As such, he attempted to leverage that connection to keep Barnabas and Paul from winning converts. When the proconsul requested to hear the gospel, the ensuing conflict set up a major power encounter event that led to the conversion of the proconsul and many other people.

In short, Paul called the Jewish sorcerer a child of the devil when he opposed God. His deeds showed his true allegiance. For the same reason, Jesus told the Jewish leaders that the devil was their father since they opposed him (John 8:44). Because the children of God reject sin and live in the light (John 1:12–13, and 1 John 3:7–12), the goal of the evangelistic mission was to lead people from the domain of darkness into the kingdom of God's light (Col 1:13). In this sense, spiritual warfare was a vital component of the church's mission to defeat Satan and advance God's kingdom.[39]

After calling the sorcerer a child of the devil, Paul cursed him to neutralize his opposition and win over the proconsul. When he did, darkness came upon Bar-Jesus, and he lost his ability to see. Ironically, sorcerers manipulate spiritual power to curse people that threaten them. In this sense, Paul did what others expected the sorcerer to do. In the eyes of the onlookers, Paul was the more powerful sorcerer in the same way that Moses was more powerful than the sorcerers in Egypt (Exod 7:8–13) and Phillip was more powerful than the sorcerer in Samaria (Acts 8).

Even though blinding a person was not common, there are biblical examples of it. Previously, angels struck the people of Sodom with blindness (Gen 19:11); God cursed the Egyptians with darkness (Exod 10:21–23);

---

39. For a theological survey of spiritual warfare and kingdom conflict in the New Testament, see Payne, *Satan Exposed*, 5–7, 151–65.

Applying the Missional Hermeneutic to Acts

Elisha blinded the attacking Aramean armies (2 Kgs 6:18–23); and Jesus blinded Paul when he confronted him on the road to Damascus (Acts 9:8). Yet this is the only time in Acts that a person of God cursed someone who opposed God. Later, Paul wrote that Christians should bless and not curse (Rom 12:14). Even though Jesus symbolically cursed the nation of Israel for rejecting him when he hexed the fig tree (Matt 21:18–19), he never cursed an individual. Rather, he healed those cursed by sin, disease, and Satan.

Acts refer to Barnabas and Paul as apostles (*apostolos*) while they are in Iconium because they are "sent" on God's mission (Acts 14:4 and 14). In this usage, apostle and missionary are synonyms.[40] While in the synagogue at Iconium, Barnabas and Paul spoke so convincingly that a large crowd of Jews and Greeks believed the gospel. As they evangelized, God confirmed their message by allowing them to perform great miracles, signs, and wonders (Acts 14:3). However, Satan agitated the unbelievers, so they planned to stone Barnabas and Paul. Because of this, the missionaries escaped to Lystra.

When Barnabas and Paul went to Lystra, they preached in the open air to the Greeks. A large crowd gathered to hear them. As Paul was preaching, he saw a man lame from birth. To show the people that Jesus was more powerful than the Greek gods, he shouted for the lame man to stand up. At once, the crippled man began to walk around. When the people witnessed the great miracle, they believed that Paul and Barnabas were the incarnations of Hermes and Zeus. The supernatural healing required a divine explanation. Since the people did not know Jesus, they went to what they knew. When Paul confronted them with the truth and told them that he was not a god, they stoned him to death. After the crowds dispersed, the disciples gathered around him, and he came back to life (Acts 14:20). Possibly, this is when Paul had his out-of-body experience in the third heaven. Paul states,

> I know a man in Christ who, fourteen years ago, was caught up to the third heaven. Whether it was in the body or out of the body I do not know—God knows. And I know that this man—whether in the body or apart from the body I do not know, but God

---

40. In New Testament Greek, the noun apostle is derived from the verb to send or dispatch (*apostellō*). In Matthew 10:2, the twelve are called apostles because Jesus sent them on a missionary journey. Later, the term functions as an office in the church and is used to describe the twelve. First Corinthians 15:4–8 distinguishes between the twelve apostles and the rest of the apostles. The other apostles may refer to the seventy-two that Jesus sent out in Luke 10:1. Paul calls himself an apostle because he received his commissioning and message directly from God via revelation (Gal 1).

knows—was caught up to paradise and heard inexpressible things, things that no one is permitted to tell. (2 Cor 12:2–4 NIV)

This section has demonstrated that God directed the mission and empowered the missionaries to do his work. As the missionaries followed God's lead, God accomplished his work. It also shows the pattern that missionary journeys followed in Acts. The Antioch church discerned God's will and dispatched the missionaries. Afterward, the missionary team returned to Antioch and reported to the church leaders. Often, Jewish leaders, practitioners of false religions, and persecution countered the work of God.

ACTS 15:1–35 — THE JERUSALEM COUNCIL

After Barnabas and Paul returned, Judaizers from the Jerusalem church came to Antioch to tell the gentile believers that they had to get circumcised and keep the law of Moses to be saved (Acts 15:1 and 5). When they did, Barnabas and Paul strongly opposed them. To settle the dispute, the leaders in Antioch sent Barnabas and Paul to Jerusalem to confer with the apostles.

During the meeting, Barnabas and Paul presented their case and the Judaizers made their case. As noted previously, the Judaizers believed that Israel was the chosen nation and that the Jewish believers were the reconstituted messianic community waiting for the return of the Jewish Messiah who would rule over the world from Jerusalem. For gentile believers to be saved, they had to join the messianic community by becoming Jewish proselytes.[41] On the other hand, Paul contended that the law was fulfilled in Christ and that all people became saved by means of faith in Christ. Without disputing the idea of the reconstituted Jewish community, Paul argued that the wall that separated Jewish believers from gentile believers was torn down and that all stood on equal footing in the church. For this reason, Paul did not require the gentile believers to keep the law and he did not separate the gentiles from the Jews when he formed new believers into a church.

The leaders of the Jerusalem church sided with Barnabas and Paul. Speaking for the consensus, Peter made a three-point argument. First, non-Jews could hear the gospel and be saved. Second, God proved this by giving the Holy Spirit to Cornelius and his extended family. Third, the law does not save Jews or gentiles because all believers are justified by faith in

---

41. Lietzmann identifies this mindset with Ps 17 (*History of the Early Church*, 28). For this reason, if gentiles want to enter the messianic kingdom, they must become Jews.

Jesus (Acts 15:6–11). Peter's response shows the missio Dei in action. Peter would not have come to this conclusion if God had not prepared him for it by sending him to Cornelius's house so he could witness the outpouring of the Holy Spirit on the gentiles. In this regard, the conversion of Cornelius the Godfearer opened the door to the gentile mission and enabled Paul to prevail at the Jerusalem Council.

ACTS 15:36-41 — BARNABAS AND PAUL SEPARATE

When Barnabas and Paul desired to return to the churches they had planted, they disputed because Barnabas wanted to take John Mark. John Mark deserted them during the first missionary journey (Acts 13:13). He was young and closely associated with the Jerusalem church. The conflict between Barnabas and Paul was intense. In the aftermath, Barnabas and Paul separated. Barnabas continued with John Mark and Paul took Silas (Acts 15:36–41). After this, Acts focuses on Paul and his ministry. From the perspective of the missio Dei, one could argue that God allowed Barnabas and Paul to separate because he wanted two missionary teams. This thinking harkens back to the discussion on the persecution of the Jerusalem believers in Acts 8.

When Paul and his team attempted to enter Asia Minor, the Holy Spirit forbade them. Then the "Spirit of Jesus" would not let them go into Bithynia (Acts 16:6–7). Acts does not say why God would not let them go. After the rebuke, God gave Paul a vision in which a man from Macedonia pleaded for him to come to him. Afterward, Paul's team discerned that God wanted them to go to Macedonia (Acts 16:10). Through supernatural revelation, God directed the missionary work of Paul and his team.

ACTS 16:16-40 — THE GIRL WITH A PYTHON SPIRIT

While in Macedonia, Paul went to a river in Philippi expecting to find a place of prayer. These gathering areas were common in locations that did not have a synagogue. At the river, Paul preached to the assembled people. Lydia and her family received Christ and were baptized (Acts 16:14–15). As the gospel continued its march from Jerusalem to the ends of the world, Lydia's conversion represents a milestone because she was the first convert in Europe.

Later, when Paul and Silas were returning to the place of prayer, a female slave with the ability to divine (a fortune teller) accosted them (Acts 16:16–18). The New Testament says that she had a python spirit (*pneuma puthōna*). In ancient Greece, Delphi was guarded by a giant serpent named Pythonos because Zeus designated it the navel of the world. As an immortal being, Pythonos was a large dragon of some sort. According to legend, she was the daughter of Gaia. She nurtured the great Typhon dragon when he was young.[42]

In many ancient myths, serpents guarded sacred trees and holy places.[43] For example, Ladon was a serpent-dragon that guarded the apple tree in the Garden of the Hesperides in Greek mythology and cherubim guarded the entrance to the garden of Eden in Gen 3. In the Bible, Leviathan, seraphim, and cherubim are terms for divine serpents.[44] Since most of the ancient serpents were winged, popular culture refers to them as dragons. In mythology, dragons were brilliant, powerful, and immortal. They were divine creatures. Interestingly, Revelation calls Satan the great dragon and the ancient serpent who deceives the world (12:9). The juxtaposition of dragon with serpent implies that Satan was a divine serpent, cherub, or serpent-like dragon. From this, some identify Satan with the serpent that guarded the Tree of Knowledge in the garden of Eden.[45] Like Pythonos who chased after the pregnant Leto to kill her twins, the great dragon chased after Mary to kill her child (Rev 12:13).

Greek mythology says that Apollo killed Pythonos because she tried to prevent him and Artemis from being born. When he did, Apollo took possession of Delphi. Since he was the god of prophecy, his priests erected a temple in his honor at Delphi.[46] The high priestess at Delphi was named Pythia. She is called the oracle of Delphi because she had the gift of divination. The title "Pythia" connects to Pythonos and the Greek verb to become putrid (*puthein*).

From 630 BC to AD 362, famous leaders from around the world traveled to Delphi to get messages from Pythia. For example, in 336 BC, the oracle told Alexander the Great that he would conquer the world. In AD

---

42. Henten, "Python," 1263–66. The Pythonos was a mantic dragon. The Pythia sat over his dead body when she divined.
43. Henten, "Dragon," 504–9.
44. Job 41 gives an excellent description of a sea dragon.
45. See Payne, *Satan Exposed*, 118–25.
46. Broek, "Apollo," 137–43.

302, the oracle told Emperor Diocletian that Christianity would destroy the Roman Empire. Consequently, he sought to eradicate the faith.[47]

When getting a message, the oracle would be possessed by the spirit of Pythonos. To do this, the priestess would drink from the sacred spring in the cave of Delphi, go into the lower levels, mount a special tripod chair, and chew laurel leaves. Perhaps vapors from the cave had a hallucinogenic effect on the priestess or the smell of the rotting Pythonos who was buried in the chasm may have inspired the Pythia. Then the oracle would go into a deep trance to receive the message for the one who inquired.[48] The above scenario may be conflated with practices associated with Apollo's oracle at Didyma.[49]

Joseph Fontenrose argues that the Pythia was not possessed. Rather, she was inspired like the prophets of the Bible. After examining her prophetic messages, he contends that she used her own voice and her reason to describe to consultants what had been revealed to her. Since Apollo was the god of poetry, it was reported that she often utilized poetic language when giving her messages. Never was she in a manic frenzy.[50]

The episode with the slave girl fits this description because Acts does not indicate that she spoke with a strange voice. Still, since Paul cast the spirit out of her, the narrative assumes that she was demonized. A demonized person can be "possessed" and speak with a strange voice (Mark 1:21–27, Luke 13:10–16, and Acts 19:11–17). Exorcists report that this is a routine phenomenon. When this happens, the spirits may laugh, mock, threaten, and argue with the person casting them out.[51]

The slave girl with the python spirit was not the Pythia from Delphi. Rather, Acts says that she had the python spirit because she was a fortune teller, i.e., the Pythia and the slave girl both channeled a spirit of divination.[52] That is why "spirit of the python" can be translated as diviner. Reminiscent of the demon who announced that Jesus was the Son of the Most High when Jesus preached in Capernaum (Mark 1:24), the python spirit in

---

47. Fontenrose, *Delphic Oracle*, 338–40, 425.
48. Mikoski, "Discerning Divine Direction," 307–8.
49. Broek, "Apollo," 142.
50. Fontenrose, *Delphic Oracle*, 204–7.
51. Payne, *Adventures in Spiritual Warfare*, 63–77.
52. "The Delphic dragon himself became a mantic animal and lent his name to predicting demons" (Henten, "Apollo," 1264).

the slave girl announced that Paul was a servant of the Most High God and that he preached the way of salvation.

Like the magicians in Samaria, Cyprus, and Ephesus (Acts 19:19–20), many people in the ancient world were gifted in the black arts. On the surface, Paul should have been thankful that this important soothsayer was announcing him and telling people to follow him. So why did Paul object? For the same reason that Jesus objected when the demon announced him. Darkness and light have no fellowship (2 Cor 6:14). The dark always has its own motives and its own purposes. In this case, a careful reading of the narrative shows that the Python spirit in the slave girl wanted to neutralize the work of God in that city.

When Paul turned to the spirit, he rebuked it in the name of Jesus and cast it out of the slave girl. Afterward, those who profited from the girl's extraordinary gifts became hostile because she made them a lot of money. In essence, Paul ruined their business. This led to persecution and imprisonment.

The missio Dei always accounts for the work of God and Satan's efforts to counter God. In the above story, the slave girl who announced Paul as a messenger of the true God was not giving glory to God or attempting to lead people to God. Instead, the spirit in her was trying to set up a confrontation. Most likely, the python spirit provoked Paul to cast it out because it intended to work through the ensuing persecution to kill Paul and Silas. After all, the missionaries were a huge threat to Satan's hegemony in pagan Europe. Plus, Satan did not want Christianity to gain a foothold in the area. Because God placed a covering over Paul, Satan and his demons could not harm him. They could, however, manipulate other people to do their bidding. In the same way that God has a plan and works through his people to accomplish it, spiritual warfare teaches that Satan does the same thing through his people. Similarly, as God gifts his disciples to prophesy and do miracles, Satan enables his followers to divine and do miracles. As the adulations of the slave girl show, it may be difficult to discern if divine speech points to God or is being used by Satan to accomplish his purposes. For this reason, the saints must discern the spirits so they are not deceived or accept the doctrines of demons (1 John 4:4).

After Paul and Silas were badly beaten and had their clothes ripped off, they were thrown into the inner prison and chained to the wall. Most likely, the officials planned to kill them in the morning. Like a grandmaster chess player, however, God was one move ahead of his opponent. In the night, he sent a great earthquake. The vibrating caused the jail door to unlatch and the restraints to fall off. The jailer assumed that his prisoners had escaped when he saw the open jail doors. The penalty for losing prisoners was death. However, Paul and all the prisoners remained in their open cells. Afterward, Paul evangelized the jailer. He and his entire family were baptized.

When the magistrates who had beaten Paul discovered that he was a Roman citizen, they were filled with remorse because it was illegal to flog Roman citizens without a trial. They could have been thrown into prison and executed. The city officials sent him and his team on their way after apologizing to Paul. In this case, even though the devil meant it for evil, God used it for good as he advanced his kingdom and his mission in Philippi. Interestingly, in Acts 5:19 and 12:5–7, God sent an angel to quietly free his people from prisons in the middle of the night. In Philippi, God used an earthquake! Most likely, the people of the area did not know that God sent the earthquake to free his people.

ACTS 17:1–15 — THE GOSPEL MESSAGE

When Paul and Silas left Philippi, they traveled to Thessalonica. Following the established pattern, they went to the synagogue and preached Jesus to the gathered Jews and Greeks. For three Sabbaths, Paul "reasoned with them from the Scriptures, explaining and proving that the Messiah had to suffer and rise from the dead. 'This Jesus I am proclaiming to you is the Messiah,' he said. Some of the Jews were persuaded and joined Paul and Silas, as did a large number of God-fearing Greeks and quite a few prominent women" (Acts 17:2–4 NIV).[53]

In the above text, many words describe Paul's evangelism, e.g., reasoned, explained, proved, proclaimed, and persuaded. When Paul was in Corinth, he went to the synagogue and boldly proclaimed the gospel. It says that he "argued persuasively" (Acts 19:8). As Paul was preaching, God performed extraordinary miracles through him (Acts 19:11). The miracles validated his message.

In the New Testament, the gospel (*euangelion*) is the good news and evangelize (*euangelizō*) means to "goodnews" a person.[54] In the secular

---

53. In 1 Thessalonians, Paul says that he did not preach human words to them. Rather, he preached the very word of God (1 Thess 2:13). Paul believed that his preaching came from God and was inspired by God.

54. Towns, *Evangelism and Church Growth*, 208.

world of that time, a royal herald who proclaimed good news was called an evangelist. They might enter a town square, sound a trumpet, gather the people, stand on a dais, and read a royal proclamation. For example, when the Pax Romana was realized, heralds proclaimed the good news about Emperor Augustus all over the Roman world. As representatives of the heavenly emperor, New Testament evangelists were divinely commissioned heralds who told the world the good news about Jesus and the in-breaking kingdom of God. The people were under an obligation to hear the message they preached.

Interestingly, even though the verb evangelize routinely appears in the Greek New Testament, it never appears in English translations. Instead, the verb is translated as proclaiming the gospel. Since evangelizing, preaching, and witnessing refer to the oral communication of the gospel, some scholars define evangelism as the proclamation of the good news. For this reason, they argue that evangelism does not include apologetics or the goal of converting people to Christ.[55] However, in Acts the ministry of evangelism was the total process by which the church worked to win converts and make disciples.

According to Elmer Towns, the early church did not define the ministry of evangelism as the oral communication of the gospel message. Rather, it used a mosaic of words to create a picture of how evangelism was practiced. New Testament evangelism words are witnessing, talking, testifying, evangelizing, confusing, explaining, demonstrating, teaching, reasoning, refuting, discussing, astonishing, preaching, announcing, declaring, winning, proving, baffling, discipling, demolishing arguments, replying to others, and persuading.[56]

The example of Paul demonstrates that New Testament evangelism was not a take-it-or-leave-it, dispassionate declaration of the gospel message. It included an apologetic approach that attempted to release the power of the Spirit so that people were convicted, persuaded, and converted. When people did not respond positively, Paul continued to engage them by overcoming their objections. That is why he often returned to the same synagogues on consecutive Sabbaths. Additionally, Acts shows that signs, wonders, and miracles added credence to the work of evangelism. If the

---

55. Stott represented this perspective at the Lausanne Congress on World Evangelization. He argued that *euangelizomai* means to preach the good news. The term must be defined by the message and not the goal of making converts ("Biblical Basis of Evangelism," 68–69).

56. Towns, *Evangelism and Church Growth*, 205–11.

people were not convinced by preaching, they were moved by the miracles that authenticated the message. Always, the New Testament preacher connected with the emotions, reason, and spirit of those being evangelized. In the end, the Holy Spirit was the power behind conversion. For that reason, one can affirm that God is the evangelist. The preacher is the one who gives witness to him by word, deed, and sign.

It should be noted that Satan worked through his people to impede the work of God in Thessalonica and Berea (1 Thess 2:18). After Paul fled, he feared that Satan would tempt the new believers to abandon the faith (1 Thess 3:5). In light of Satan's obstacles, Paul prayed that God would clear the way for him to return to them (1 Thess 3:11). Literally, Paul wanted God to "direct our way to you." Paul believed that Satan opposed him and his team because they were doing God's work. At the same time, he assumed that God was working to minimize Satan's influence so his mission could go forward.

Specifically, the Jews rounded up miscreants from the marketplace to form a mob that started a riot in Thessalonica. When the assembled crowd heard Paul say that Jesus was king, the masses attempted to persecute those who accepted Jesus. At night, the believers helped Paul and Silas escape to Berea. When they preached in Berea, the people examined the Hebrew Scriptures to see if Paul's teaching was correct. Many prominent people accepted Jesus. But the jealous Jews from Thessalonica came to Berea to foment another riot. When this happened, the Berean believers sent Paul to Athens and told him to wait for Silas and Timothy.[57] Evidently, Paul was the lightning rod since Timothy and Silas remained in Berea without any reported problems. Previously, the Jerusalem church sent Paul to Tarsus because his ministry stirred up persecution (Acts 9:30).

ACTS 17:16-34 — PAUL IN ATHENS

Instead of keeping a low profile and waiting quietly for Timothy and Silas, Paul became greatly distressed when he viewed all the idols in Athens. So, he did what Paul always did: he reasoned in the synagogue and debated with those in the marketplace. As he spoke in the open market, Greek

---

57. First Thessalonians says that Paul and Silas (Silvanus) sent Timothy back to Thessalonica while they stayed in Athens (3:1–3). Since it is a part of the undisputed Pauline corpus and predates the writing of Acts, its description is preferred. That means that Silas was with Paul while he was in Athens.

philosophers engaged him. According to Silvia Montiglio, itinerant philosophers wandered all over the Roman world in the time of Paul. They were erudite men who spread their teachings and intervened in religious quarrels. In essence, they were sophists—experts on all things related to intellectualism and religion. They had charisma and a high social status. Like Paul and the missionary bands, the wandering philosophers were mendicant preachers. Unlike Paul, wandering was a means by which they acquired more knowledge in the same way that a well-traveled person gains a crosscultural perspective and has experiential knowledge not available to those who have never traveled.[58] In any case, the philosophers who debated with Paul were his intellectual equals.

The philosophers were not impressed with Paul. Some referred to him as a babbler (*spermologos*). The term refers to a lazy person who lacks substance. Empty talker and buffoonery are synonyms. Others said that he preached foreign gods because Paul spoke of Jesus and the resurrection (*anastasis*). Anastasia is a popular Greek name that means resurrection. Evidently, they thought that "Resurrection" was Jesus' consort goddess. Since the philosophers wanted to know if Paul was preaching a new god, they took him to the Areopagus.

The Areopagus represented the cultural center of that world. In early Greece, a great council met there to advise the king and make rulings. In Paul's time, the Greek council focused on philosophy, learning, and religion and did not advise the Roman government. As a religious hub, it contained altars for the various gods and goddesses in the empire (Acts 17:23). Representatives of the gods were also present so the leaders could understand the gods and render homage to them. History taught the Romans that neglected gods caused problems.

Rome was religiously tolerant. As it expanded, it did not destroy the gods of the people it conquered. Rather, it assimilated them into its pantheon. As long as subjects paid tribute to Caesar, they could worship their native deities. In contrast, Hellenism attempted to force its culture and its gods on the people it controlled. This led to the Jewish uprising that is chronicled in 1 and 2 Maccabees.

Paul changed his preaching style when he spoke to those at the Areopagus because they were not Jews, they did not know about the Jewish

---

58. Montiglio, "Wandering Philosophers," 86–92. For an interesting study of the wandering, charismatic teachers in the Didache, see Draper, "Weber, Theissen, and 'Wandering Charismatics,'" 541–76.

messiah, and they did not care about miracles. Four points will show how Paul evangelized the religious elite.

One, he said that they were very religious (*deisidaimonesterous*). That is, the leaders had anxiety about the gods and did not want to get any of them angry. As such, they showed devotion to the gods by honoring their altars (Acts 17:22).

Two, Paul found a common point of reference by preaching about the altar to the unknown god. Missiologists refer to this as a redemptive analogy—a native practice or belief that is a bridge by which a missionary can connect a people to the gospel story so they can be evangelized.[59] The altar to the unknown god existed because the religious elite did not want to offend any god. Also, the existence of the altar showed that the leaders were open to learning about new gods or an unknown god. Building on that point, Paul said that Jesus was the unknown god for whom they built the altar (Acts 17:23).

Three, to personalize his message about the unknown god, Paul used their literature to make his point when he quoted from Epimenides and Aratus. Paul could do this because he was a bicultural person who understood their culture.[60] In verse 26, he also referred to Deut 32:8: "When the Most High gave to the nations their inheritance, when he separated the sons of men, he fixed the bounds of the peoples according to the number of the sons of God" (RSV). In other words, when God chose the Jews and identified with them, the sons of God were given stewardship over the nations. Paul identifies the sons of God with the nation gods. Since the resurrection of Jesus, the church has been sent to the nations to bring all the peoples back to the true God (Matt 28:19). In large part, freeing people from their bondage to the gods is a primary mission of the New Testament missionaries. According to Paul, Jesus is above every ruler, authority, power, dominion, and the spiritual forces of evil in the heavenlies (Eph

---

59. Richardson, *Peace Child*, 268–71. The Sawi people would kill and eat their enemies. To stop the killing, two families within the warring tribes had to exchange babies and raise them as their own. The baby was called the peace child. As long as it lived, there was no war. Killing the peace child was the greatest sin. Don Richardson won the people over when he showed them that Jesus was God's peace child, and he was murdered.

60. Missiologists refer to this as contextualization. "Nor need we say that he was simply stooping to accommodate himself to his age; rather he was imbibing its atmosphere, growing strong in faith and mighty in spiritual stature as he worshiped and served his crucified and risen redeemer in the language and under the inspirations furnished by the religious world of his day" (Case, "Christianity and the Mystery Religions," 15).

1:23 and 6:12). Paul came to this theology largely because of his surpassing revelations and his trip to the third heaven.

Finally, Paul segued to the heart of his message when he deconstructed the Greek faith and told the leaders that God would judge the world through Jesus.[61] According to Paul's message, Jesus was the only true Lord, the time of ignorance has passed, and everyone must repent and accept Jesus. In this way, Paul preached for a response. He did not lecture to inform the leaders about his faith. Paul did the same thing when he was on trial before King Agrippa.

Today, many in the West do not think that people need to repent or turn to Jesus to be saved since the democratic impulse avers that all religions offer equally valid pathways to God. This notion connects with postmodern thought. The underlying assumptions lead to theological universalism—the belief that a loving God will save all good people. When people internalize this belief, they imagine that Christian missionaries are arrogant and insensitive people who insult and disrespect practitioners of other faiths or no faith. Modern universalism reflects the entrenched influence of humanism. When the spirit of humanism controls how Western Christians think and live their lives, they are unable to win others to Christ or have a clear testimony to share with the world.[62]

ACTS 18 — CORINTH

When he left Athens, Paul went to Corinth. After he spent many Sabbaths trying to persuade the Corinthian Jews to come to Christ, the Jews became abusive and began to persecute him. In response, Paul rejected them and said he would focus on the gentiles. Nevertheless, prominent Jews and Greeks converted to Jesus.

---

61. "Paul's apocalyptic mission shapes his apocalyptic gospel, which, in turn, finds its contingent expression in the particular setting of Paul's letters. Or to say it a little differently, Paul's missionary call and ministry are fundamentally shaped by an apocalyptic perspective that influences the theological expression of Paul's gospel" (Carriker, "Missiological Hermeneutic," 45).

62. "The loss of evangelistic potency corresponds to the surging growth of secular humanism in post-Christian America. Furthermore, as evangelicals own secular humanism and the narratives that accompany it, they become inclusivists and cease to own the evangelistic mandate of the church. If the process is not reversed, they become Christian humanists. Christian humanism is a syncretistic faith orientation that is contrary to the teachings and practices of traditional Christianity" (Payne, "Assessing the Student Shift," 17).

Applying the Missional Hermeneutic to Acts

To assuage Paul's anxiety about the ongoing persecution, God spoke to him in a vision. He said, "Do not be afraid; keep on speaking, do not be silent. For I am with you, and no one is going to attack and harm you, because I have many people in this city" (Acts 18:9–10 NIV). For this reason, Paul rightly discerned that God wanted him to stay in Corinth because it was a strategic place that God wanted to win for his kingdom. Consequently, for eighteen months, Paul successfully evangelized Corinth. While he was there, Aquila and Priscilla were added to his team. After Paul left Corinth, Apollo joined his team. Like Paul, Apollo was an adept apologist. He vigorously refuted the Jews who opposed Jesus in public debates while proving from the Scriptures that Jesus was the Messiah (Acts 18:28).

When considering the missio Dei, one should note that Paul wrote many letters to the Corinthian church (the church of God at Corinth). The letters addressed critical issues about church discipline, in-fighting, immoral behavior, practical theology, the Eucharist, spiritual gifts, food sacrificed to idols, the superiority of love, right worship, the resurrection, the second coming, and stewardship. Paul wrote the letters in response to questions that the Corinthian believers asked. As a missionary apostle, Paul continued to give pastoral oversight to this church when he traveled. Because of his correspondence with the Corinthian church, Christians have benefitted from Paul's inspired communication for two thousand years. If Paul had not stayed to grow the Corinthian church and if it had not been a problematic church, 1 and 2 Corinthians would not have been written.

ACTS 19 — EPHESUS

Ephesus has an interesting backstory. According to legend, when Androclus wanted to establish a new Greek settlement, he turned to the oracle at Delphi for guidance. The oracle told him a boar and a fish would show him the new location. One day, as Androclus was frying fish over an open fire, a fish flopped out of the frying pan and landed in the nearby bushes. A spark ignited the underbrush, and a wild boar ran out. Recalling the oracle's prophecy, Androclus built his new settlement where the bushes stood. He called it Ephesus.[63]

---

63. Fant and Reddish, "Ephesus," 179.

Artemis

From the sixth century BC, Ephesus was dedicated to the goddess Artemis. She was the daughter of Zeus, the twin of Apollo, and one of the three virgin goddesses (Hestia, Artemis, and Athena). Normally, the Hellenistic Artemis was surrounded by young virgins who hunted with her. She was also called the goddess of the moon and the Queen of Heaven.[64] The Queen of Heaven designation continued into the Roman era when Artemis was renamed Diana. The temple to Artemis in Ephesus was so renowned that it was listed as one of the seven wonders of the ancient world. Pilgrims from all over Asia Minor flocked to the temple. It contained a holy relic in the form of an Artemis statue.[65] The statue's image is depicted on Roman coins. In Acts 19:35–36, the citizens of Ephesus claimed that the statue of Artemis fell from the sky. Since "from the sky" is ambiguous, other translations say it fell from Jupiter (Zeus) because he is the sky god. Regardless of the translation, the people saw it as a divine gift.

The Artemis in Ephesus wore a robe of many breasts.[66] Other statues and pictures show her as a young woman engaged in one of the activities associated with her many conflated identities, e.g., Hecate and Selene.[67] In that society, Artemis was the ideal for the virtuous woman. Similarly, Isis with Horus on her lap became the ideal for motherhood after her cult was imported from Egypt. When the Roman masses flooded into Christianity after the Edict of Tolerance in 311 and the Edict of Milan in 313, the new Christians did not abandon their old faith. Rather, they syncretized them. When they did, the Virgin Mary combined both attributes and became a functional substitute for Diana and Isis.[68] In some cases, the goddess temples and statues were merely repurposed to accommodate the Virgin Mary cult.

---

64. Mussies, "Artemis," 170–71.

65. "The image was carved in ebony. It represented a woman standing bolt upright. Her body was bound from head to foot by wrappings between which a number of metal bosses can be seen. At a later period, sculptors reproduced these bosses as the numerous breasts of the goddess of fertility. A crescent moon was shown behind her head" (Lietzmann, *History of the Early Church*, 158).

66. Lietzmann, *History of the Early Church*, 174.

67. Lietzmann, *History of the Early Church*, 172.

68. Benko, *Virgin Goddess*, 213–16, 257. Today, Mary is called "Blessed Virgin, Holy Mother, Mother of God, Bride of Christ, Bride of the Spirit, and Queen of Heaven" (Lloyd, "Rise and Rise"). Lloyd recounts how Mary became associated with the titles. He also shows the connections to ancient goddesses. He regrets that Mary rivals Jesus. See also Weigall, *Paganism in our Christianity*, 124–32 and Houtman, "Queen of Heaven," 1278–83.

Interestingly, the statue story about Artemis in Ephesus closely parallels the statue story about the Virgin Mary in Cuba (the Virgin of Charity). Both came from heaven and were given to devotees on earth; both were black; both were made of wood; and both resided in great religious buildings to which people made pilgrimages. Also, both Artemis and Mary were called the Queen of Heaven. Artemis was the moon goddess. The statue of the Cuban Mary stands on a half-moon. It is conflated with a West African orisha (goddess) called Oshun. Artemis is conflated with Selene and Hecate.[69] The Virgin Mary was dedicated as the Patroness of Cuba in 1916 by Pope Benedict XV. In 1998, Pope John Paul II crowned her as the Queen of Cuba.

The Virgin Mary statue came to Cuba when three fishermen prayed to her for help during a violent storm. When the storm was over, they saw a statue of the Virgin floating in the water. When they picked it up, it was dry. It had a note that said, "I am the Virgin of Charity." The statue kept disappearing from locked buildings. Soon it moved to the place where it wanted to be, enshrined in a great church. Today people crawl to the statue and ask the Virgin Mary for blessings like pilgrims went to the virgin Artemis's temple in Ephesus and asked for blessings. Cubans believe that the statue of Mary is a gift from God and they keep it as a holy relic. They also think it is a powerful object through which they can gain healing, blessings, and help.[70]

Kingdom of God

When Paul arrived at Ephesus, he went to the synagogue and preached the kingdom of God boldly for three months. In Acts, Jesus referred to the kingdom of God twice (Acts 1:3, 6). Philip connected the kingdom of God to Jesus (Acts 8:12). Paul mentioned the kingdom of God five times (14:22, 19:8, 20:25, 28:23, and 28:31). Because of the shifting focus from the Jews to the world, Acts does not mention the kingdom of God as often as Matthew, Mark, and Luke. In those books, it is the primary theological construct. For example, Matthew refers to the kingdom of heaven, the kingdom of God, and the kingdom forty-six times.

Since the message that Paul and his companions preached is enumerated in Acts, one can assume that preaching the kingdom of God meant teaching that Jesus was the Messiah and that people must come to him to

69. Benko, *Virgin Goddess*, 214.
70. Espin, "Mary in Latino/a Catholicism," 22–23.

get right with God. In the Gospels, the kingdom of God is the reign of God. As the long-awaited Messiah, Jesus revealed the kingdom and was the face of God's reign. As the Son of God, he preached the kingdom, healed the sick, cleansed the unclean, cast out demons, reconciled the outcasts, forgave sinners, and performed miracles that showed his divine pedigree. When preaching God's righteousness, he invited others to enter the kingdom by becoming his disciples. Jews who turned to Jesus accepted the gospel of the kingdom, put faith in King Jesus, turned from their sins, and submitted to God's rule as it was mediated through Jesus. Most of Jesus' hearers believed that he would usher in the messianic kingdom and sit on the throne of David as the ruling monarch of the world.

When the Ephesian Jews rejected Paul and his message, Paul separated himself from the synagogue and relocated to Tyrannus Hall (Acts 19:8–10). The new believers went with him. Then Paul spent twenty-four months preaching and doing miracles in Ephesus. By means of this, he gained great notoriety. People from all over Asia Minor became aware of him and his ministry because the pilgrims who came to see the temple of Artemis also learned about Paul. In a centripetal way, Ephesus was a vortex where masses of potential converts heard the gospel.

Conflict with Artemis

While talking to the Greeks in Ephesus, Paul urged them to reject their idols and embrace the true God. He told them that idols were worthless. Through miracles, he showed the Artemis pilgrims and the residents of Ephesus that the God he preached was more powerful than the idols the people grasped. His ministry was a direct assault on Artemis. When the keepers of the Artemis cult realized the threat, they said, "There is danger not only that our trade will lose its good name, but also that the temple of the great goddess Artemis will be discredited; and the goddess herself, who is worshiped throughout the province of Asia and the world, will be robbed of her divine majesty" (Acts 19:27 NIV). Afterward, they and the entire city began to shout, "Great is Artemis of the Ephesians!" (Acts 19:28). Later, when they realized Paul was a Jew, they started the "Great is Artemis of the Ephesians" praise for another two hours (Acts 19:34).[71] The unified praise was intended to stir up and empower the goddess so that she would

---

71. The Jews and Artemis faithful had a history of conflict in Ephesus because Jews did not pay the temple tax to Artemis or worship her (Mussies, "Artemis," 178–79).

overcome Paul and the followers of Jesus in Ephesus. Imagine how much spiritual power was released when the entire city shouted praise to Artemis for such a long time.[72]

The keepers of Artemis were upset for many reasons. First, Paul displayed great spiritual power when God did extraordinary miracles through him. For instance, handkerchiefs and aprons that had touched Paul cured illnesses and drove out demons when they were taken to the sick and demonized (Acts 19:11–12). This idea is widely accepted in animism. According to the law of contagion (sympathetic magic), a spiritual link connects people who have been in contact with each other. The link can be established by passing personal objects from one person to another. When this happens, the spiritual power in the first person passes to the other person.[73] This is illustrated in the Old Testament when a dead body that touched the bones of Elisha the prophet came back to life (2 Kgs 13:21). Also, the Roman Catholic notion of holy relics reflects this idea. Things can possess spiritual power. In black magic, a practitioner can use hair, nail clippings, or other personal items to curse a person. In Ephesus, the pilgrims believed that the small Artemis idols that were blessed by the priests and sold in the temple contained spiritual power.

After describing the miracles that Paul did, Acts says that the word of the Lord spread widely and grew in power (19:20). The emphasis on power demonstrates that Luke understands the animistic context in Ephesus. When the mission moved from Jews to polytheistic pagans who had an animistic worldview, God moved from apologetics to power ministry.

Second, the episode about the sons of Sceva demonstrated that the Jesus Paul preached was mightier than the demons the religious specialists tried to cast out. Most likely, the sons of Sceva were itinerant exorcists from a Levitical family who received money for their services. They must have had some success and notoriety because they were far from Jerusalem. Perhaps they only worked with Hellenistic Jews. Regardless, after they witnessed that Paul was a superior exorcist, they modified his approach to suit their purposes. According to the text,

> Some Jews who went around driving out evil spirits tried to invoke the name of the Lord Jesus over those who were demon-possessed.

---

72. A similar thing happened in 1 Kgs 18:26–29 when the prophets of Baal engaged in frenzy prayer and self-mutilation from morning until afternoon to release spiritual power, but Yahweh checked the power of Baal.

73. Frazer, *Golden Bough*, 12–55.

> They would say, "In the name of the Jesus whom Paul preaches, I command you to come out." Seven sons of Sceva, a Jewish chief priest, were doing this. One day the evil spirit answered them, "Jesus I know, and Paul I know about, but who are you?" Then the man who had the evil spirit jumped on them and overpowered them all. He gave them such a beating that they ran out of the house naked and bleeding. (Acts 19:13–16 NIV)

The story became widely known in Ephesus and the surrounding areas. When Greeks and Jews heard it, they were seized with fear. Since the name of Jesus was more powerful than the demons that the people feared, they held his name in high honor (Acts 19:17). In a culture that valued spiritual power, the name of Jesus was a real threat to Artemis and those who profited from her.

Third, because of the surpassing power of Jesus, a large group of local sorcerers turned to Christ. Per the power encounter model, when they believed that Jesus was more powerful than the spirits they served, they burned their magical scrolls. Like Boniface cutting down the sacred tree or a missionary eating the sacred totem, they demonstrated that they rejected their gods when they destroyed their scrolls.[74] Assuming an average person makes $50,000 a year, the scrolls were worth $6,849,315 in modern America.

Fourth, if Satan attempted to use the riot to destroy the work of God in Ephesus, it did not work. The power of the ruling spirits was not released, the work of God was not curtailed, and the desired riot did not materialize. Likewise, the cult of Artemis was not vanquished. In the aftermath, Paul and company had to leave because of the persecution. In fact, the church leaders would not allow Paul to speak to the assembled crowds during the commotion. Later, Paul met the leaders of the Ephesus church in Miletus, thirty-six miles from Ephesus (Acts 20:17–38). Finally, the letter to the church of Ephesus in Revelation shows that the Ephesus church remained faithful to the gospel and God.

ACTS 21–23 — JERUSALEM

While in Ephesus, Paul said he planned to go to Jerusalem and then to Rome (Acts 19:20–21). However, he did not leave for Jerusalem until the Ephesian protest ended. During his extended farewell discourse with the

---

74. Kraft, *Power Encounter*, 1–13.

Applying the Missional Hermeneutic to Acts

Ephesian leaders, he said the Spirit compelled him to go to Jerusalem (Acts 20:22). He reminded them that prophets in every city told him that persecution and imprisonment awaited him. Knowing this, he informed the Ephesian leaders that he would never see them again (Acts 20:25 and 38).

En route to Jerusalem, Paul stopped in Tyre. Through the Spirit the local prophets urged him not to go to Jerusalem (Acts 21:4). When he reached Caesarea, Paul stayed with Philip the Evangelist and his four daughters who were prophetesses. During his stay, Agabus, a prophet from Judea, told him that the Jerusalem leaders would bind him and hand him over to the gentiles (Acts 21:10–11).

Clearly, the gift of prophecy was accepted and practiced in the New Testament church. First Corinthians 11–14 refers to the gift of prophecy twenty times. Paul taught that prophecy was a spiritual gift that should be utilized in the local congregation. Christians should desire the gift of prophecy (1 Cor 14:5). In fact, the ministry of the prophet is second only to the apostles (1 Cor 12:28). From a missional perspective, God works through prophecy to guide the church into his mission.

James was in charge when Paul arrived in Jerusalem (Acts 21:18). He told Paul what to do. At the Jerusalem Council, the apostles were present. However, like Paul, they did not stay in Jerusalem. Rather, they itinerated (1 Cor 9:5). In their absence, James, the brother of Jesus, served as the default leader of the Jerusalem church.[75] For example, when the angel released Peter from jail, Peter told the gathered believers to tell James and the other leaders of the Jerusalem church what had happened (Acts 12:17). Most likely, the apostles were not mentioned because they were not there. During the Jerusalem Council, James rendered a verdict on behalf of the whole church (Acts 15:13–21). James was so significant that he had a personal encounter with Jesus after the resurrection (1 Cor 15:7). Paul referred to James as an apostle (Gal 1:19). He said that "James, Cephas, and John" were the pillars of the church (Gal 2:9). In the Gospels, Peter was always listed first. Based on the order in Gal 2:9, one could argue that James superseded Peter. Also, when Paul had his intense controversy with the Judaizers, he said that they came from James (Gal 2:12).

The succession debate in early Islam was similar. The leadership of the Islamic community (Ummah) was divided between the rightfully guided

---

75. Lynch, *Early Christianity*, 40. There is no reliable evidence that James, the brother of Jesus, was a disciple during Jesus' ministry. Certainly, he was intimately familiar with Jesus and his ministry. Perhaps he became a believer and leader when Jesus appeared to him after the resurrection (see 1 Cor 15:7).

ones who were Muhammad's close companions (disciples) and those who were his biological descendants. The Shia argued that the leader of Islam had to be a direct descendant of Muhammad (Ali). In the same way, prima facie evidence hints that there was tension between the brother of Jesus and the apostles. As the leader of the Jerusalem church, did James believe that he was the leader of the church?

As was previously noted, the Jewish believers in Jerusalem wanted Paul to separate the Jews from the gentiles when he formed new churches during his missionary journeys. The new Jewish believers were to keep the law in the same way that the Jewish believers in Jerusalem kept the law (Acts 21:20) and the gentile believers were to obey the purity code given to them by the Jerusalem Council (Acts 21:25). The Jerusalem leaders refer to the purity code as "our decision." In their minds, they were the ones who made the decision that gentiles did not have to become Jews even though they opposed it until Peter gave his testimony. However, God told Paul that he should not distinguish between Jewish believers and gentile believers before the Jerusalem Council met. The author of Ephesians calls this revelation a mystery: "This mystery is that through the gospel the Gentiles are heirs together with Israel, members together of one body, and sharers together in the promise in Christ Jesus" (Eph 3:6 NIV).

Paul's revelation put him in direct conflict with the Judaizers who believed that they were the reconstituted messianic community waiting for the return of the Messiah so that God's promises to Israel could be fulfilled in them. When Paul came to Jerusalem, the church leaders correctly said that Paul told the Hellenistic believers not to circumcise their babies or keep the law. The Letter to the Galatians chronicles Paul's reasoning for this and his conflict with the Judaizers. If the missionary congregations were to be united, all the members had to follow the same script. If the Jewish believers kept the law and the gentiles did not, they could not form one congregation. The Judaizers understood this. That is why they wanted Paul to separate the Jews from the gentiles.

Instead of arguing with the Judaizers when he arrived in Jerusalem, Paul went along with them following his teaching in 1 Corinthians:

> Though I am free and belong to no one, I have made myself a slave to everyone, to win as many as possible. To the Jews I became like a Jew, to win the Jews. To those under the law I became like one under the law (though I myself am not under the law), so as to win those under the law. To those not having the law I became

like one not having the law (though I am not free from God's law but am under Christ's law), so as to win those not having the law. To the weak I became weak, to win the weak. I have become all things to all people so that by all possible means I might save some. (9:19-22 NIV)

So to show the Judaizers that he was a true Jew who kept the law and that the reports about him were not true, Paul took a purification vow. Afterward, he shaved his head and went to the temple to set the date for the required sacrifice (Acts 21:24-26). While Paul was waiting, Hellenistic Jews from Asia Minor were filled with rage when they recognized him. Like the silversmiths in Ephesus, they stirred the crowd into a frenzy by saying Paul taught against their customs and that he brought gentiles into the temple (Acts 21:28). The entire city was in an uproar. During the commotion, Jews from every quarter ran to the temple. The angry mob seized Paul and beat him as they dragged him from the temple to kill him.

Fortunately for Paul, Roman soldiers intervened. After quelling the riot, they arrested Paul and bound him with chains. However, they had to carry Paul because the mobs continued to pull at him. Before going into the barracks, Paul asked if he could address the mob. Then he evangelized the crowd by sharing his testimony (Acts 22:1-21). This is the second time that Acts recounts Paul's conversion.

The crowd listened to Paul until he told them that God sent him to preach to the gentiles. At that point, they resumed rioting. Because the commander assumed that Paul had caused the riot, he took him into the barracks to flog him. At that point, Paul told the soldiers that he was a Roman citizen and that they were not allowed to flog him.

The next day, the commander took Paul to the Sanhedrin so he could figure out why the Jews wanted to kill him. When Paul spoke, he intentionally pitted the Sadducees against the Pharisees. This diverted the conversation and took the attention off him. At that point, the Pharisees advocated for Paul. When the dispute became violent, the commander used force to remove Paul. After this, the Lord stood near Paul and gave him a special message. "Take courage! As you have testified about me in Jerusalem, so you must also testify in Rome" (Acts 23:11 NIV). According to the internal organization of Acts, Rome was the last barrier that he had to cross. Because Rome was the heart of the Roman Empire, it was a political barrier.

ACTS 24–26 — VARIOUS TRIALS

To get to the political center of the Roman Empire, Paul had to go through governors and kings. First, he went before Felix. After being accused of various Jewish infractions, Paul brilliantly countered the charges that the Jews brought against him. He also used his trial to give a testimony about Jesus. Later, Felix came to Paul with his Jewish wife. They listened as Paul preached. This became Paul's modus operandi. Whenever he went before officials, he used his defense as an opportunity to preach Jesus. In this way, the Roman leadership heard the gospel from a chief apologist.

Next, Paul went before Festus. When Paul contended that he was innocent, Festus asked him if he would go to Jerusalem and stand trial there. The Jews had requested this so they could ambush him while he was being transported. Since he was a Roman citizen, Paul asked to be tried before Caesar (Acts 25:11). Appealing to Caesar was how Paul planned to get to Rome per the word that God spoke to him.

A few days later, Paul had to stand before King Agrippa so he and Festus could determine the charges since a prisoner could not be sent to Caesar without a charge (Acts 25:27). Their conversation underscores that Paul did not do anything deserving of imprisonment or punishment. King Agrippa appeared in the court with high-ranking military officers and a crowd of prominent people (Acts 25:23). They were the people that Paul wanted to evangelize.

For the third time, Paul gave his testimony. Each retelling differed from the previous version. However, the message and the essential events remained the same. This shows that preaching contextualizes the message to an intended audience. Since Paul was evangelizing an erudite group of important people, he customized his message like he did when he spoke to the philosophers on Areopagus (Acts 17).

A testimony is a personal story that contains a message that points people to God. It is hard to argue with a person's testimony. In Paul's case, the king could say that he did not believe the content of his testimony. Yet Paul made a strong case for it. In fact, the specifics of his testimony were well known. Plus, the radical change in his life gave evidence of his encounter with Jesus. For these reasons, Agrippa did not disparage his story.

Paul separated his testimony into three parts.[76] The first part talked about his life when he lived as a passionate Jew. During this time, he was an

---

76. Mittelberg et al., *Becoming a Contagious Christian*, 126–30.

overachieving Jew who surpassed his contemporaries. In his zeal, he gladly persecuted the Jewish believers. Like his accusers, he voted to put them to death (Acts 26:9–11).

In the second part, Paul described his encounter with Jesus. His testimony emphasized the supernatural aspects of the encounter. He saw a brilliant light, fell from his horse, and heard a voice from heaven. The voice scolded him. Then, Jesus commissioned him to rescue people from the power of Satan and turn them to the light of God (Acts 26:12–18).

In the third part, he described his response. Without going into excessive detail, he said that he obeyed the heavenly voice by telling people to repent and turn to God. For this, he said he was wrongly seized and arrested in the temple. Based on Paul's testimony, King Agrippa did not discern any charges. He and Festus agreed that he would have been released if he had not appealed to Caesar (Acts 26:32).

Finally, Paul gave an "altar call." Since the king and Festus knew about Jewish theology, Paul made the case that Jesus was the Messiah and fulfilled the Jewish prophecy about the Messiah. Specifically, he emphasized that the salvation message included the gentiles (Acts 26:23). When Festus called him insane, Paul retorted that his message was true and reasonable. Then he appealed directly to King Agrippa because Agrippa knew his message was true. Since the king knew that Paul was evangelizing him, he asked Paul if he could make him a Christian in such a short time (Acts 26:28). Paul then cast the net wide. He turned toward the crowd and said that he hoped that all who heard him would be saved (Acts 26:29).

The court scene is reminiscent of Jesus' words to the disciples when he said, "On my account you will be brought before governors and kings as witnesses to them and to the Gentiles. But when they arrest you, do not worry about what to say or how to say it. At that time, you will be given what to say, for it will not be you speaking, but the Spirit of your Father speaking through you" (Matt 10:18–20 NIV).

ACTS 27 — BATTLING A "TYPHOON"

Acts does not specify the charges that were placed on Paul. However, it says that he was sent to Rome to stand trial there. Paul foresaw that the trip would be disastrous and that the ship, cargo, and the lives of his shipmates could be lost. The prescience could have come from a revelation. Most likely, it was based on experience since people were always trying to kill him. Why would the trip to Rome be different?

Soon, the ship was hit by a hurricane-force wind that made it impossible for the coxswain to steer it. Because the crew feared that the pounding waves would break the ship, they wrapped ropes around it. In short order, they had to throw the cargo and tackle overboard. No one ate while the violent storm raged for fourteen more days. The passengers and crew thought they would die.

Amid their hopelessness, Paul shared an explicit message that he received from an angel. He told the crew and passengers that they would be saved because he had to stand before Caesar. Then Paul told them what would happen and what they had to do to remain alive. At one point, some tried to escape on the lifeboat. Because the centurion trusted Paul, he ordered the soldiers to cut the ropes and set the lifeboat adrift. After this, Paul told them to eat because they would need strength to get ashore. When they had eaten, all the remaining food was thrown overboard. Finally, the ship ran aground and began to break apart.

The soldiers planned to kill the prisoners so none would escape. Perhaps Satan was behind this. The centurion, however, spared the prisoners to save Paul. With that, they abandoned the ship. Some swam to shore, and others floated on pieces of wood. In the end, all the crew and passengers made it to shore.

What does this text mean? First, in Genesis, God planned to destroy the world because of rampant sin. The sin went back to Satan's fall, Adam's disobedience, and the transgression caused by the delinquent sons of God who mated with women to sire Nephilim offspring. As God contemplated the destruction of all life, Noah found grace in God's sight because he was a righteous man who was unblemished and faithful (Gen 6:7–8). Unblemished may refer to his human ancestry.

Before God destroyed the world, he told Noah to construct an ark. Like Abraham, when Noah believed God and did what God told him to do, he showed that he was righteous. If he had disobeyed, God would have judged him with those who perished. Noah and his family were spared because God does not destroy the righteous with the unrighteous.

Second, when God said that he would destroy the cities of Sodom and Gomorrah because of their great sin, Abraham bartered for the people by asking if God would destroy the righteous with the unrighteous (Gen 18:24). God was willing to save everyone if he could locate ten righteous people in those cities. In the end, God delivered Lot and his family before he destroyed the cities.

Third, Satan may use persecution and natural disasters to kill the righteous, but God does not kill the righteous through his judgment. Nothing can estrange the righteous from God's grace. For this reason, God separates the righteous from the unrighteous before he judges. During the shipwreck, the angel told Paul that the people on the ship would be spared because of him (Acts 27:22–23). This is a great truth and a reason why the world needs to be salted with godly people.

Fourth, the hurricane wind is called a Northeaster (*Eurakulon*). The term combines Greek and Latin roots (Acts 27:14). It refers to a seasonal storm that had high winds. Acts describes the Northeaster as tempestuous wind (*anemos typhōnikos*). Literally, it was a "typhon wind." In Greek mythology, the *Anemoi* were minor gods. They were named Zephyros, Notos, Boreas, and Euros. They represented the cardinal points. They were the winds that blew the sails on the ships. For this reason, sailors prayed to the winds before they set sail. In contrast, Typhon was a terrible monster. He is described as a giant serpent with wings. Pythonos was a smaller version of Typhon. Typhon was the offspring of Gaia and Tartarus. He was the most terrible of all the monsters. When Typhon attempted to overthrow Olympus, an epic battle ensued. Finally, Zeus's lightning bolts threw Typhon down to earth and cast him into Tartarus.[77] Ironically, Jesus uses the same language to describe how Satan was cast from heaven (Luke 18:10). Like Typhon, in Revelation Satan was called the great dragon who was cast down from heaven (12:7–12). As his name implies, Typhon was associated with violent winds and cyclones since they are destructive forces in nature.

Usually, English Bible translations hide overt references to terms associated with Greek mythology. Even if the sailors did not think that the typhoon winds emanated from Typhon, they would have believed that they were associated with the gods because they did not have a naturalistic or scientific worldview.[78] For example, the sailors who were battered on the sea in Jonah automatically prayed to discover which god was upset with them because they believed that the violent storm was of divine origin (1:5). This was a normal response in the precritical world in which Paul

---

77. Henten, "Typhon," 1657–62.

78. "Virtually everyone believed that the unseen powers, some good and some evil, were active in human life. In the Greco-Roman world, the good and evil spirits were thought to be numerous and everywhere" (Lynch, *Early Christianity*, 126).

lived.[79] For this reason, Michael Heiser argues against scholars who demythologize biblical texts when they ignore, reject, or fail to comprehend the supernatural worldview of the biblical authors.[80]

The Gospel writers understood the mindset of the ancient sailors. For example, when Jesus was in a boat on the Sea of Galilee, a life-threatening storm (lit., a mega-storm of wind) suddenly fell on him and his disciples. After assessing the problem, Jesus stood up and cast out the spirit that manipulated the storm by commanding it to be still and be quiet. The storm immediately stopped when the spirit was dispatched (Mark 4:35–41). All who witnessed Jesus do this miracle were amazed because the wind (*anemos*) and the sea (*thalassa*) obeyed him.

The use of "obey" (*hupakouei*) in Mark 4:41 shows that the Gospel ascribed will to the natural forces that attacked the disciples. In classical times, people believed that supernatural spirits could manipulate the natural elements. In this story, Jesus personified the storm when he spoke to the spirit that was using the wind as a weapon. The storm spirit was sent to stop Jesus. Consequently, Jesus confronted the storm spirit like he did ordinary demons that possessed people.

Additionally, when Jesus approached the disciples while walking on the troubled waters (Matt 14:22–33), they thought he was a ghost (*phantasma*). They came to this conclusion because their worldview led them to it, i.e., they believed in nature spirits and knew that people do not walk on water.[81] It was a predictable response that showed critical analysis. Under the same circumstances, most modern people would come to the same conclusion. Once again, in this story, Jesus proved his mastery over the natural elements.

Since the Gospels aver that spirits can manipulate natural forces, the storm that threatened Paul on the sea could have been the same kind of storm that tried to destroy Jesus on the Sea of Galilee.[82] If that is the case, it points to the need for divine protection and divine covering. The first-century reader of Acts might conclude that Satan targeted Paul via a terrible

---

79. Martin says, "As a Pentecostal, I seek to enter the world of the living, dynamic, charismatic word of God, a world that is manifested through encounter with the God who is in, around, above, below, and in front of every text. In this charismatic encounter, the text is no longer the object of my critical critique, but I become the object of critique to the voice of God that speaks from the midst of the fire" ("Hearing the Voice of God," 205–6).

80. Heiser, *Unseen Realm*, 13.

81. Payne, *Satan Exposed*, 19–24.

82. Henten, "Typhon," 1660.

storm because he wanted to kill him. Paul was a high-value target who was on a mission for God. To thwart Satan's malice, God told Paul he would save him and the passengers. In this case, Paul did not cast the spirit out of the storm. Instead, he waited for God to give him a path through the storm. Sometimes, God destroys the storm. At other times, God enables his people to pass through the storm. In both cases, God is a fortress for those in peril and a companion for those who are attacked by evil spirits.

As has already been shown, Paul's theology acknowledged powers, principalities, authorities, and thrones in the heavenly places. He does not believe that the gods are real, but he does believe that spiritual forces are at work in the world. The corrupted sons of God, Satan, nation gods, and demons are examples. The gods may be the faces of these powers. They are connected to Satan's ongoing efforts to dethrone God and corrupt the world.[83] In the ancient world, storm gods were the strongest gods. For example, Baal Zephon, the head god of the Canaanite pantheon, was a storm god. So was Zeus. They are referred to as sky gods.[84] Scholars have argued that there is a strong connection between Baal Zephon, Typhon, Seth, and Satan.[85] For example, while pursuing the woman who gave birth, the great dragon (Satan) poured a river of water from his mouth to overtake the fleeing woman (Rev 12:15). Typhon is an antigod who opposes God. The spirit behind the Typhon winds would qualify as a storm god.[86] So would the spirit that used a storm to attack Jesus on the sea.

ACTS 28:1-10 — ON THE ISLAND OF MALTA

Sid Roth moderates a Christian television show that interviews people who have encountered God in remarkable ways. Guests contemplate visions, miracles, profound healings, incredible evangelism, and angelic visitations. Appropriately, the show is titled *It's Supernatural!* The same could be said about Acts. Apart from the resurrected Jesus, the blinding of Paul, and the visible presence of the Holy Spirit at Pentecost, Acts is filled with villains, sorcerers, a fortune teller, gods, goddesses, demons, oracles, exorcists, divine healings, raising people from the dead, miracles, prophets, shaking buildings, angelic interventions, and power evangelism. A word search

83. Payne, *Satan Exposed*, 63–86.
84. Payne, *Satan Exposed*, 134–36.
85. Henten, "Typhon," 1657.
86. Henten, "Typhon," 1659–60.

for "angel" in Acts fills two full pages. They are at the ascension, they free people from jails, they give people messages, they kill a bombastic Herod, and they work behind the scenes to enable God's mission. Also, Acts mentions Artemis, Jupiter, Hermes, Lady Justice, Typhon, Castor, Pollux, the python spirit, and the gods in the Acropolis. In Acts 8, a sorcerer called the Great Power of God realized that Jesus' power was greater than his power. So he converted to Jesus. When an evil sorcerer in Cyprus tried to stop the work of God, Paul cursed him by calling down blindness on him. When the Ephesian sorcerers saw that the demons brutalized the Sons of Sceva and that Paul could cast demons out, they converted to Jesus.

When reading Acts, one will realize why early Christians embraced the Christus Victor theology that emphasized Jesus' triumph over the evil powers in the heavens and on earth.[87] Acts shows that Jesus is more powerful than all the gods, goddesses, and demons in this world; no power can match his power or defeat him. Because his throne is higher than the thrones of the heavenly powers, principalities, and world rulers who seek to bring people into spiritual bondage, spiritually oppressed people want to align with him.

Not only is Acts supernatural; it is pure and unadulterated spiritual warfare. In Acts, God fights on behalf of his people. When an evil governor tried to kill Peter, God sent his angel to rescue him from prison. When Paul was in prison waiting for the morning, God sent an earthquake to rescue him. During a time of intense persecution, the church cried out to God. He responded by shaking the building in which they prayed and pouring out his Spirit more abundantly so they could do more signs and wonders. In Acts, people were not filled with the Spirit. Rather, they were constantly being filled with the Spirit.

The narrative about Malta continues the same storyline. After everyone reached dry land, the Maltese inhabitants made a fire to warm up the castaways. When Paul threw a stick into the fire, a deadly viper latched onto him. It did not strike and retreat. Instead, it emptied all of its venom into Paul's body. The people thought the great Typhon did not kill him, but the small serpent would. In other words, Paul escaped from the sea torment, but the goddess of justice (Lady Justice) has now claimed his life. In their minds, the deadly snake bite proved that Paul was an evil man. Once again, this episode demonstrates the supernatural worldview of the people that Paul and the early church evangelized.

87. For more information on Christus Victor, see Pugh, *Atonement Theories*, 1–25.

In Acts, everything and everyone tried to kill Paul. The following texts record times when someone or something tried to kill Paul in Acts: 9:23, 29; 14:5, 19; 16:23; 17:5; 19:29; 21:31; 23:12; 24:3; 27:14; and 28:3. From a spiritual perspective, the pattern points to spiritual warfare. Simply put, Satan wanted to neutralize Paul. Paul says,

> [I have] been in prison more frequently, been flogged more severely, and been exposed to death again and again. Five times I received from the Jews the forty lashes minus one. Three times I was beaten with rods, once I was pelted with stones, three times I was shipwrecked, I spent a night and a day in the open sea, I have been constantly on the move. I have been in danger from rivers, in danger from bandits, in danger from my fellow Jews, in danger from Gentiles; in danger in the city, in danger in the country, in danger at sea; and in danger from false believers. (2 Cor 11:23–26 NIV)

On Malta, Paul shook the snake into the fire. When the inhabitants realized that he was immune to the full venom of a deadly snake, they changed their thinking. They now believed Paul was a god. Previously, when Paul healed the lame man (Acts 14:5–6), the adoring crowds declared that he was Hermes before they stoned him to death and proved that he was not a god. That story did not repeat itself in Malta. This time, Paul evangelized the people through his anointed ministry. Specifically, when he healed the father of the island's chief officer, all the sick people on the island came to Paul so he could heal them (Acts 28:9). Normally, Paul would have established a church. However, his status as a prisoner prevented him from doing that. Plus, he was bereft of his traveling companions.

ACTS 28:11–31 — ROME

Three days after Paul arrived in Rome, he asked to speak to the Jews residing there. After identifying himself as a brother, he attempted to gain access to their community. On an appointed day, Paul shared the gospel with the gathered Jews. Some believed it. For the next two years, Paul continued to preach the gospel without hindrance in the heart of the final frontier—Rome.

In his letter to Rome, Paul told the Roman Christians that he wanted to visit them (Rom 1:8–12). Obviously, he did not start the Roman church. Roman Catholic tradition says that Peter founded the church in Rome and that he was the Bishop of Rome. He is buried at Saint Peter's Cathedral in Rome.

However, Peter is not mentioned when Paul lists all the notable people in the Roman church (Rom 16). In Acts 8, the believers fled in all directions when the Jerusalem church was persecuted. As they fled, they preached the gospel. Based on this, one should assume that Jewish believers who went home to Rome following the persecution seeded the church in Rome.

There is an interesting side note to Paul's time in Rome. While in Rome, he was allowed to live on his own, although a Roman soldier had to guard him at all times. Over the two years that Paul lived in Rome, hundreds of guards must have sat with Paul. In his letter to the Philippians, Paul said that his imprisonment resulted in the great progress of the gospel because he evangelized the entire Praetorian Guard one soldier at a time (1:12–13). The members of this elite unit served as bodyguards for the emperor. Previously, the New Testament reported that other Roman soldiers and centurions accepted Christ. Certainly, Paul hoped that his work with the Praetorian Guard would influence the Roman Empire. Sadly, no historical evidence substantiates that the Praetorian Guard was converted to Christ or that Paul's mission to them changed how they treated Christians.[88] Nonetheless, the anecdote in Phil 1 shows Paul's missiological thinking. As he was writing to the saints at Philippi, he believed that the guards that he tried to evangelize would push God's mission forward.

THOMAS'S MISSION TO INDIA

Acts mostly follows the journey of Paul as he was converted and became the face of New Testament missionary activity. Both history and tradition confirm that other apostles itinerated as missionaries, too. As such, the story of Thomas is a fitting way to conclude this chapter.

In their diaspora, Jews traveled as far as India and settled in modern-day Kerala. Until they returned to Israel in 1952, many lived in Jew Town, a community in Kerala. Jews living in other areas of India were called Bene Israel, Tribal Jews, and Baghdadi Jews. During the intervening years, many forgot that they were Jews. They nonetheless held onto their Jewish way of life.[89] Evidence suggests that the Jews reached Kerala as early as 1000 BC. They were traders from King Solomon. Through the centuries, other Jews immigrated to Kerala.[90]

   88. Smith, "Paul and the Praetorian Guard."
   89. Pradhan, "Jews of India."
   90. A tradition says that Jews immigrated to Kerala during the time of King Solomon.

Since Jews lived in India during the first century, one should expect that Christian missionaries would have evangelized them since the Jewish believers attempted to regather the Jews who had been driven to the nations. In this vein, tradition teaches that Thomas went to Kerala in AD 52 to evangelize the Indian Jews. According to Samuel Moffett, the early missionaries prioritized ministry to the Jewish diasporas. For that reason, it is fitting that Thomas's first Indian convert was a Jewish girl who attended to the local ruler (Acts Thom. 6).[91]

Legend says that a Brahmin priest killed Thomas while he was witnessing to Christ in AD 72. Today, pilgrims pay homage to Thomas while viewing his coffin in Chennai, India. Personally, I believed the legend when I stood before Thomas's coffin. Regardless, the existence of the Mar Thoma Church is a visible reminder that the gospel went throughout the known world during the apostolic era.[92] It is also a testimony to the church's commitment to obey Christ's command to witness to him to the "ends of the earth" (Acts 1:8).

CONCLUSION

This study of Acts has demonstrated that God had a mission and that he directed the church to fulfill it. In tangible ways, Acts shows that God partnered with the church just like he partnered with Moses to lead the Israelites out of Egypt. For example, as God confronted the powers who attempted to stop his mission, he neutralized them by enabling his church to do signs and wonders. Indeed, the parallels between Moses in Egypt and the church in Acts are striking.

Another tradition says that Jews went there during the Babylonian exile to escape forced deportation. Others say that they went there after the Romans destroyed the Second Temple. "There is evidence of a long-standing Jewish community in the city of Cranganore (present-day Kodungallur), identified with Muziris, which was an important medieval port. It was the capital of the powerful Chera kingdom in 1000 CE, the year in which an inscription was engraved there on copper tablets, recording a set of privileges granted to Joseph Rabban, leader of a Jewish trade guild" (Eliyahu-Oron and Johnson, "Kerala Synagogues," 118).

91. Moffett, *History of Christianity in Asia*, 27–36. Moffett refers to the Acts of Thomas. After considering coins, engraving, local histories, and other forms of hard evidence, Moffett concludes that it is highly likely that Thomas traveled to India.

92. Puthiakunnel, "Jewish Colonies."

Moses was prepared for his ministry when he was saved from the Nile and raised in Pharaoh's house. When Moses realized his calling, he got ahead of God by trying to intervene before God told him to act. Afterward, he spent forty years tending sheep in the wilderness. At the right time, God revealed himself to Moses in a burning bush and commissioned him to do his work. Everyone resisted Moses. Nonetheless, the signs and wonders that he performed confirmed his calling and his leadership.

God prepared Paul for his calling by allowing him to be born a Roman citizen. In addition, he was raised as a strict Pharisee at the feet of Gamaliel. God called Paul by blinding him with a bright light. Like Moses, Paul received a verbal commissioning from God. Like Moses, Paul acted prematurely. For that, the early church sent him away. During this time, he learned more about his calling and the gospel he would preach. At the right time, Barnabas retrieved Paul. Ultimately, Paul spoke with authority and did great signs and wonders as he became the face of God's mission in Acts.

Acts portrays a supernatural story in which God confronts Satan as the evil one works through false religion and bad people to disrupt God's mission. To best understand the interplay between God and Satan, one needs to "remythologize" Acts by reading it in its original context. To do this, one must accept the supernatural worldview of the participants. One must also employ the spiritual warfare hermeneutic because it connects the mission of the church with the kingdom of God theme in the Gospels. Through the mission of the church in Acts, God defeats Satan and displaces his kingdom.

This chapter has also shown that the mission of God crossed social, geographic, and political boundaries as it moved from Jerusalem to Rome. Often, boundary crossing was accompanied by internal conflict and the giving of the Holy Spirit. The giving of the Spirit showed God's approbation and neutralized internal quarreling. Nevertheless, an in-house battle between the Judaizers and Paul proved that the church was not of one mind. In fact, Paul disputed with Barnabas, the churches he planted, members of his missionary team, the Jews, and the gentile world. The intensity of his faith and his strong convictions led him to this. Paul believed that he was on mission with God, God was guiding him, and he needed to be true to the special revelation that God gave to him.

6

Analyzing the Current Immigration Debate in the US with the Missional Hermeneutic

PREVIOUS CHAPTERS HAVE DESCRIBED the missional hermeneutic and applied it to the interpretation of Scripture. This chapter shows that a missional reading of Scripture can guide Christ-believers as they seek to discern God's will about a controversial current issue—immigration. This is warranted because the Bible has much to say about the topic.

Evangelicals believe the Bible shows God's mission, God's character, God's truth, God's justice, and God's ways. Moreover, they avow that the inspired Scriptures mediate God's authority. Disobeying what the Scriptures command is sin. As such, when considering current affairs, evangelicals should discern what the Bible affirms and seek to understand what God is doing so they can align themselves with God. To this end, this chapter asks a fundamental question: How should the Bible's teaching about strangers and foreigners in ancient Israel inform an evangelical theology of immigration today? More specifically, how should a missional reading of Scripture influence how evangelicals respond to the current immigration debate in the US? Instead of giving a definitive answer, the chapter explores the larger hermeneutical issues surrounding the question.

This chapter is divided into four parts. The first section examines the Jewish idea of land. The second explores the foreigner in the Hebrew Scriptures. This is important because many Christians who advocate for immigration reform look to these texts to build a theological foundation that informs their ethical position. The third section reviews the New Testament teaching related to "the least of these" in Matthew and the command to love your neighbor. The final section examines the current immigration situation in light of the missio Dei and the mandate to evangelize the nations.

SECTION 1—THEOLOGY OF THE LAND

If you keep up with the news, you will know that local farmers in Okinawa, Japan have fulminated against military bases on their island.[1] I witnessed the rallies during the three years I lived in Okinawa. At first glance, the issue appears to be political. Certainly, environmentalists and peace activists do not want any military presence in Japan. They are connected to the media and are well funded. Upon closer scrutiny, however, one will discover that those who lost ancestral land to the US occupation after World War II are the most vocal and the most aggrieved. Even though Japan compensated them for the lost land, they still feel an emotional and spiritual attachment to their land and desperately want to reconnect with it.

Indigenous peoples throughout the world have a similar relationship with their lands. Those familiar with African spirituality will immediately recognize this point. Dr. Beauty Maenzanise, the former dean at Africa University's Faculty of Theology, told me that her Zimbabwean students had to take a course on the theology of the land. Surprisingly, it is one of the most popular classes at Africa University. Maenzanise also told me that Africans want a working theology of the land. For them, this is bigger than mere environmentalism. It is practical and spiritual because rural Africans feel deeply connected to the land where their ancestors lived. According to the theology, people are made from the earth. Like a mother, the land cares for them. Tending the land and remaining connected to it are sacred obligations.[2]

Not surprisingly, Jews also feel an attachment to their ancestral land. Some who have never lived in the modern state of Israel call it their spiritual home. Of course, the Palestinians who were displaced when the modern state of Israel was created also want to reoccupy the land. Throughout the world, people self-identify in four primary ways: God, family, ethnicity, and land. Often, all four categories intertwine.[3]

1. Tong, "Our Land, Our Life."
2. Beauty Maenzanise, personal communication with author.
3. Block, *Gods of the Nations*, 162–68. Block offers an exegetical overview of the intricate relationship between God, land, and people in the Hebrew Scriptures.

Analyzing the Current Immigration Debate

The following three biblical anecdotes show how Israelites understood land. According to the Book of Jubilees, when Canaan was looking for a place to settle, he stole the land allotted to Shem's descendants (Jub 10:27–34). When Canaan wrongly claimed the promised land and desired to establish his family there, his family warned him not to take the land of Shem because it came to him and his sons by lot. After Canaan took the land, his family told him that he would be cursed more than all the children of Noah because of the oath they swore before the holy judge and Noah (Jub 10:32). Canaan disregarded his family's chiding. His malfeasance became a justification for the Israelites to reclaim the land of Canaan after they left Egypt.

In Gen 12, God promised to give the land of Canaan to Abraham and his descendants. Abraham was a son of Shem through Arphaxad (Gen 11:10–27). According to God, those who bless Abraham and his descendants will be blessed. Those who curse him and his family will be cursed (Gen 12:1–3). When God finally returned the children of Abraham, Isaac, and Jacob to the land of Canaan (the promised land) after hundreds of years in Egypt (Exod 12:40), it was divided by lot. Afterward, the allotted portions perpetually remained with the families to whom it was given (Josh 14:2–5). It cannot be taken from them. Even if it is sold, the property must be returned to the allotted family during the jubilee year (Lev 25:13). The Torah stipulates the levirate law because the allotted land must be maintained. Under the levirate law, if a man dies before he sires a son to whom he may bequeath the family inheritance, a brother must marry his widow and father a son on his behalf (Deut 25:5–10).[4]

In 1 Kgs 21, King Ahab attempted to buy Naboth's vineyard, but Naboth would not part with it. He said, "The Lord forbid that I should give you the inheritance of my ancestors" (1 Kgs 21:3). After Jezebel had Naboth stoned, Ahab confiscated his property. After King Ahab wrongly confiscated Naboth's land, God cursed him with no descendants and said that dogs would lick up the blood of his wife. Retaining one's allotted ancestral land is a sacred obligation in the Hebrew Scriptures. Not even a king can steal the ancestral land from an Israelite.

Additionally, the Hebrew Scriptures personify the land. Since Adam was an earthling made from the ground, his physical body depended on the land for survival. After Adam and Eve sinned, the earth no longer

---

4. For a good overview from an Orthodox Jewish perspective, see Faust, "Jubilee Real Estate Law."

cooperated. In fact, God cursed the land because of their sin (Gen 3:17–19). Furthermore, God warned the Israelites not to commit abominations or the land would vomit them out in the same way that it vomited out the Canaanite nations that occupied it before them (Lev 18:24–25). Also, the Torah stipulated that the Jews could not sow on the land during the seventh year because the land needed to rest (Lev 25:4–5). Joel 2 promises that the land will rejoice when God brings salvation. When that happens, it will bear rich harvests and feed its inhabitants. Paul connects with Joel's promise when he writes that creation waits for human redemption. While waiting, it moans and groans under the curse. In the consummation, it will be set free from its bondage (Rom 8:19–22).

George Otis's research has demonstrated that God blesses the land and minimizes some effects of the curse when the people who occupy the land turn to God and renew their covenant with God.[5] His idea is based on a realized understanding of kingdom of God theology. Otis's thesis is too complicated to explore in depth. Suffice it to say, in the Bible people have an intrinsic linkage to the land. When they live righteously, God blesses them and their land.

I offer the following observations. First, God assigned the promised land to the Jews when they came out of Egypt. It was a blessed land that flowed with milk and honey. Second, the land was not their private possession because it belonged to God. They were caretakers of the land. As caretakers, they enjoyed its blessings to the extent that they remained faithful to the Creator who gave the land to them. Third, the earth is the Lord's (Exod 19:5 and Ps 24:1). All the lands belong to God. The idea of adverse possession does not exist with God. No matter how long a population occupies a territory, it still belongs to God. For example, in Lev 25:23 God says the land is his and that the Israelites are strangers and foreigners in the land. Fourth, God can give land to a people or take it away from a people. For example, he told the Israelites that he would drive them from the land if they defiled the land by abandoning the covenant through sin. In the parable of the tenants, Jesus portrays God as a landowner and Israel as God's vineyard. Because they reject God's Messiah and do evil, God takes the vineyard from

---

5. This concept threads its way through all of Otis's writings. See especially Otis, "Community Transformation" and *Twilight Labyrinth*, 311–14. The Almolonga, Guatemala renewal is often cited as evidence that Otis's thesis is correct. See Winger, "Almolonga, the Miracle City," 9–20. His books and documentaries offer a plethora of examples to demonstrate his thesis.

them and gives it to another (Matt 21:33–45). The destruction of the temple and the Jewish diaspora validate Jesus' parable.

In sum, a deep respect for the land as a gift from God over which people have a stewardship obligation is embedded in the Bible's personification of the land. Without moving into pantheism or animistic thinking, the personification reflects the "Mother Earth" and "Father God" theology of the ancient religions. For example, in the Canaanite religion, Asherah was the mother goddess and El was the father god. As a fertility goddess, Asherah had an exaggerated influence on Jewish religion. Because of a syncretistic commingling of El with Yahweh, at times the Israelites connected Asherah to Yahweh.[6] Despite occasional personification of the land, the Hebrew Scriptures do not present a Mother Earth goddess. Instead, Yahweh is a father who cares for the earth and his people.

SECTION 2—THE PEOPLE OF THE LAND

This section moves from land to people. In some ways, a parallel exists between how the ancient Israelites referred to non-natives and how Americans refer to the undocumented immigrants in their midst. In various English translations of the Hebrew Scriptures, non-Jews are distinguished by the following terms: stranger, sojourner, settler, guest, foreigner, neighbor, temporary resident, foreign worker, heathen, uncircumcised pagan, gentile, and the nations. Some of the terms are positive. Others are neutral. A few reflect hostility and contempt.

Bible scholars may use many English words to translate the Hebrew words for immigrants and foreigners. For example, translators employ nations, gentiles, pagans, and heathens for the same Hebrew word. When translating texts, Bible scholars have to pick an English word based on their knowledge of the context without allowing bias or personal theology to influence their choice of words. What did the Hebrew writer mean when he employed a given word? Words are dynamic. As such, one must translate for meaning. For instance, in the King James Version (KJV), Lev 25:44–45 directs the Jews not to treat fellow Jews as slaves when they are in servitude,

---

6. "An eighth-century B.C.E. inscription from Khirbet el-Qom, about twenty-five miles southwest of Jerusalem, contains similar language in 1 Kgs 15:13 and 2 Kgs 18:4, 21:7, and 23:6 (with parallels in 2 Chronicles) indicate that at least during certain points in the ninth, eighth, and seventh centuries B.C.E., Asherah's sacred pole was perceived as an appropriate icon to erect in Jerusalem, even in YHWH's temple" (Ackerman, "Ashera," para. 6).

but it allows them to make slaves of the heathens who dwell among them. Most modern translations, however, refer to bondservants and the strangers that sojourn among them instead of slaves and heathens.

When the KJV was published, heathen was a pejorative term that the English used to describe indigenous peoples from other parts of the world. It meant non-Christian and uncivilized person. One had to extend personhood and rights to a Christian but one could do as one pleased to a heathen. For example, the English depersonalized the African slaves that they imported to the Caribbean and British North America by calling them heathens. As late as the 1790s, William Carey had to flee from the jurisdiction of the East India Company because it did not approve of evangelizing the heathen natives in India. If the Indians became Christian, the mercantile class would have to treat them like real people.

The same attitude has dominated Christian interactions with Muslims. Even John Wesley stereotyped Muslims as heathens and used the terms Saracen and Mohammedan as bywords. Because the Muslims were dehumanized by negative rhetoric during the Crusades, Christian pilgrims, knights, and monks did not try to evangelize them. Rather, hostility colored their engagement with them.

A closer examination of Lev 17:8, Lev 25:45, and Ezek 47:22 shows that "heathen" does not fit the scriptural context because the stranger living amid the Jews may have been a circumcised God worshiper. The Torah makes frequent reference to circumcised God worshipers. Such foreigners may partake in the Passover, make offerings, and have the rights of a native-born.

For these reasons, "strangers who sojourn among you" is a better translation. It's not pejorative and isn't colored by the graphic ethnocentrism of previous times. It also feels neutral and avoids the judgmental nature of the harsh terms. Even so, since they were a kinship-based society, one should assume that biblical Israelites had ethnocentric prejudices because the notion that the Jews were the "chosen people" led to a corresponding notion that gentiles were not chosen. Xenophobia is demonstrated in the rebuilding of Jerusalem and the putting away of foreign wives (Ezra 10:3). Also, the surrounding nations repeatedly attempted to destroy Israel and carry its people off as slaves. The nations were their enemies. Finally, many of the foreigners who resided in Israel were not noble God worshipers deserving of a protected status.[7]

---

7. In the 1970s, many Israelis did not want to extend the right of return to Ethiopian

Analyzing the Current Immigration Debate

In sum, evangelicals should not impose personal biases on the text by forcing a preferred translation. At the same time, they should be aware that the English xenophobia of the seventeenth century may have colored how KJV-reading evangelicals developed negative ideas about American immigrants because the KJV overly uses derogatory terms to refer to them in the Old Testament (heathen and pagan).[8] Of course, a type of American nationalism that normalizes the "white" experience may feed into this problem.

Israel's Hospitality Codes

The Old Testament approaches the foreigner in many ways. Many Americans fixate on the negative approach: that is, the inhabitants of the Canaanite nations were evil, vile, and idolatrous. God destroyed them and gave their lands to the Hebrews because they were an abomination and a source of temptation to the Israelites. Their mere existence in the land was a continued source of contamination and defilement. Furthermore, God sent the Jews into Egypt so that the meager line of Jacob would not assimilate into the heathen Canaanite nations because he detested the Canaanite ways. When they returned to the promised land from Egypt, the Jews were commanded to destroy the inhabitants and avoid any social intercourse with them. They had defiled the land (Lev 25:18). In this regard, the Jewish invaders were the tools by which God cleansed the land of its wretchedness. In fact, God drove the Canaanite nations from the promised land so Israel could possess it (Deut 7:1). This theme is emphasized in Leviticus, Numbers, Deuteronomy, Joshua, and the other historical books in the Old Testament.[9]

Jews because they were not biologically Jewish, even though they had practiced Judaism for two thousand years. After an intense debate, in 1977 they were given the right of return.

8. The NIV rightly captures the meaning of Lev 25:44–45 when it states, "The male and female slaves which you have are to come from the surrounding nations; you are permitted to buy slaves from them. You may also buy the children of foreign workers who are living among you temporarily and from their clans which are living among you and have been born in your land." Rich sojourners also had the right to buy Jews as long as they treated them well, allowed them to be redeemed by a kinsman, and released them at the jubilee. The Message attempts to capture the meaning of the Hebrew by using both heathen and stranger.

9. "When the Lord your God brings you into the land you are entering to possess and drives out before you many nations—the Hittites, Girgashites, Amorites, Canaanites, Perizzites, Hivites and Jebusites, seven nations larger and stronger than you—and when the Lord your God has delivered them over to you and you have defeated them, then you

The theme is also picked up in Ezra and Nehemiah when God cleanses the Jews of their foreign wives, pagan influences, and unlawful interactions with gentiles before he reconstitutes the people in Israel after the Babylonian captivity (see Ezra 10; Neh 9:2 and 10:28–31). Accordingly, Jews were not to learn the ways of the nations or be joined to them. Also, ritual purity laws enabled social boundaries that kept the Jews from having intimate contact with foreigners.

The savage imagery of the conquest narratives and the seeming hostility with which the Hebrew texts refer to the Canaanites rightly repulse many evangelicals.[10] It sounds like genocide. How could a loving God condone the killing of men, women, and children because they occupied a land that he selected for himself and his people? The answer is complex.

First, when God chose Israel to be a holy nation on whom he placed his name, he separated his people from the surrounding peoples (Exod 19:3–6). In this regard, allegiance to the covenant defined holiness and formed a barrier that kept Israel from being contaminated by pagan nations. Second, God called Israel to be a light unto the nations and the mechanism by which they would be drawn to him (Isa 49:6). At first, the two ideas seem contradictory. But if one views the problem through the lens of God's mission in the world the solution becomes clear. That is, when one uses the mission of God as a grand narrative to read and interpret the Bible, the two extremes are connected via a missional tension.

In brief, in the beginning, God desired that all people should be properly related to him and that God would have a positive relationship with all people. Through the fall and the subsequent rebellion, sin alienated peoples from Yahweh. Through Israel, God sought to establish a beachhead in the world. This is seen in Exod 19:4–6: "You have seen what I did to the Egyptians, and how I bore you on eagles' wings and brought you to myself. Now therefore, if you will obey my voice and keep my covenant, you shall be my

---

must destroy them totally. Make no treaty with them, and show them no mercy. Do not intermarry with them. Do not give your daughters to their sons or take their daughters for your sons, for they will turn your children away from following me to serve other gods, and the Lord's anger will burn against you and will quickly destroy you. This is what you are to do to them: Break down their altars, smash their sacred stones, cut down their Asherah poles and burn their idols in the fire. For you are a people holy to the Lord your God. The Lord your God has chosen you out of all the peoples on the face of the earth to be his people, his treasured possession" (Deut 7:1–6 NIV).

10. See Hawk, *Joshua in 3D* and Hawk, *Berit Olam*.

own possession among all peoples; for all the Earth is mine and you shall be to me a kingdom of priests and a holy nation" (RSV).

Importantly, the covenant was predicated upon Israel keeping God's commandments and remaining a holy nation consecrated to God. At the same time, it says that Israel would be a kingdom of priests. In common practice, a priest has special access to God to mediate God to others. Through the priest, Jews gained access to God when the priest acted on their behalf to offer a sacrifice or a blessing. Collectively, Israel is called a priestly nation. Israel was not called to evangelize the nations. Rather, it was called to be God's special people who lived in harmony with the covenant God made with them. When this occurred, the nations would see Israel and take notice of Israel's God. When they did, they would be drawn to God. In this way, the Jews could mediate Yahweh to the nations. For this to work, Israel had to adhere to the covenant. When Israel fell into sin and abandoned the covenant, the missional purposes of God were at risk. For that reason, God had to judge Israel to bring them to repentance and renewal. God's missional purposes depended on Israel being faithful to him.

Many biblical examples illustrate Israel's missional nature. First, in 2 Kgs 5, General Naaman from Syria has leprosy. None of his gods could heal him. Through an Israelite slave girl, Naaman heard that he could get healed in Israel. This drove him to seek the God of Israel. Eventually, Elisha showed the foreign general that Yahweh was superior to the other gods by healing him. In the aftermath, the general became a God worshiper and took Israelite soil back with him so that he could stand upon God's land when worshiping Yahweh in his foreign land. Through Naaman, we may presume that other Syrians heard about God.

Second, because of the name of Yahweh, the Queen of Sheba came to Jerusalem to query King Solomon (2 Chr 9). In the end, she departed a changed person, overwhelmed by the greatness of God. A Jewish midrash states that she was converted to Yahweh and became the founder of the ancient Ethiopian Jewish community.[11]

Third, while dedicating the temple, Solomon's prayer demonstrated his belief that strangers from foreign lands would come to the temple to seek God because of God's great fame. In the prayer, Solomon petitioned

---

11. Kadari, "Queen of Sheba." According to the *Kebra Nagast*, an Ethiopian legend says that the Queen of Sheba and King Solomon had a child named Menilek I. According to the legend, he became the king of Ethiopia and founded a Solomonic dynasty that lasted until Haile Selassie took over in 1974.

God to grant whatever foreign seekers prayed for so that they would tell their people that the God of Israel was the great God who answered prayers:

> As for the foreigner who does not belong to your people Israel but has come from a distant land because of your name—for they will hear of your great name and your mighty hand and your outstretched arm—when they come and pray toward this temple, then hear from heaven, your dwelling place. Do whatever the foreigner asks of you, so that all the peoples of the Earth may know your name and fear you, as do your own people Israel, and may know that this house I have built bears your Name. (1 Kgs 8:41–43 NIV)

This expectation is further illustrated when God directed Solomon to build a court for the nations in the temple. It is the same outer court that Jesus cleansed when the Jewish high priest turned it into an animal market and a place to exchange money. Jesus understood the missional purpose of the outer court and was enraged that the Jewish leaders desecrated it. Quoting Isa 56:7, Jesus said, "My house will be called a house of prayer for all nations." In other words, since the Lord intended for the nations to come to the temple to pray, make offerings, and encounter God, he created space for them in the temple.

Considering this, the hospitality codes in Israel take on a new perspective. Through sojourning in a holy Israel that worshiped Yahweh and kept the law, foreigners came to know God and to be delivered from their bondage to false gods and evil practices. When they returned to their homelands, they became a means by which God could spread his name and eradicate evil among the nations.

This theme is greatly magnified in Second Isaiah and the Psalms. For example, Ps 67 petitions God to bless Israel so the nations would see the greatness of Israel's God and be drawn to God through Israel. Repeatedly, it talks about the salvation of the nations and states that the nations should praise God. From this, one can say that Israel was blessed to be a blessing! This harkens back to God's original covenant with Abraham in Gen 12:2–3: "I will make you into a great nation, and I will bless you; I will make your name great, and you will be a blessing. I will bless those who bless you, and whoever curses you I will curse; and all peoples on earth will be blessed through you" (NIV).

Analyzing the Current Immigration Debate

From the Outside to the Inside

Because of its missional purposes, Israel had a moral obligation to care for the strangers and foreigners in its midst. The following is a summary of statements given to the Israelites about foreigners and strangers:

1. The Israelites are not allowed to mistreat the foreigner. They are told that the law equally applies to the native-born and the foreigner.
2. They must care for strangers. This includes rules about leaving a portion of the harvest in the fields for them to glean.
3. Circumcised strangers are to be treated as native born.
4. Because God loves the foreigner in the midst, the Israelites must also love him.
5. They are to share the tithe with the foreigner so that he may eat and be satisfied. When they obey this, the Lord will bless the Israelites.
6. The foreigners are grouped with the widows and the orphans throughout the Torah and Prophets. As such, Jews have a special obligation to them. Specifically, they are told not to abuse the foreign worker. In Ezek 22:29, God says that he has poured out his indignation upon the Jewish people and has consumed them with the fire of his wrath because they have oppressed the poor and needy and have extorted from the stranger without redress.

The book of Ruth aptly illustrates God's perspective on hospitality, family, and inclusion. Because of a severe famine, a Jewish family relocated to Moab. From the story, one may assume that the Moabites treated the Jewish sojourners well. They prospered to the extent that they had enough social standing so their two sons could marry Moabite women. In time, Naomi's husband and two sons died. Afterward, Naomi and her two Moabite daughters-in-law decided to go to Israel. On the way, Naomi encouraged the Moabite women to return to their country. Orpah returned but Ruth would not. Instead, Ruth bonded herself to Naomi and Yahweh.

Upon their return to Israel, Ruth gleaned in the field of Boaz. When Boaz discovered who she was, he told her to join with his women and glean behind the men. He also vowed to protect her since she was a vulnerable widow and sojourner in their midst. Soon after this, Boaz invited her to eat with the harvesters. He provided food and water for her throughout the harvesting season and ensured that she had enough grain to support herself and Naomi. When Boaz redeemed Ruth by marrying her, he brought her into the community of Israel as an insider.

In sum, foreign sojourners moved from the outside to the inside of the community by invitation of native people. In the process, they discovered Yahweh. Ultimately, by God's design, Ruth became a direct ancestor of Jesus. Clearly, God did not reject righteous gentiles who came to Israel to seek him.

SECTION 3—THE LEAST OF THESE

Matthew 25 connects to the Jewish conversation about tending to the needs of foreigners and strangers. Furthermore, it shows how Jesus feels about those who ignore them.

> Then he will say to those at his left hand, "Depart from me, you cursed, into the eternal fire prepared for the devil and his angels; for I was hungry and you gave me no food, I was thirsty and you gave me no drink, I was a stranger [alien] and you did not welcome me, naked and you did not clothe me, sick and in prison and you did not visit me." Then they also will answer, "Lord, when did we see thee hungry or thirsty or a stranger or naked or sick or in prison, and did not minister to thee?" Then he will answer them, "Truly, I say to you, as you did it not to one of the least of these, you did it not to me." And they will go away into eternal punishment, but the righteous into eternal life. (Matt 25:41–46 RSV)

The Judgment of the Nations in Matt 25

On the surface, the judgment of the nations in Matt 25 perfectly illustrates the Jewish moral code related to foreigners and strangers. At the return of Christ, the gentiles will be rewarded or condemned based on how they treated the "least of these" who had physical, material, and emotional needs.[12] Those who care for the least of these will receive rewards and those who do not will be sent to eternal punishment. Additionally, this irrefutable prooftext cajoles American evangelicals to care for the undocumented immigrants in their midst. After all, they do not want God to judge their country because they do not care for the poor.

---

12. A non-Jewish person is a gentile. When the term is plural, it refers to the non-Jewish nations.

Certainly, I am sympathetic to this reading and believe that the New Testament teaches believers to care for the poor and needy. I would also include the undocumented immigrant in that category. Nevertheless, the church has too quickly commandeered this text for the above purposes. Exegetically, the "least of these" in Matt 25 refers to the wandering mendicant apostles mentioned in Matt 10 and was not intended to be applied to the generalized poor.

In speaking to his apostles when he sent them out on their first mission, Jesus states, "He who receives you receives me, and he who receives me receives him who sent me.... And whoever gives to one of these little ones even a cup of cold water because he is a disciple, truly, I say to you, he shall not lose his reward" (Matt 10:40–43 RSV). This reiterates what Jesus says in Matt 25:46. In Matt 10, "little ones" refers to the apostles whom he sent out. The word for little ones is *micron*. It can be translated least of these. Based on the missionary context of Matt 10, the wandering apostles had no support and were fully dependent on God and others for their survival when Jesus sent them out on their mission (Matt 10:9–13). In Matt 10, they are an extension of Jesus. What people did to them they did to Christ. Even the simple act of giving one of them a cup of cold water will not go unnoticed by God.

After Jesus' ascension, teams of wandering preachers scattered throughout the world, living in poverty while preaching the kingdom of God and doing signs and wonders. Paul is an example of this. When referring to the wandering apostles, the Didache encourages the churches to support them provided they do not overstay their welcome of two days (1:1–7). When an apostle or prophet left, the church was not to give them any money. They had to live in poverty following Jesus' instructions in Matt 10:9–11.[13]

These missionary apostles had little social status in the eyes of the world and could be easily abused. In fact, they gave up their earthly privileges when they became itinerant evangelists. Such people have a preferential place in God's kingdom. Based on this interpretation of the "least of these" in Matt 25, Jesus tells the nations that he will hold them responsible for the way they treated his apostles when they came to them. To receive an apostle and his message of salvation will lead one to eternal life. To reject them is to consign oneself to eternal punishment.

---

13. The Didache is a first-century church manual that was highly influential in the early church.

Who Is My Neighbor?

In Matt 22:35, a lawyer asked Jesus to name the greatest commandment. Based on popular rabbinic teaching, Jesus indicated that the law could be reduced to two primary categories. First, people must love God with their total being. This refers to the first four commandments of the Ten Commandments. Individuals could not please God, be right with God, or fulfill their moral obligations if they did not put God first. Second, if people truly love God, they will show it by loving their neighbors because the love of neighbor is the fruit that manifests that one loves God.

First John says people should love others because God loves them. Practically, people cannot claim to love God if they do not love others (1 John 4:19–21). James makes the same point when he says that believers must care for those in need if they truly believe in God (Jas 2:14–17). For Paul, loving others is a fruit of the Spirit (Gal 5:22). Furthermore, religious people who make great personal sacrifices for their faith gain nothing if they do not have love (1 Cor 13:4). In the end, the opposite of love is not hate—it is self-focus.

When reading the following Scripture, think about the example of Christ. Then think about the spiritual perils of ethnocentrism and the need to demonstrate love to immigrants. "Love is patient and kind; love is not jealous or boastful; it is not arrogant or rude. Love does not insist on its own way; it is not irritable or resentful; it does not rejoice at wrong, but rejoices in the right. Love bears all things, believes all things, hopes all things, endures all things" (1 Cor 13:4–7 RSV).

In Luke 10, a lawyer asks what he must do to inherit eternal life. After the lawyer quotes the great commandment to love God and one's neighbor, Jesus tells him that he will obtain eternal life if he does this (Luke 10:28). Not satisfied with the answer, the lawyer asks, "Who is my neighbor?" (Luke 10:29). This was not a philosophical question. He wanted Jesus to define neighbor as a closed set that only included righteous Jews and excluded other classes of people. In his mind, God's command to love your neighbor should not extend to Roman soldiers, tax collectors, winebibbers, prostitutes, and Samaritans. Instead of giving him a direct answer, Jesus told him the parable of the good Samaritan (Luke 10:25–37).

In the parable, a pious Jew is robbed and left for dead. A priest and a Levite saw him and did not intervene. If they were going to the temple to perform official duties, touching blood or a dead person would have disqualified them from serving in the temple. If this were the case, it would indicate that they prioritized sacerdotal duties over the care of a hurt neighbor.[14] In other words, they loved serving God in the temple, but they did not love the injured Jew because love requires action on behalf of an injured person.

In contrast, when the Samaritan traveler saw the injured Jew, he was filled with pity. Then he provided emergency first aid and transported him to an inn. When the Samaritan left the inn, he paid the injured Jew's medical bills in advance and promised to pay additional fees. In terms of the lawyer's mindset, Jews and Samaritans were not neighbors. Yet, the Samaritan treated the Jew like a neighbor by caring for him. The lawyer wanted to draw a line around the idea of a neighbor so he could limit it to his own people. Jesus erased the line and said that anyone you encounter with a need is your neighbor and you must love that person.

In the gospels, Jesus is the good Samaritan. In radical and socially unacceptable ways, he modeled God's love of neighbor by casting demons out of a gentile who lived in the tombs, by reaching out to a Samaritan woman who lived with a man to whom she was not married, by forgiving a woman caught in the act of adultery, by healing a Samaritan leper, by eating with notorious sinners, by touching impure people, by honoring a ritually impure woman who touched the hem of his garment, by interacting with Roman soldiers to include healing a centurion's child, by calling a tax collector into his intimate circle, by helping the Syrophoenician woman, by leading a revival in a Samaritan village, by dying for the world, and by sending his church out to the ends of the earth as his representatives to witness to his love in word and deed. Whenever evangelicals attempt to skirt the obligation to love one's neighbor in tangible ways by redefining the term to fit their biases, they transgress the great commandment to love God and one's neighbor as oneself.

Missiologists have noted that people tend to divide their world into three categories. The first is family, friends, and colleagues. These are the people with whom one has intimate contact and reciprocal social obligations. One knows them by name and cares for them. The second is machinery. These are people with whom one has a working relationship. They may be the person who cuts the grass, harvests the crops, cleans one's house, delivers the mail, or serves tables in the restaurant where one eats. Many

---

14. "If any one touches an unclean thing, whether the uncleanness of man or an unclean beast or any unclean abomination, and then eats of the flesh of the sacrifice of the Lord's peace offerings, that person shall be cut off from his people" (Lev 7:21 RSV).

are nameless even though one may interact with them regularly. They have value to the extent they meet one's needs. The third category is scenery. This includes migrant farm workers, construction workers, the homeless, and others. They are the masses of people that one passes daily. Since they are not in one's social circles and one does not do direct business with them, the person tends to ignore them. In other words, one sees them but does not notice them. In terms of Jesus's command to love our neighbor, these are the neighbors in the parable.[15]

AMERICAN IMMIGRATION TODAY

In October 2023, 49.5 million American residents (15 percent of the total population) were foreign-born immigrants. This is the highest percentage since America became a nation.[16] In December 2023, US officials processed 302,000 immigrants. That does not count the immigrants who bypassed the checkpoints or never left when their visas expired.[17] Credible estimates claim that 8,062,646 immigrants have crossed America's southern border since January 2021.[18] Some claim the number is above ten million.[19] They come from Africa, Asia, and Latin America. Most are fleeing failed governments, escaping persecution, or seeking a better life in America. Others are associated with human trafficking, drug cartels, and violent gangs. Some are agents of foreign governments. Places with large concentrations of new arrivals have experienced increased crime and a steady drain on local resources.[20]

    15. Smalley, "World Is Too Much with Us," 234–36.
    16. Camarota and Zeigler, "In October 2023."
    17. Garver, "Huge Number of Migrants."
    18. Blankley, "Illegal Aliens Since 2021."
    19. Blankley, "Retired FBI Execs," reports on a letter from ten retired FBI directors. The letter states, "In 2021, the demographics of those crossing the porous southern boundary started to shift. Young men from around the world traveling alone and holding questionable motivations dramatically increased in number to become the most common profile of those breaching the nation's borders. A startling number have been found on the terrorist watchlist or are from countries designated as State Sponsors of Terror distinctly unfriendly to the United States. . . . The surge in numbers of single, military-aged males descending upon American cities and towns is alarming and perilous. Additionally, they are not just from terror-linked regions, but from China and Russia as well—hostile adversaries of the U.S. with aspirations to devastate national infrastructure" ("America's Border Security," H331).
    20. Rappaport, "Massive Burden."

Analyzing the Current Immigration Debate

Allow me to put a face on the immigration debate. In recent years, twelve to fifteen thousand Haitian immigrants have settled in Springfield, Ohio.[21] Affordable housing, low crime, and job opportunities attracted them to the city. Most came by word of mouth or were invited by family and friends who had previously relocated to Springfield.[22]

Since the traditional population of Springfield is about sixty-five thousand, the Haitian influx is a source of cultural change. Typically, people resist rapid change and those who cause it. Furthermore, even though the Haitians are a working population, they still strain local resources and must be accommodated in public schools. Latent racism plays into the negative stereotyping since the local population is mostly white and the Haitians are Afro-Caribbean.[23]

During the 2024 presidential campaign, the situation in Springfield received a lot of attention. Some politicians negatively stereotyped the Haitians by reporting that they eat pets. Presumably, because of hunger in parts of Haiti, Haitians have eaten dogs. In the aftermath, Springfield officials debunked and rejected this unfortunate claim. The ensuing debate led to a national conversation about prejudice and American hospitality.

The overwhelming majority of Americans affirm legal immigration. Nonetheless, most want the open border with Mexico to be closed. They worry that many of the undocumented immigrants will hurt America and are a threat to the American way of life. Reports about *Tren de Aragua*, an armed gang from Venezuela that is terrorizing parts of America, have legitimized the fear and stereotyping of undocumented immigrants.[24]

Tyrone Muhammad captures the sentiment when he states, "When the black gangs here get fed up with the illegalities and criminal activities of these migrants or non-citizens, the city of Chicago is going to go up in flames and there will be nothing the National Guard or the government

---

21. Haitians are fleeing their homeland because of the unstable government, abject poverty, lawlessness, and gangs. Recently, 210,000 have been paroled into the United States. Approximately 852,000 Haitian immigrants live in America.

22. Shoichet, "Why Springfield?"

23. Haitian immigrants who live in large cities have complained that Black Americans also discriminate against them because of vast cultural differences. In 1998, while I was conducting a research project with the Haitian diaspora in Boston and Florida, Haitian leaders emphasized that they were not African Americans and that they did not want to be absorbed by the Black community.

24. Salinas and Salhotra, "What You Need to Know."

can do about it when the bloodshed hits the streets. It'll be blacks against migrants."[25]

Law-abiding immigrants who come to the southern border want to get processed and released into America because it gives them benefits and opens the door for asylum. Plus, according to the United States Citizenship and Immigration Services, the average wait time before asylum seekers have their first immigration hearing is ten years. During that time, they are free to work, buy homes, go to school, raise families, and pursue the American dream.[26]

Besides the law-abiding immigrants, officials know that bad people are crossing into America. According to the House Homeland Security Committee, "The number of individuals apprehended illegally crossing the Southwest border and found to be on the terrorist watchlist has increased 2,500 percent" since 2021.[27] Some have been apprehended and deported multiple times. As soon as they are deported, they return. The gotaways, i.e., people not stopped and checked when crossing the border, pose the greatest danger because they are invisible until caught. Officials do not know how many of the gotaways are jihadists, foreign agents, sex offenders, murderers, criminals, spies, and national enemies.[28] A recent letter from ten retired FBI directors says, "It would be difficult to overstate the danger represented by the presence inside our borders of what is comparatively a multi-division army of young single adult males from hostile nations and regions whose background, intent, or allegiance is completely unknown."[29]

In 2024, the House of Representatives issued two articles of impeachment against the head of Homeland Security because he is not enforcing immigration laws.[30] Even though President Biden says he can stop the flow across the border, the federal government seems unwilling to do so. This has caused great frustration for big-city mayors who do not have the resources or the will to absorb the large number of immigrants that have come to them. Governor Abbott of Texas has likened the problem to a foreign invasion. Since President Biden has not stopped the massive influx of

---

25. Lee, "Chicago Gangs."
26. "Asylum Quarterly Engagement."
27. "Border Sector Chiefs."
28. Camarota and Zeigler, "In October 2023."
29. Blankley, "Retired FBI Execs," para. 4.
30. "Impeaching Alejandro Nicholas Mayorkas."

unauthorized travelers, Abbott has deployed the Texas National Guard and erected a razor wire fence in places where Trump's wall is not completed.[31]

Speaking of Texas, Spanish is the dominant language in the border areas and many of the large cities.[32] Because of the shifting demographics, one must be bilingual to work in a public service job. The same is true in South Florida and large parts of California.

Those who focus on the benefits of immigration say that America has always been an immigrant country. Plus, immigration drives America's economy and fuels job growth in sectors that need more workers. According to the Brookings Institute, "Immigrants boost economic activity, promote innovation, and improve the productivity of native-born workers. Increases in immigration raise both tax revenues and fiscal costs."[33] The US government and many independent sources support what the Brookings Institute says about the economics of immigration.

Immigration influences the religious landscape in America. Since immigrants bring their faith with them, their place of origin is important. The surge on the southern border is global. Sixty-three percent has come from Latin America, 11 percent from Sub-Sahara Africa, 10 percent from East Asia, and 6 percent from the Middle East. Ironically, only 2 percent of the immigrants are from Mexico. The majority are from Central America.[34] Latin America is 87 to 90 percent Christian. However, over recent years, Evangelical-Pentecostalism has grown three times faster than the population.[35] The growth of Evangelical-Pentecostals is so rapid that Brazil and Guatemala should have an Evangelical-Pentecostal majority by the end of the decade.[36] Already there are more Evangelical-Pentecostals in Honduras than Catholics. In total, 19 percent of Latin Americans are Evangelical-Pentecostal.[37]

In 1970, there were 62.7 million global Evangelical-Pentecostals. By 2020, the number had grown to 709.8 million. Experts say that the number will increase to 1 billion by 2050. Most of the growth comes from Africa,

---

31. Beitsch, "Speaker Johnson."
32. "Background on the Colonias."
33. Edelberg and Watson, "More Equitable Distribution," para. 6.
34. Camarota and Zeigler, "In October 2023."
35. Tennent, *Invitation to World Mission*, 286.
36. Bidegain and Soler, "Religion in Latin America," 5.
37. "Religion in Latin America."

Latin America, and Asia.[38] It is the fastest-growing faith in the world. In addition to Evangelical-Pentecostals, the Roman Catholic Church is being renewed by the growth of Spirit-filled Charismatics. From 1970 to 2020, Catholic Charismatics grew from 2,000,000 to 160,000,000.[39] According to Philip Jenkins, as the Western church diminishes and the global church grows, the "Next Christendom" will be Evangelical, Pentecostal, and Charismatic. Furthermore, Evangelical-Pentecostal immigrants are carrying their fervent faith to the West.[40]

WHAT IS GOD DOING?

When considering the changing religious composition of Latin America and the other places in the world that are sending immigrants to America, one should ask what God is doing. Is God working through immigration to further an unknown purpose? A previous chapter demonstrated that God has always worked in history to push forward his missional objectives. Is God sending the immigrants to America because he wants to use them to change America, revive America, or equip America to evangelize the nations who are sending immigrants to America?

According to "reverse mission" theorists, renewalist churches in Africa, Asia, and Latin America are sending immigrants to Western countries so they can plant churches and minister to the immigrant populations.[41] In essence, some immigrants are Christian missionaries. The concept argues that the West is a mission field because of the growth of the unchurched, the massive numbers of new arrivals from non-Christian lands, and the de-Christianizing influence of secular humanism. Throughout the West, immigrant churches are pastored by immigrants. Many of the immigrant churches also evangelize native-born Americans and start congregations with them. For example, a former student from a Pentecostal church in Ghana is a hospital chaplain during the week. On the weekend, she leads a language-specific service for people from her tribal community. Afterward, she conducts an English service. Her husband is a bishop from her home

---

38. Center for the Study of Global Christianity, "Christianity in Its Global Context."
39. Nucci, "Charismatic Renewal."
40. Jenkins, *Next Christendom*.
41. Olofinjana, "Dummies Guide" and Galadima and George, *Africans in Diaspora*, in particular chapter 1, "Beyond Empire: Global Migrations and New Approaches to Christian Mission."

denomination. He travels between Texas and New York giving leadership to Pentecostal immigrant churches. When I preached at the English service, I saw large numbers of African Americans, whites, Hispanics, and anglophone Africans from other countries. One Hispanic couple told me they attended the church because it was like their home church in the Dominican Republic.

When immigrants from countries that do not permit Christian evangelism come to America, they can be evangelized. Usually, they are evangelized by immigrants from their home country. After coming to know Jesus, some of the converted immigrants return to their home countries to evangelize friends and family members. In time, they start churches in hard-to-reach countries. Seeding the gospel in unreached places allows the church to grow where traditional missionaries cannot go. This process is a corollary to reverse missions and may be God's strategy for evangelizing people in closed countries.

PERSONAL EXAMPLES THAT POINT TO THE MISSIO DEI

While in college, I worked for a Cuban newspaper in Orlando, Florida. I took pictures, delivered papers to local businesses, and worked in the office. One night, the boss's Pentecostal wife introduced herself to me. Over a period of months, I began to attend the small church she pastored. Ultimately, she baptized me. I am indebted to the Cuban immigrants who loved me, accepted me, and evangelized me.

From 1994 through 1995, I pastored a Cuban refugee camp in the jungles of Panama. The refugees were plucked from the Gulf of Mexico as they tried to get to Florida. Hundreds of them packed our worship services and participated in daily ministry events. During a two-week period, I baptized eighty-seven of them. A large portion of the camp population wanted to come to America so they could practice their faith and evangelize Cuban Americans without Communist persecution.[42]

From 1998 through 2000, I pastored a large church in West Central Florida. One Saturday evening, Reyes and Olivia came to my office saying that God had called them to start a ministry with the large number of unchurched Hispanics who worked in our area. The ministry that we began soon outgrew a chapel that seated 120. In time, we had off-site services in migrant camps, homes, and local churches. Baptisms were constant. We

42. Payne, "Religious Community," 141–54.

estimate that three hundred participated in our Spanish-speaking ministry for immigrants in a given week. As the new Christians followed the crops to other states, they continued to share their faith. We called them our missionaries.[43]

In 2018, I hired a Peruvian language coach to help me teach at an evangelical seminary in Colombia. Soon, I realized that she lived in abject poverty. So, my wife and I invited her to live with us for two years. Her mother came with her. During that time, she became a sister to my daughter. While living with us, she actively participated in a local evangelical church. Since graduating from college, she has become a Spanish teacher in a public school, bought a home, got married, and is allowing other Peruvian immigrants to live with her. She stipulates that everyone who lives in her house must attend church and Bible study.

In the last two years, I have become friends with a group of immigrants from Honduras. One of them started a Spanish ministry in the church I pastored. Before she left Honduras, her family owned a home and a coffee farm. When she and her family became evangelicals, the Honduran army began to harass them. During her encounters with soldiers, she was violated, had her jaw badly broken, and was repeatedly threatened. When soldiers killed her first cousin, they told her that her family would be next. In desperation, she and her husband grabbed their papers and some money before fleeing toward the US border. They left everything behind. While coming to America, they endured countless hardships and daily deprivations. Last year, they were granted asylum. Now, she is a bivocational minister within the Hispanic community. Instead of giving in to bitterness, she thanks God that he has let her family live in America. By the way, her son is an honor student in gifted classes even though he did not speak a word of English when they crossed the border.

CONCLUSION

The Old Testament told the Israelites to care for the immigrants who came to them. It assumes that gentiles will come to find God and join themselves to Israel. For this reason, the pro-immigration laws in the Old Testament have a missiological focus. As a secular nation, America is not inviting people to immigrate to get evangelized. Therefore those laws cannot be unilaterally applied to the American context. Nonetheless, the command to love

---

43. Payne, *American Methodism*, ix–xiv.

one's neighbor obligates evangelical Americans to care for poor immigrants with the same intensity that the good Samaritan cared for the injured Jew.

When American immigration is viewed through the lens of the missio Dei, one can assume that immigration will play into God's mission. This chapter explores ways in which that might happen. For this reason, evangelicals should remain optimistic about immigration and not seek to argue against it even though there are serious problems associated with it. Rather, they should seek to discern how God is using it so they can align themselves with God's work.

7

The Divine Preparation for the Gospel

THE ANCIENTS OBSERVED REPEATING seasons and the forward movement of ordinary time. Additionally, they read the stars, looked for omens, and consulted oracles to foresee specific events that portended exaggerated significance. For anxious people, certain moments in history were pregnant with anticipation. In English, when all the antecedents have been satisfied, those waiting for the big event can say that the time is ripe. Examples of ripe moments in American history are D-Day, the 1963 march that launched the civil rights movement, landing on the moon, and the Jesus revival that instigated a resurgence in evangelical faith at a time when the mainline churches greatly waned (1966–1978). Likewise, in the Bible, the birth of Jesus came at a ripe moment.

When the Magi witnessed Jesus' natal star, they came to Jerusalem because they realized that it signaled the birth of a great king (Matt 2:2). For Zoroastrian astrologers, the star served as a divine omen. Since Daniel had been a Wiseman, the Wisemen in Matthew may have been observing the prophetic timetable noted in Dan 9:24–27. If so, they would have been waiting for a heavenly sign to announce the arrival of the "anointed one" (*mashiach*) about which Daniel prophesied since his timetable pointed to it (Dan 9:25).

According to Hans Lietzmann, Daniel's "right time" was the great telos—the goal to which all time was moving. He states, "Daniel . . . comprehended all earthly history as a great unity which moves towards a final

The Divine Preparation for the Gospel

goal according to a divine plan."[1] The divine plan is the missio Dei, and the goal is the renewal of all things through God's direct intervention at the appointed time (Dan 11:35).[2]

When a special event disrupted the normal movement of history, Greek thought called it a *kairos* moment.[3] In addition to *kairos*, Greek speakers used other words to describe time events. For example, the "day" of the Lord (Acts 2:20) and the "hour" of his coming (Matt 24:36) refer to *kairos* moments that will punctuate and highly disturb the sequential flow of chronological time. According to Luke 21:24–26, when the time (*kairoi*) of the gentiles ends, people will faint from fear and expectation when they see what is coming on the earth.

In the Greek New Testament, *kairos* can be translated as an opportune time, the right time, or the fullness of time. According to Paul, at the fullness of time, Jesus was born (Gal 4:4).[4] In Matt 8:29, the demons ask Jesus if he had come to torment them before the time. They were referring to the day of judgment—a special event that would forever change the course of human history. Following Jesus' triumph over Satan in the wilderness challenge (Matt 4:1–11), the evil spirits were waiting for him to inaugurate the day of the Lord in preparation for his divine rule in alignment with the kingdom of God he preached. Often, *kairos* pointed to an event related to something that God had determined by his will. For instance, because the *kairos* was fulfilled, Jesus told people to repent and believe the good news of the kingdom (Mark 1:15). In the Gospels, the timing of Jesus' ministry perfectly aligned with God's mission and God's timeline.

The divine timing of Jesus' birth and the successful implementation of the church's mission in the world were closely linked. In the early fourth century, Eusebius wrote an apologia to argue that Christianity was superior to Greek religion and Greek philosophy. He titled his treatise *Praeparatio evangelica*.[5] The title means the preparation for the gospel. Scholars have

---

1. Lietzmann, *History of the Early Church*, 25.

2. Daniel refers to the appointed time (*mo'ed*) four times. In Daniel, the word signals the fulfillment of God's plan. That is, when something transpires in accordance with God's determined plan, it is the appointed time.

3. Smith, "Time," 1–2.

4. One should be careful not to exaggerate the distinction between *kairos* and *chronos*. For example, in Gal 4:4 Paul uses the fullness of *chronos* and Mark 1:15 uses the fullness of *kairos*.

5. Eusebius of Caesarea, *Preparation for the Gospel*.

used the phrase to describe the providential circumstances that facilitated the growth and success of the early church.[6]

Since the time of the apostles, Christians have noted that their faith entered the world at a propitious time. In particular, Origen (AD 185–254) argued that God prepared the nations for Christ's teaching and the subsequent flourishing of the faith when he caused Jesus to be born under the reign of Caesar Augustus during the Pax Romana.[7] In other words, the timing was not an accident of history. As a fulfillment of prophecy, it occurred in accordance with God's determined timetable and sovereign will. More importantly, God worked behind the scenes to prepare the world for what he was doing. When all the conditions were right, God launched his plan. Like the events surrounding Joseph and Moses, the timing pointed to the missio Dei.

When referring to the *praeparatio evangelica*, Michael Green states, "No period in the history of the world was better suited to receive the infant Church than the first-century AD."[8] In alignment with *kairos* thinking, Green mentions the role of "divine providence."[9] Adolf Harnack makes the same point when he analyzes the conditions that enabled Christianity to grow and flourish during the first three centuries.[10] Succinctly stated, Christianity would not have become the dominant faith in the West or the largest religion in the world without the favorable conditions that existed when the church's mission began.

When God launched the church, did he take advantage of a favorable moment in history, or did God work behind the scenes to shape history to accommodate his unfolding plan? Secular historiographers argue that a divine will does not shape history, and history has no plan. Conversely, the missiologist contends that God is always working his mission (John 5:17). His plan may suffer setbacks because evil is fighting against it. Still, a careful review of history, including the fulfillment of biblical prophecies, reveals how God works to accomplish his sovereign plans. For this reason,

---

6. In a similar way, Wesley refers to prevenient grace. For Wesley, prevenient grace is what God does in the unbeliever to prepare the person to receive Christ. Prevenient grace and *praeparatio evangelica* are synonymous ideas since God works to steer both individuals and nations toward an encounter with him.

7. Fowler, "Origen." Michael Green explains how the Roman Peace served the cause of Christianity (*Evangelism in the Early Church*, 30–31).

8. Green, *Evangelism in the Early Church*, 29.

9. Green, *Evangelism in the Early Church*, 30.

10. Harnack, *Expansion of Christianity*, 1:1–83.

missiologists can examine the favorable factors that positively influenced the successful launch of the church in the first three centuries to understand how God was at work in history. Saying that God works in and through history does not mean that God condones every facet of history or causes evil. Rather, an omniscient God knows what will happen and has a strategy to work around it or through it to fulfill his mission.

JEWISH INFLUENCE

Judaism was the most significant factor that enabled the church's growth in the first three centuries. Rodney Stark, a noted sociologist of religion, argues that the close relationship between early Christianity and Judaism enabled the church's successful evangelism of Jews and those who were attracted to Judaism. First, many of the early converts mentioned in the New Testament were Hellenistic Jews. They offered a cultural bridge between temple Judaism and the Greek world. Second, the New Testament era church grew best with gentiles who were familiar with the Septuagint because the evangelists preached that Jesus was the promised Messiah who fulfilled Jewish prophecies. Like Luther's publishing of the Bible in the language of the people, the publishing of the Septuagint in 250 BC allowed the Greek-speaking masses around the world to read the Jewish Scriptures.[11] By itself, this factor greatly facilitated the mission of the Jews to the world and the work of the Christian apologists who built upon their efforts.[12] Also, the Greek translation led to the Hellenization of Jewish thought. For example, substituting Hades for Sheol in the Septuagint changed how Hellenistic Jews thought about the afterlife.[13] Third, the early missionaries mainly preached in the Jewish synagogues scattered throughout Europe. Fourth, because of the close relationship between early Christians and Hellenistic Jews, many churches were constructed in the Jewish sections of the towns.[14] Fifth, since the Hellenistic Jews in the Roman provinces enjoyed a special status that exempted

---

11. To understand how the Septuagint informed the Christian mission, transformed Judaism, and adapted Jewish thinking to the Greek world, see Gonzalez, *History of Christian Thought*, 1:39–42.
12. Lietzmann, *History of the Early Church*, 91.
13. Payne, *Satan Exposed*, 37–40.
14. Stark, *Rise of Christianity*, 63.

them from military service and allowed them to practice their faith, e.g., keep the Sabbath, many Christian converts wanted to identify as Jews.[15]

Stark's careful research challenges the conventional idea that the Jewish mission ended soon after the destruction of the Second Temple. In fact, as temple Judaism came to an end, emigrating Jews from Palestine were more likely to consider Christianity because it was a quasi-Jewish sect that connected them to their faith, gave them hope, and allowed them to lower the wall of contention that had separated Palestinian Jews from the pagan world without giving up the essentials of their identity. Also, the Hellenistic Jews who had previously converted paved the way for them.[16] Stark states, "Contrary to the received wisdom, Jewish Christianity played a central role until much later in the rise of Christianity—that not only was it the Jews of the diaspora who provided the initial basis for church growth during the first and early second centuries, but that the Jews continued as a significant source of Christian converts until at least as late as the fourth century."[17]

Additionally, the ongoing Jewish mission was important because the ubiquitous Jews lived everywhere from Babylon to Spain.[18] Harnack estimates that 4.5 million Jews lived throughout the Roman Empire.[19] Wherever they lived, the Jews gathered in synagogues and practiced a distinct lifestyle that set them apart from the pagans. As has been noted, the Christian missionaries infiltrated the Jewish communities and specifically targeted the Jews with their evangelistic message. For this reason, the evangelization of the diaspora Jews laid the foundation for the church's mission to the world.

The Jewish mission to the nations also prepared the world for the gospel. During the Babylonian exile, the Jews recognized the universality of their faith. They concluded if Yahweh was the only true God, the gods of the nations were false gods. As the guardians of the divine truth, they believed that they needed to share it with the nations. Living in exile among the nations punctuated the urgency of this point.[20]

The following Scriptures from Psalms show how the Jews began to change what they thought about the nations and the universality of their

---

15. Green, *Evangelism in the Early Church*, 44.
16. Green, *Evangelism in the Early Church*, 66.
17. Stark, *Rise of Christianity*, 49.
18. Green, *Evangelism in the Early Church*, 44.
19. Harnack, *Expansion of Christianity*, 1:8.
20. Hedlund, *Mission of the Church*, 25–27.

faith: "Sing the praises of the Lord, enthroned in Zion; proclaim among the nations what he has done" (9:11 NIV). "Therefore, I will praise you, Lord, among the nations; I will sing the praises of your name" (18:49 NIV). "I will praise you, Lord, among the nations; I will sing of you among the peoples" (57:9 NIV). "Give praise to the Lord, proclaim his name; make known among the nations what he has done" (105:1 NIV). "I will praise you, Lord, among the nations; I will sing of you among the peoples" (108:3 NIV).

> Sing to the Lord a new song; sing to the Lord, all the earth. Sing to the Lord, praise his name; proclaim his salvation day after day. Declare his glory among the nations, his marvelous deeds among all peoples. For great is the Lord and most worthy of praise; he is to be feared above all gods. For all the gods of the nations are idols, but the Lord made the heavens. Splendor and majesty are before him; strength and glory are in his sanctuary. Ascribe to the Lord, all you families of nations, ascribe to the Lord glory and strength. Ascribe to the Lord the glory due his name; bring an offering and come into his courts. Worship the Lord in the splendor of his holiness; tremble before him, all the earth. Say among the nations, "The Lord reigns." (96:1–10 NIV)

Jesus recognized the zealous nature of the Jewish mission to the world when he said that the Jews went all over land and sea to make a single proselyte (Matt 23:15). When doing this, the Jewish missionaries deconstructed Greek religion and challenged conventional ideas about religion and ethics. Emphatically, they preached monotheism. Paul modeled their approach when he preached to the religious elite at the Areopagus (Acts 17:22–34).

The large numbers of Jewish sympathizers, Godfearers, and proselytes show that the Jewish mission to the world during this era was successful. Unfortunately for the Jews, the harvest they prepared was stolen by the Christian missionaries. Indeed, the Jewish sympathizers, Godfearers, and proselytes were the first to accept Christ because Christianity gave them the benefits of Judaism and full participation in the covenant community without making them convert to cultural Judaism.[21]

Harnack summarizes how the Jews seeded the growth of the infant church and prepared the world for the church's evangelism:

> The Christian mission was indebted, in the first place for a field tilled all over the empire; in the second place, for religious communities already formed everywhere in the towns; thirdly, for "the

---

21. Hedlund, *Mission of the Church*, 142.

help of materials" furnished by the preliminary knowledge of the Old Testament, in addition to catechetical and liturgical materials which could be employed without much alteration; fourthly, for the habit of regular worship and a control of private life; fifthly, for an impressive apologetic on behalf of monotheism, historical theology, and ethics; and, finally, for the feeling that self-diffusion was a duty. The amount of this debt is so large, that one might venture to claim the Christian mission as a continuation of the Jewish propaganda.[22]

Finally, from the perspective of the missio Dei, Christianity benefited from the destruction of the Second Temple and the scattering of the Palestinian Jews. The events pushed Jewish Christians to embrace Hellenistic Christianity and caused the church to push past the sectarian controversies that Acts and Galatians chronicle. Also, the transition that followed the dispersion of Jewish believers from Judah enabled a contextualization that accommodated the Christian mission to the world. Without the ongoing contextualization that attended the gentile mission, Christianity would not have become a cultural option for the gentile masses.

As I write elsewhere, "Contextualization is a theological imperative and a mission strategy. Succinctly, in the same way that God incarnated the divine self in Jesus by taking on the culture of a specific people, God calls the church to incarnate the faith into the cultural categories of the peoples that it seeks to reach as it 'makes disciples of all nations.' Biblical faith is always a culture-specific faith [when it is carried to a new people]."[23]

The Hellenization that accompanied the Jewish diaspora and the translation of the Hebrew Scriptures into Greek is an example of contextualization. In the same way that it enabled the flourishing of Hellenistic Judaism, the contextualization of Christianity permitted the flourishing of the Christian faith in the Roman world. The contextualization of the Christian faith happened so quickly that the surviving source documents are in Greek.[24] Even though Jesus taught in Aramaic and the Jews wrote in Hebrew, the universal message of the gospel was written in Greek and carried

---

22. Harnack, *Expansion of Christianity*, 1:15.

23. Payne, "Contextualization," para. 1.

24. After discussing the current debate associated with the language of the source documents, George Howard makes a convincing argument that Matthew was originally written in Hebrew. Others argue that the Hebrew Matthew was a later translation that enabled the evangelization of Palestinian Jews or that Rabbi Shem Tov translated it from existing copies of Matthew ("Was the Gospel," 15–25).

throughout the Roman Empire by Greek-speaking witnesses who made it sound like a native religion.[25] This fact points to the missio Dei because it was a favorable factor that facilitated the spreading of the Christian faith.

DISCIPLING THE EMPIRE

Modern missiologists have noted the positive correlation between good contextualization and the growth of Christianity with one exception. In the modern West, to the extent that biblical Christianity has attempted to win humanists by accommodating humanism, the Christian faith has compromised its core and failed to win humanists to the faith.[26] Instead, a syncretistic faith called Christian humanism has emerged.

In America, liberal Protestantism is the prime example of Christian humanism. In the 1960s, when liberal Protestantism identified with the values, beliefs, and practices of Christian humanism, its membership began to plunge.[27] Today, only 2 percent of Americans actively participate in a mainline Protestant church. American humanists do not embrace Christian humanism because they reject moralistic theism, do not like Christianity, and do not value membership in progressive churches. What does the liberal church offer that a humanist cannot get from another voluntary organization? Without winning the humanistic masses, the process by which liberal Protestantism identified with humanism caused it to lose its soul. Nonetheless, liberal Protestantism has an exaggerated social influence because of its conflation with humanistic values and liberal politics.[28]

Modern humanism is not compatible with biblical Christianity to the extent that it attempts to minimize biblical Christianity's influence and displace it from the cultural core while making itself the dominant social force in society. The ongoing process that pits humanism against traditional Christianity is called the cultural war. Still, even though humanism rejects the notion of creation, human depravity, divine revelation, the need for

---

25. Cairns, *Christianity Through the Centuries*, 38–39.

26. Payne, "Probing Reasons."

27. See Payne, "Deal with the Devil," 18–22, to understand the need for critical contextualization.

28. Critics would contend that American evangelicals seek an exaggerated influence through an alignment with patriotism, American exceptionalism, and Christian nationalism. To some extent, this fails because evangelicals seek to align America with the witness of Scripture and the calling of God by bringing the nation to Christ. Humanists, on the other hand, want to align America with secularism and practical atheism.

salvation, and the supremacy of God, like Christianity, it has a high view of reason, morality, and human flourishing. The fact that humanism grew out of Christianity is the main reason why it is immune to Christian evangelism. Today, it functions as the "anti-Christian" faith.

In many ways, Christianity was the antithesis of the religions that dominated the Roman world in the first centuries. It was monotheistic, intolerant of other gods, had a universal message, and believed that Jesus was Lord. The "Jesus is Lord" declaration was a political statement since it directly contradicted the "Caesar is Lord" (*Kaisar kurios*) statement that Romans had to pledge to live a normal life in the empire. When the "Jesus is Lord" statement was combined with the kingdom of God theology that Jesus taught, believers became a threat to emperors and cultures.

Indubitably, early Christianity wanted Jesus to be the Lord of the Roman Empire. Before the mission to the gentiles, the Jewish believers were waiting for Jesus to set up his kingdom in Jerusalem and establish his universal rule over the nations. Even though Jesus did not return as a global monarch (messiah), the vision did not disappear.

When the Jewish believers spread across the world, Christianity existed as a small, insignificant, and fragile religion in a very cosmopolitan world that was dominated by other religions. Since a returning Christ did not conquer the Roman world and establish a theocracy as the Jewish believers expected, the church had to win the world through evangelism and persuasion. Before this could happen, Christians needed to affirm the culture without compromising the faith. In other words, Christianity had to become a viable option for the masses by lessening its "Christ against culture" mentality.[29]

Hellenistic Judaism offered a template. The Greek Jews who had spread across the empire embraced the Roman world and had cultural influence without compromising their religion. In this way, they had peace with the social environment without endorsing it. On the other hand, the Judean Jews who resisted Roman culture lived with tension and mistrust of Rome.

Since Christianity started in Judea, it shared the prejudices of the Judean Jews. However, if it was to become a world religion, it had to become more like the Hellenistic Jews and less like the Judean Jews. The "Christ against culture" approach can grow an alternative society around the church

---

29. In *Christ and Culture*, H. Richard Niebuhr argues various positions. One is "Christ against Culture." The countercultural position draws a sharp distinction between the world and the church. Rejecting the world is necessary to embrace Christ in this life.

as the New Jerusalem, but it will not transform the pagan society. Still, the "Christ for culture" approach would lead to negative outcomes when the church became too affirming of the culture. To walk the tightrope, the church had to acknowledge that the culture bore the marks of the fall and that people needed to be saved while affirming the Roman way of life.

Discipling the society emphasizes a long-term process by which the Holy Spirit slowly transforms the culture through lifestyle evangelism, apologetics, disciple-making, and church planting. As increasing numbers of people receive Christ, the culture begins to take on the character of Christ. At first, the attitude toward Christianity changes. Then the Holy Spirit convicts people regarding societal vices. For example, people should care for the poor and not treat slaves badly. In time, the entire society is convicted by the salty lifestyles of the Christians who live in their midst (Matt 5:13). In this way, one can speak of cultural sanctification. It is a by-product of saturation evangelism and the discipling of the people in the society. It is not the main goal. Yet, when believers leaven the society with Christ, it should be expected.

RELIGION IN THE EMPIRE

The Christian mission did not enter a religious vacuum when it engaged the Greco-Roman world because every aspect of life was tainted by religion. In fact, during this period a religious revival spread across the land. It was not a revival of a specific religion. Rather, it was a revival of personal religion in response to psychological stressors, anxiety, fear, and oppressive fatalism.[30] Through the many mystery religions, people of every social class sought to find meaning in life, transcend the mundane, and build community with like-minded seekers. Cultural anthropology and psychology have noted that religion alleviates individual and corporate anxiety. Also, revitalization theory has shown that revivals of religion usually parallel times of stress and anxiety.[31]

Before the flourishing of the mystery religions that pandered to individuals, Greco-Roman culture employed religion to bind society together. By honoring the gods, the leadership hoped that the gods would preserve the state. In this era, honoring the gods became a civic duty. When state bureaucrats officiated at public ceremonies in opulent temples supported by

30. Lynch, *Early Christianity*, 24–25.
31. Payne, *American Methodism*, 248–53.

public coffers, the masses watched with approval. The ceremonies defined the positive relationship between Rome and state religion. This is called civil religion. Good citizens supported the state cult because state religion benefited them. Nonetheless, the state cult was inadequate because it did not satisfy the spiritual needs of the individual.[32]

This omission opened the door to personal religion. Externally, the state religion bound the people to the gods, Rome, and each other. Internally, personal religion fed the inner soul and gave their lives meaning. As long as the people honored the state cult and did not use personal religion to subvert the state or work against its values, Rome completely tolerated private faiths. In fact, emperors, senators, generals, and leading citizens happily participated in the mystery religions. Polytheism extended beyond the recognized gods of the Roman pantheon. It also included worshiping foreign gods, minor gods, and spirits.[33] This is why the caretakers of the Areopagus wanted to question Paul about the strange gods he was preaching when he spoke about Jesus and the resurrection (Acts 17:18–21).

Like Judaism, Christianity did not conform to state expectations because believers worshiped a jealous God who would not conjoin himself to other gods.[34] Christians could not deify the emperor, worship the goddess Roma, or participate in state ceremonies that invoked the gods.[35] This led to periods of sporadic persecution. To mollify the problem, Christians prayed for the state leadership, including the emperor (1 Tim 2:1–4), and encouraged their members to obey the laws like good citizens (Rom 13:1, Titus 3:1, and 1 Pet 2:13). Also, they were not to foment slave revolts or act in ways that contravened established cultural practices to the extent that they did not sin (1 Pet 2:12).

Paul maintains a utilitarian view on this issue when he says, "I urge, then, first of all, that petitions, prayers, intercession and thanksgiving be made for all people—for kings and all those in authority, that [*hina*] we may live peaceful and quiet lives in all godliness and holiness. This is good, and pleases God our Savior, who wants all people to be saved and to come to a knowledge of the truth" (1 Tim 2:1–4 NIV).

---

32. Lynch, *Early Christianity*, 25.
33. Harnack, *Expansion of Christianity*, 1:21–22.
34. Lynch, *Early Christianity*, 25–26.
35. Roma was the goddess of Rome. She represented the values and ideals of Roman culture, personifying Roman culture and its rule. Her image is on many coins. When everyone worshiped Roma, it bound everyone in the empire together. See Mellor, "Goddess Roma," 956.

The *hina* clause can be translated as "so that." It indicates a purposeful relationship between the first part of the sentence and the second part. As such, this text tied faith in God to good citizenship because the latter enabled survival and allowed the church to attract the masses of unchurched people who would have been disinclined to unite with a personal religion that did not support Rome. When detractors said that the Christians were atheists (against the gods and the Roman way), the Christians could rejoin that they prayed for the emperor, diligently practiced a moral life that reflected the civic virtues, and were dutiful citizens. In terms of Roman categories, even though they did not worship the gods, they lived exemplary lives. That was the point of religion—it equipped people for moral behavior. Much of Paul's controversial teachings about culture-specific behavior reflect his attempt to align Christianity with the positive elements of the Roman culture so others would not speak badly about the Christians.

Even though aspects of the epistles admonished Christians to follow the Roman way when possible, the New Testament was not of one voice on this issue. For example, Rev 2–3 excoriated the Roman way. Furthermore, the New Testament taught that the many social constructions that dominated life in the Roman Empire did not define life in the body of Christ. For instance, the Jew/Greek, man/woman, free/slave, and rich/poor binaries did not exist in the egalitarian church where all believers were equal before Christ and each other (Gal 3:27–28). In fairness, the initiates entering the mystery religions would have heard a similar message. In principle, through philosophy and Roman law, the empire taught the same thing.

Roman law was fair and every person was equal before the courts. Citizens were privileged, but everyone had access to fair laws. Over time, this fed into the notion of democracy.[36] In classical Greek political thought, democracy was not a virtuous form of government because the philosophers did not believe that the masses could separate their self-interest from the common good. Nonetheless, in AD 212 the Edict of Caracalla granted Roman citizenship to all the freemen in the empire, spreading the ideal of democracy and equality. The spirit of democracy emboldened Christians to contend publicly with the established religions.

First Peter was written to a minority community of Christians who had little recognition and no power. It tells them how to live for Christ without compromising their faith. After urging Christian women to submit to mean husbands, he tells Christian husbands to treat Christian wives

---

36. Cairns, *Christianity Through the Centuries*, 35–36.

like Christ treated the church, with dignity, honor, and a sacrificial heart (1 Pet 3:1–7). He tells slaves to serve their masters with respect as unto the Lord even though they do not merit it (1 Pet 2:18–24). Christian slave masters, however, are to treat slaves like brothers in Christ (Phlm 16). Also, when Christians give honor and due respect to government officials, they demonstrate that Christians are good people (1 Pet 2:13–17). This behavior lessened persecution and laid a foundation for evangelism.

First Peter 3:15–16 makes this point when it states, "Always be prepared to give an answer to everyone who asks you to give the reason for the hope that you have. But do this with gentleness and respect, keeping a clear conscience, so that those who speak maliciously against your good behavior in Christ may be ashamed of their slander" (NIV).

THE TRIUMPH OF CHRISTIANITY IN THE ROMAN EMPIRE

Christianity grew slowly in the first two centuries. By AD 100, there were 7,530 Christians in the Roman Empire. The numbers jumped to 40,495 by AD 150. In AD 200 there were 217,795 believers.[37] That was not a fast growth rate.[38] However, in the third century, Christianity showed an exponential growth rate increasing from 217,795 to 6,299,832 adherents. More significantly, the percentage of Christians in the Roman Empire grew from 1.9 to 10.5 percent. Much of the extraordinary growth occurred during times of sporadic persecution.[39]

So, what happened? How does history account for the rapid growth of Christianity in the third century? From an institutional perspective, the church was well organized, had expanded to every part of the empire, had a compelling message, and had fully adapted to the Roman world. In some

---

37. Stark, *Rise of Christianity*, 6.

38. By contrast, in a land filled with competing denominations, early American Methodism grew from 361 members in 1770 to 883,709 members by 1840. The membership numbers do not count the total number of participants. Incredibly, American Methodism equaled 33 percent of the total population in 1820 (Payne, *American Methodism*, 5–6). A positive combination of institutional, contextual, and spiritual factors accounts for Methodism's meteoric growth. In short, early American Methodism became so American that it embodied its values and gave voice to its ideals without compromising its message or its emphasis on faith and experiential religion. Of course, it rode the waves of the Second Great Awakening.

39. Stark, *Rise of Christianity*, 6.

pockets, it was extremely well placed, influencing the government and the army.[40] Sustained growth does not happen without evangelism, discipleship, and church planting. Augustine of Hippo contended that "Christianity must have reproduced itself by means of miracles, for the greatest miracle of all would have been the extraordinary extension of the religion without any miracles."[41] Adolf Harnack contends that Christianity's triumph was inevitable. Even though Constantine was the one who pushed Christianity to the front, another would have done the same thing if he had not because the time was ripe.[42]

Leading up to the fourth century, the empire was split between lesser rulers. The army was the power behind the throne. After a quick succession of rulers, turmoil swirled. External forces threatened the empire and internal forces threatened to pull it apart. Rome needed stability, a national vision, and a strong leader to unite it together. Because of this, Emperor Diocletian disbanded the Senate and determined to bring religious unity to the empire by returning the traditional gods to their place of dominance.[43] He "believed that Christians were disloyal, disrupted social unity, and displeased the gods."[44] According to early church fathers, the impetus for the ensuing persecution of Christians began when believers made the sign of the cross at official functions to ward off demons and prevented the priests from divining the future. The power encounter infuriated Diocletian.[45] In 303, Diocletian purged Christians from the army and his court. He also prohibited Christian meetings, destroyed churches, deposed church officers, imprisoned those who still practiced the faith, killed others, and ordered that all the Scriptures be burned.[46] This started a virulent and dev-

---

40. Harnack, *Mission and Expansion*, 2:52–53.
41. Quoted in Harnack, *Expansion of Christianity*, 2:466n1.
42. "It is idle to ask whether the church would have gained her victory apart from Constantine. Some Constantine or other would have had to come on the scene. Only as one decade succeeded to another, it would be all the easier for anyone to be that Constantine" (Harnack, *Expansion of Christianity*, 2:465).
43. Diocletian realized that the Roman Empire was too large to be ruled by one person. He therefore split it between the East and the West. He stayed in the East and appointed a Western emperor. He remained the chief emperor. Also, each emperor had a Caesar under him. The Caesar would become an emperor when one of the emperors died (Lynch, *Early Christianity*, 126–27).
44. Lynch, *Early Christianity*, 123.
45. Lynch, *Early Christianity*, 123.
46. Cairns, *Christianity Through the Centuries*, 93.

astating persecution. In some parts, it lasted until AD 309. Still, it was ill conceived. By AD 303, Christianity was too ingrained and respected to be destroyed. Realizing the error, Galerius, the Eastern Augustus, issued the Edict of Tolerance in AD 311. The Edict did not make Christianity a state religion. Rather, it gave Christians the same rights as the other religions in the empire.

In AD 306, Constantine's father was killed in battle. He was one of two "Augusti" (emperors). When he died, Constantine took his place. In AD 312, Constantine reunited the empire under one ruler after winning the Battle of Milvian Bridge. The night before, while in prayer, Constantine had a vision that told him to conquer in the name of Christ. Afterward, he issued the Edict of Milan. This legalized Christianity everywhere and required that the property, churches, and wealth of persecuted Christians be restored.[47] Through this, Constantine allied the state with the church. Afterward, he used his position to unite the divided Christians and bring theological unity to the church. Even though he did not make Christianity the state religion, he favored it. Because of his patronage, the church grew to 33,882,008 by 350. At that time, it equaled 56.5 percent of the population.[48]

One can argue that Constantine's actions ultimately hurt the vitality of the church, wrongly aligned it with the state, led to power struggles that excommunicated Christians for wrong beliefs, caused massive syncretism with Roman religions, and institutionalized the faith under ecclesial rulers who acted like religious emperors (popes). Despite these issues, today Christianity is the largest religion in the world because of Constantine's actions. Furthermore, throughout history, God has continued to reform the church by sending theological renewal and periodic revivals. For better or worse, God worked behind the scenes to make Christianity the dominant faith in Europe in the fourth century.

ADDITIONAL FACTORS

Regarding external factors that facilitated the spread of Christianity, Adolf Harnack emphasizes exceptional facilities. First, the road system was phenomenal. They were well made. Literally, a person could go anywhere within the empire on the roads. Second, the flourishing of interstate commerce

---

47. Lynch, *Early Christianity*, 127.
48. Stark, *Rise of Christianity*, 6.

permitted merchandise to travel in all directions. This led to a blending of cultures and a sharing of ideas. Third, soldiers guarded the roads to ensure that everyone could travel safely. This allowed Christian missionaries and wandering philosophers to travel from one side of the empire to the other without fear.[49]

Christianity's encounter with Greek philosophers and philosophy helped it sharpen its apologia against polytheism and refine its message. For instance, Lynch maintains that Christian evangelists repurposed Cynic attacks on the gods when they denounced the pagan world around them.[50] Christian evangelists borrowed heavily from the philosophers. For example, the relationship between Augustine of Hippo and Plato is very evident. One could argue that apologists Christianized Plato and Aristotle. The process of borrowing from the philosophers was called "spoiling the Egyptians."[51]

The willingness of Christians to suffer for Christ when persecuted is an important factor. Since Christians lived as moral people who adopted abandoned babies and buried the poor, many believed the attack on them was unjustified. The growing public sympathy helped the church brand itself as a minority religion that merited protection. When a person bravely dies a horrific death for the sake of faith and conscience, others take notice.[52] To be sure, some Christians renounced the faith and others tried to find ways to skirt persecution. For example, in the first century, some circumvented persecution by claiming to be Jews because Jews had legal exemptions. Nonetheless, throughout the Roman Empire, Christians refused to say that Caesar was Lord or to compromise their faith by participating in pagan worship. Ultimately, this led to numerical growth and the termination of persecution with the Edict of Tolerance.

CONCLUSION

The Old and New Testaments contend that God works in and through history to accomplish his mission, i.e., history testifies to God's plan. Despite reversals and the presence of evil, God is always at work. By examining numerous contextual, institutional, and spiritual factors, this chapter has

---

49. Harnack, *Expansion of Christianity*, 1:20–21.
50. Lynch, *Early Christianity*, 34.
51. Green, *Evangelism in the Early Church*, 35–38.
52. Lynch, *Early Christianity*, 124.

argued that God prepared the Roman Empire for the birth of Jesus and the propagation of the gospel according to his divine will, as it was presaged by prophecies and Jesus' teaching. The "preparation for the gospel" shows the missio Dei.

8

Applying the Missional Hermeneutic to History

THE PARABLE OF THE tenants (Mark 12:1–12) assesses the history of Israel through a theological lens. According to the parable, Israel is God's vineyard. The tenants are the corrupted spiritual leaders with a divine mandate to manage God's vineyard. The servants are the repulsed prophets who God has sent to correct them. And the owner's son is Jesus (the heir). In the parable, the religious leaders did not give God's prophets what God required when they came to them. Instead, they rejected them and harmed them. Their defiance will cause them to kill God's Son. Throughout Israel's history, God's attempts to pastor his flock via his under shepherds or religious leaders have failed.

As Jesus delivers the parable in the temple, the religious leaders (the tenants) are about to condemn him (the heir) because he is a threat to their system of control even though the people believe he is the Messiah, the Holy One sent from God (Mark 11:8–9). In the story preceding this parable, Israel is likened to a fig tree that will be destroyed because it did not bear fruit for the Messiah when he came to it (Mark 11:12–14). In the story immediately following the parable, the Jewish leaders do not render to God what belongs to God (Mark 12:17). When Jesus calls the leaders back to God by telling them to submit to his lordship, they rebuff his authority (Mark 11:27–28). Jesus tells them that he is the Stone that the builders rejected (Mark 12:10 and Ps 118:22). The rejection of Jesus is the rejection of God. In the end, the leaders believed that Roman rule was better than a theocracy that took away their privilege.[1]

Knowing what will happen, Jesus tells the leaders that God will reject them and give the vineyard to others. According to Matthew's version, God will destroy the tenants and rent the vineyard to others who will pay him his due (Matt 21:41). This happened when the Romans destroyed the Second Temple and scattered the Jewish leadership. In common interpretation, Jesus' followers are the "others" to whom God has given the vineyard and the benefits of the covenant (Mark 12:9).

The parable affirms three things. First, Israel is God's portion, the people belong to him, and the leadership should serve him. Second, God has worked through the events of Israel's history to call the people to him by sending them prophets and incarnating himself in the Son. Third, those who reject God's rule will be punished by God and those who embrace God's lordship will be accepted by him.

Regarding point two, since the resurrection of Christ, God's mission has been universal. Using the language of the parable, one could say that the world has become God's vineyard, and the church is his steward. The church bears fruit by discipling the nations and expanding God's kingdom (Matt 28:18–20). God wants the church to evangelize the nations (Matt 28:19, Mark 16:15, Luke 24:47, and Acts 1:8). As God pursues his global mission through the church and other means, one can expect that history will reveal God's activities in tangible ways. As such, one should be able to talk about God's activity in history like Jesus talked about God's past activity in the parable of the tenants. Succinctly, if the missional hermeneutic properly captures God's missional character and if the Bible reveals how God has acted in accordance with his missional intentions during biblical times, then one may assume that an examination of history will also reveal God's unfolding mission. For this reason, one should interpret history like Jesus interpreted Jewish history since they both reveal God's mission.

SALVATION HISTORY

Church history, sacred history, profane history, salvation history, the history of missions, and missional history are interpretive approaches to

---

1. John's Gospel captures their sentiments when it says, "If we let him go on thus, every one will believe in him, and the Romans will come and destroy both our holy place and our nation" (John 11:48 RSV).

Applying the Missional Hermeneutic to History

understanding the past. Church history focuses on the church's expansion, the great councils, theological debates, biographies of significant Christians, the growth of denominations, revivals, ecclesial conflicts, and the Crusades. On the other hand, sacred history analyzes how God has interacted with humanity in the Old and New Testaments by reading the Bible as history. The great flood, the destruction of Sodom, the exodus from Egypt, the Davidic monarchy, the return to Jerusalem after the Babylonian exile, the defeat of the Greeks by the Maccabees, the life of Jesus, and the missionary journeys of Paul are examples of how God has acted in history.[2] Profane history is what one reads in a school textbook. Ideally, profane history should be a disinterested and dispassionate retelling of history from a value-neutral and rationalistic perspective. In actuality, profane history is a social construct since it promotes carefully shaped narratives that are informed by cultural and political partialities.

Every history tells a story. The content depends on the perspective of the people who recount it. Since every approach to history produces biased narratives, one should not conclude that profane history is fairer and more accurate than sacred history. Owning one's bias and understanding the prejudices of those who write and deconstruct history will enable a critical reading of history.

Salvation history is a subset of sacred history. It seeks to understand how God has revealed his redemptive activity within human history. The Bible is its primary source document. Five theological convictions undergird salvation history. One, humanity needs to be saved because the fall is a real event with tangible consequences. Two, God loves humanity and desires to save lost people. Three, God is saving humanity. Four, salvation flows through Jesus since he is the mediator of God's salvation and the fulcrum of his salvation plan. Five, salvation history begins in the garden of Eden and will end at the consummation of all things.

According to Christian Ceroke, the Bible is a historical record that shows how God works in history to bring about the salvation he desires. Specifically, salvation history is a hermeneutic that reads the Bible in light of the successive steps by which God is saving humankind. Unlike exegesis,

---

2. Minimalists argue that the early histories of the Bible are national myths because they lack evidence to support what the Bible says. Recent scholarship, however, has strongly argued against this argument from silence by referencing a plethora of physical evidence to support the historicity of the Hebrew Scriptures (Garfinkel, "Birth and Death"). Expedition Bible is a popular YouTube channel that goes throughout the Bible lands demonstrating the historicity of the biblical texts.

it does not seek to discern the deeper meaning of any given text. Rather, it reads the Bible to identify the forward movement of God's salvific work in history. In this regard, the Bible is like a tapestry and each book is like a colored thread. When woven together, one sees the big picture of salvation. Ultimately, salvation history points to Jesus and his ongoing work to save humanity through the church.[3]

H. Dale Hughes notes the progressive nature of salvation history. When one sees the big story that the Bible reveals about salvation, one should come to a three-part conclusion. First, God is always at work in history. Second, God is seeking to establish his kingdom. Third, Jesus inaugurated God's kingdom. The third point has eschatological implications since God's earthly kingdom will not be fully realized until the return of Christ.[4]

Bill Arnold emphasizes that salvation is the overriding theme of the entire Bible—a grand unifying theme that holds the Bible together. It is a spiritual reality that is played out in human history. History has a beginning and an end. Always, salvation is a relational concept. God is saving humankind because he wants a relationship with people.[5]

Even though the salvation hermeneutic is seen in history, most scholars only apply it to sacred history. According to Joseph Pathrapankal, sacred history is derived from an informed reading of the inspired Bible. It interprets history from the perspective of God's revealed truth. Sacred history affirms that the salvific acts of God are revealed in history and that the process will conclude when Jesus returns. History has a telos and the Bible points to it.[6]

According to the Roman Catholic catechism, salvation history reveals humankind's perfect creation, fall into sin, deliverance from sin, and restoration by God through the redemptive work of Jesus Christ.[7] J. P. Nunez summarizes the Catholic understanding of salvation history as "the story of

---

3. Ceroke, "Principles of Salvation History," 29–32.

4. Hughes, "Salvation-History as Hermeneutic," 81–84.

5. Arnold, "Salvation," 701.

6. Pathrapankal, "World History," 97–117. Pathrapankal laments that contemporary theology has not furnished the categories necessary to apply the concept to the current context. For that reason, he believes that the humanization process offered through liberation theology should be embraced as the current reflection of God's saving grace in history. He favors liberation theology because he believes that God is working in other religions and in secular society. He notes that God is not limited to the church or Christian history. He believes that all religions reveal the Divine mind and the saving acts of God.

7. "Lesson One" from Our Lady of the Assumption Parish.

Applying the Missional Hermeneutic to History

how God created a good world, how we messed that world up by sinning, and how God plans to save his children and bring us back to him. Simply put, the Bible is the story of salvation history."[8] In other words, the Bible tells the history of God's dealings with humanity and chronicles his activities to bring his children to the goal for which he created them.

While assessing the theological notion of salvation and the mechanisms by which Protestant structures helped people get saved, Stanley Skreslet asserts that Reformation leaders and mission strategists derived a particular doctrine of salvation from the Bible. For example, early Protestants believed that Adam's sin was a historical fact and that people were alienated from God because of original and personal sin. Reformation theology avers that people need to be saved by faith through grace, Jesus came to save people, and the church continues Christ's salvific mission as it preaches the pure word of God and creates believing communities that enable discipleship. In this age, God works in concrete ways to save humankind. Employing a careful reading of history, those results can be assessed and measured. The political and social consequences can also be seen and measured.[9] Profane history studies the social influences of religion but fails to discern how God works in history.

Kenneth Scott Latourette also espouses a salvation history hermeneutic by contending that world history shows God's efforts to save humanity.[10] He defines salvation history as the record of God's redemptive dealings with humankind.[11] He says that the distinction between world history and salvation history contradicts the gospel message and betrays the heart of God. According to Latourette, God has been active in history in ways consistent with the salvation history thesis. Additionally, he expands salvation history to the entire universe because God's purposes extend to all of creation (Rom 8:22).[12]

Latourette's wave theory of history is core to his salvation history paradigm. As he examines the highs and lows of Christianity from its inception through the modern era, he observes that the "Christian impulse" goes forward and then recedes. Nonetheless, every new impulse outpaces the

---

8. Nunez, "Story of Our Salvation," para. 2.

9. Skreslet, *Constructing Mission History*, 47–58.

10. Standard histories reject the "divine hand" approach to history because they believe history should evaluate religion as a social phenomenon.

11. Latourette, *Christianity Through the Ages*, xi.

12. Latourette, *Christianity Through the Ages*, ix–xi.

previous recession. In this way, he believes that the Christian faith is moving toward a culmination and that God is divinely guiding that process. His theory has a triumphalist emphasis.[13]

As a hermeneutic and theological conviction, salvation history affirms four biblical teachings. First, people need salvation, and God is attempting to save them. Second, in Christ, God decisively entered history to become the world's Savior. Third, Christ's salvific work continues through the church. Fourth, his work will be fulfilled when the redeemed are remade in Jesus' divine image.

From the perspective of the missio Dei, salvation history is too narrowly focused since the missional hermeneutic emphasizes that God's mission is everything that God does per his will and purposes. It extends to the heavenlies as Jesus subdues all the dominions, authorities, and cosmic powers aligned against the Father (1 Cor 15:24). It also includes the eternal punishment of those who reject God or war against him. To limit the missio Dei to the story of how God saves humans (salvation history) assumes that God exists for the salvation of people. Such a notion aligns with Christian humanism because it promotes a utilitarian theology that can devolve into salvific universalism. Jesus sends the church to evangelize the nations because the nations are lost. He wants them to turn to him and be saved (John 3:16 and 1 Tim 2:4). However, only those who come to him in faith and obedience will be saved (Heb 7:25 and 9:28).

Furthermore, the purposes of God (missio Dei) continue beyond the eschatological horizon of the Scriptures and are larger than the salvation of humankind. Ponder the following three questions. Why is God saving people? What is God's big plan? Is the salvation of humanity a part of a larger plan—one that God has not revealed?

I sense that the salvation of humanity is penultimate to a greater goal—one foreshadowed in the garden of Eden before humans sinned. God created humans because he wanted to partner with them in the management of his physical creation. In this case, Latourette is correct when he extends salvation history to the entire universe because God's big plan includes humanity but is not limited to it.

Salvation history has a larger problem. While affirming that God works in history to save humanity, most who utilize it do not move beyond the biblical text. If God worked in biblical times, he continues to work in history to accomplish his mission. As such, a careful reading of profane

---

13. Latourette fully uncovers his wave theory in *Unquenchable Light*, x.

history should show the sacred contours of God's gracious interventions as he acts through history to reveal himself and accomplish his will.

INTRODUCING MISSIONAL HISTORY

The history of missions tells the story of the advancement of Christianity by examining the spread and growth of the church from synchronic or diachronic perspectives. On the other hand, missional history evaluates history via a missional metanarrative. It offers an overarching account or interpretation of history from the perspective of God's unfolding mission to discern a pattern or structure that illustrates how God has acted through history to accomplish his mission. In essence, it applies the missional hermeneutic to the task of reading profane history.

History of mission is objective.[14] It deals with facts. Missional history is subjective. It views history through the lens of theological convictions. In so doing, it sees the broad story that sacred history reveals about the unfolding of God's mission. Briefly stated: a missional lens allows missiologists to approach the historical task with a set of assumptions that color how they interpret the historical data in accordance with the missio Dei.[15]

The following assumptions capture the missional approach. First, throughout history, God has intervened in decisive ways and at critical times to fulfill his purposes. Historians ask if history changes through evolution or revolution. The Bible shows that God works through both. In the Old Testament, evolution is the slow process by which the people of God gradually fall away and reject God's covenants. Then, God dramatically intervenes to enable the people to repent and renew the covenant. That is revolution. Those who do not repent suffer judgment. At times, judgment is how God intervenes. Afterward, the process repeats itself. In American

---

14. Skreslet exemplifies the history of mission approach by examining "master narratives of mission history." A master narrative is a story about Christianity and its spread. They are hermeneutical approaches to Christian history. He considers three master narratives: promise and fulfillment, mission as a form of colonialism, and the lens of world Christianity. Each uncovers an important aspect of mission history. In his critiques, however, he avers a more value-neutral approach that reflects how scholarly historians evaluate history as a social phenomenon (*Constructing Mission History*, 1–29).

15. Tennent examines the role of the Holy Spirit in directing and unfolding the missio Dei in Acts. By extension, one could use the same approach to examine the role of the Holy Spirit in the expanding mission of God in the totality of church history (*Invitation to World Mission*, 409–39).

history, the Second Great Awakening is an example of a divine revolution and a massive cultural reset by which God called America to himself.

The Old Testament records many historical benchmarks that show how God has worked through history to accomplish his mission at critical points. The stories of Noah, Abraham, and Moses are obvious examples. The Babylonian captivity, the Maccabean revolt, the scattering of the church (Acts 8), and the Pax Romana (27 BC–AD 180) also show how God intervened in concrete ways to enable his mission.[16]

Not only has God worked to shape the flow of history per his missional purposes, he entered history at the right time. In this light, the incarnation is a seminal event that ties God's mission to his salvific purposes. When the incarnation is viewed with the giving of the Holy Spirit (Acts 2) and the mission mandate to witness to Christ from Jerusalem to the ends of the earth (Acts 1:8), it becomes clear that God empowered the New Testament Church so that he could work through it to continue his mission of reclaiming the nations. In this case, the commission to make disciples of all nations (Matt 28:19) is the solution to the Babel story in which God scattered the nations and chose Israel to be his portion (Deut 32:9).

Sadly, from the Edict of Milan (AD 314) until the Battle of Tours (AD 732), Christian institutionalism, the commingling of church and state, ecclesial corruption, the rise of the Dark Ages, religious syncretism, political infighting, lukewarm faith, plagues, and a conquering Islam greatly hampered God's missional plans. During these long years, a shrinking Christendom and the diminishing influence of the Holy Spirit in the everyday life of the church produced a languid Christianity that was largely devoid of apostolic character and personal piety. In Europe, the rise of the Celtic mission was God's response to the decline of apostolic Christianity. Through the Celtic mission, God re-evangelized Europe, revitalized the institutional church, and reclaimed biblical Christianity. It was a revolution.[17]

A second assumption comes from the first. History points to a divinely ordained telos. That is, history is purposeful (not random) and God is moving it forward in a determined way according to the prophetic vision of the Old and New Testaments.[18] In making this statement, I assert

---

16. For more information on the external and internal causes for the expansion of early Christianity, see Harnack, *Expansion of Christianity*, 1:1–85, or Green, *Evangelism in the Early Church*, 29–49.

17. Hunter, *Celtic Way of Evangelism*, 38–41.

18. I affirm a linear model of history. Nevertheless, within the forward progress there are cyclical movements. For example, history shows the rise, growth, and fall of nations.

Applying the Missional Hermeneutic to History

that God continues to interface directly with the world through the church, angels, and the Holy Spirit per his mission as he guides it to a time when his will and his kingdom are established on earth in the same way that they are established in heaven (Matt 6:10).

As a corollary to this, I affirm that Scripture reveals Satan's work to disrupt God's purposes, e.g., the fall, the corruption of the antediluvian world, the killing of the babies, the corruption of Israel, the temptation of Jesus, the giving of false revelation, and the persecution of the church. The spiritual warfare hermeneutic supposes an ongoing cosmic battle between God and the gods. In this case, the nation gods are the Sons of God who rebelled against God. Afterward, they used their stewardship to turn the nations from God (Deut 32:8–9 and Ps 82).[19] In the New Testament, Paul refers to them variously as thrones, powers, dominions, world rulers, spiritual forces of evil in the heavenlies, rulers in heavenly places, authorities, demons, and the god of this age. The language of rulership assumes the reality of an evil realm. When Jesus refers to the gates of Hades, he is not talking about human death (Matt 16:18). Rather, it is a metaphor for Satan's kingdom and his rule.[20]

In his earthly ministry, Jesus pushed against the kingdom of darkness. Every demon he cast out, every person he healed, and every disciple he made was a blow against Satan. In the Scriptures, Satan and the hosts of evil are not God's equal. Rather, God has permitted the spiritual revolt to happen even though he did not instigate it.[21]

Often, history reveals God's hand when God pushes against the work of Satan to bring some good out of his malice. The miraculous establishment of modern Israel, its survival after the combined militaries of many

---

Also, there have been technological resets. In Eastern thought, progress is an illusion. Everything is born, lives, dies, and is reborn. The law of death and rebirth overshadows everything, including the cosmos and the gods. But in biblical faith, notwithstanding the work of Satan to corrupt God's mission, the Scriptures assume a chronological progress toward a divinely ordained goal. The setbacks do not thwart the progress. Interestingly, some theories about the Big Bang do not say that the expanding universe will collapse and be reborn because the force of outward expansion is greater than the pull back toward a center. In fact, the expansion rate of the universe is accelerating. Destruction is not inevitable.

19. Payne, *Satan Exposed*, 72n3 and 83–84, and Heiser, "Deuteronomy 32:8."

20. Payne, *Satan Exposed*, 41–47. There was a grotto of Pan (the goat god who symbolizes Satan) and a "bottomless pit" that some believed went down to hell at the bottom of Mount Herman in Caesarea Philippi where Jesus spoke about the gates of Hades.

21. Payne, *Satan Exposed*, 63–86.

nations attempted to destroy it, and the continuing return of the Jewish diaspora to Israel exemplifies this notion. God did not cause the Holocaust that killed six million Jews or make the Arab nations fight against Israel before the Jews had a standing army to defend themselves. Even though God judges, evil is contrary to his nature. In this case, Jewish history shows that Satan has always worked through anti-Semitic tyrants and evil governments to destroy and corrupt Israel. The hosts of evil hate Israel because God chose Israel and is still working through Israel in some mysterious way. The ubiquity of anti-Semitism is a historical fact that reason cannot explain. Regrettably, at times, it is easier to see how Satan works in history to foment evil than it is to see God's mission.

THE EXAMPLE OF ISRAEL

In the Old Testament, God called Israel to be his special agent (Exod 19:5–6). From the beginning, God intended to work through Israel to bless all the families of the earth (Gen 12:3). Israel bore God's name, carried his covenant, and shined his light on the nations. As the nations encountered faithful Israel, God drew them to himself. The stories about Naaman and the Queen of Sheba show this. When God allowed Solomon to construct the temple, God directed him to build a court for the nations because he anticipated that the gentiles would be drawn to him and desire to worship him in the temple (1 Kgs 8:41–43). The Old Testament foresees a time when the nations will come to Jerusalem to seek the Lord and be saved by him (Isa 60:3 and Zech 8:20–23). Israel is to be a light to the nations so that God's salvation will reach the world (Isa 49:6).

When Israel chased after foreign gods and did evil, they ceased to be God's light to the nations and threatened the progress of his missional plan. Since God chose Israel as his portion (Deut 32:9), he did not have a backup plan. So, he sent prophets to call Israel back to the covenant. When Israel refused to be corrected, he reconstituted his covenant with a holy remnant and moved forward with his purposes.

The exile served God's missional purposes. During the exile, the Jewish diaspora became more serious about preserving the faith and witnessing to God among the nations (see Dan 1–6). As a result, it established synagogues and Jewish enclaves in major population centers around the world. These gave the nations easy access to God's people and his revelation. The Psalmist declares to the exiled Jews, "Sing unto the Lord, bless his name; show forth his salvation from day to day. Declare his glory among the heathen, his wonders among the gentiles. . . . Say among the peoples that the Lord reigns" (Ps 96:1–2, 10a).[22] The faithful witness of the Jews when they lived among the nations also prepared the world for the church's missionary activity.[23]

Ultimately, God's missional purposes were consummated when Israel gave birth to Christ. Jesus is the holy remnant. He satisfied the missional calling that God gave to Israel. In his resurrection, God defeated Satan and claimed the nations as his own. The day of Pentecost declares this. Today, God wants the entire world to live under his gracious rule so it can be in a proper relationship with him.

In the same way that God selected Israel to carry forth his mission in a previous age, during this age Jesus has empowered and dispatched his church to witness to him and make disciples of all nations (*missio ecclesiae*). In short, the church is the primary means by which God accomplishes his missional purposes for the nations. When the church becomes corrupted, God's missional purposes become threatened. At such times, God calls the church back to the covenant. Often, he accomplishes this by calling forth reformers who function like the prophets of the Old Testament. However, when the institutional church thwarts the purposes of God by blocking reform, God will claim a holy remnant and work through it to advance his cause.

A MISSIONAL ASSESSMENT OF THE REFORMATION

In the same way God sent prophets to call Israel back to its covenant so his mission could move forward through them, he raised up sixteenth-century reformers to check the corruption in the medieval church so he could work through a restored church to continue his mission in the world. That is, the Reformation movement was a means by which God cleansed a church that had lost its way so that he could realize his larger purposes related to his global mission. But the Reformation was only one step along the path to the

---

22. Author's translation.

23. "Judaism during the intertestamental period expresses the latent centrifugal mission found in Isaiah and other prophets. It was only in their dispersion that the Jews turned toward the Gentile world, not only to defend its own faith with apologetics but even more to commend it to the people in a time of religious uncertainty. Some Jewish leaders felt that Judaism was destined to become the universal religion, and so they engaged in fervent missionary activity and won many converts and a larger listening public" (Hedlund, *Mission of the Church*, 142).

rediscovery of apostolic Christianity. Subsequent reformation events show that God continues to reform the church so he can use it to move history toward his divinely ordained telos.

Without a doubt, the Reformation's emphasis on salvation by faith triggered a transformation in Christian ecclesiology, soteriology, and orthopraxy. No longer was the church a Latin-speaking institution that sold indulgences to spiritually anxious people who wanted to ensure that they would not get stuck in purgatory when they died. Equally significant was the Reformation's emphasis on the final authority of Scripture. Coupled with the translation of the Bible into the vernacular languages, the invention of the printing press, and the wide distribution of the Scriptures, Bible-reading people all over Europe forever changed the face of Western Christianity. Religious oligarchs of all sorts did not want the laypeople to read the Bible because they knew that it would liberate them from ecclesial control and allow the Holy Spirit to speak directly to them. In short, giving the peoples of Europe a Bible in their own languages started a spiritual revolution.

Of course, the Reformation was a mixed bag in that the evil one sowed weeds among the wheat God planted. Except for the Anabaptists, the emerging Protestants continued the unfortunate marriage of church and state. Spiritual abuse, legalism, intolerance, infighting, civil religion, and spiritual lethargy were long-term consequences of this practice. The current spiritual topography of the Reformation lands shows that vital piety has been replaced by secular materialism and agnostic rationalism. Also, Luther's idea of the priesthood of all believers died before it altered the ecclesial character of institutional Christianity. Even today, the exaggerated divide between clergy and laity perpetuates false notions related to the practice of ministry.[24]

The lack of missionary zeal is one of the most glaring deficits in the early Reformation. For sure, the leaders wanted to reform northern Europe. However, they did not have a vision for the world or believe that the Great Commission's mandate to evangelize the nations obligated them to go to the world. Perhaps, their lack of missional vision would have changed if they had had easy access to the world. Fortunately, the Pietists maintained a heart for world missions.

---

24. For a helpful conversation on ordination and the priesthood of all believers, see Snyder, *Radical Renewal*.

THE RISE OF PROTESTANT MISSIONS, THE SECOND REFORMATION

God augmented the Reformation with other "reformation" events that pushed forward his missional purposes. One was the nineteenth-century mission revolution that propelled the Protestant churches to the ends of the world. In the same way that Roman Catholicism followed the great explorers from southern Europe to exotic places that had not been evangelized, Protestant clergy in the seventeenth century also rode the coattails of colonialism. Most went as chaplains and did not see the Great Commission as a personal mandate when interacting with the native populations. Often, their association with the colonial enterprise caused them to act in ways that compromised the gospel message. Civilizing the natives as they spread the gospel is a case in point. In time, civilizing became a synonym for subjugating and westernizing. In its aftermath, anemic growth, state entanglements, denominational extensions, dependency, split-level Christianity, and abuse imperiled apostolic missions and prevented the indigenization of national churches. Still, God used colonialism to take the Reformation to the world.

Fortunately, the eighteenth-century rise of missionary societies and the deployment of faith-based missionaries throughout the world pushed global missions beyond the confinements of the colonial powers. William Carey modeled this. Heroic men, women, and students took the gospel to unreached peoples. Many died in the lands where they journeyed. They were motivated by a vision, a calling, and a hunger to participate in the Great Commission.

Even though most never saw the expanded fruit of their work, they planted the seeds for a future harvest. For example, the translation of the Bible into the languages of native peoples, the training of indigenous leaders, and the emphasis on three-self churches helped the emerging global church of the twentieth century to break free from the colonial powers and the national denominations that attempted to regulate the shape of global Christianity. Often, the rise of the indigenous church in any given location was accompanied by a revival, the discovery of the Holy Spirit as the living presence of God in the faith community, the empowering of lay leaders, and the contextualization of the faith.

THE RISE OF PENTECOSTALISM, THE THIRD REFORMATION

Without a doubt, the twentieth-century Pentecostal revival was the greatest reformation event since the giving of the Spirit in Acts 2. Unlike previous reformation events, the Pentecostal renewal flowed directly from the throne of God. The long-term consequences of this divine intervention in human history are incomprehensible. More importantly, they show the direction of God's evolving mission.[25]

It began in 1901, at Bethel Bible School in Topeka, Kansas, when students received the baptism of the Holy Spirit. As they spread the Pentecostal message in America, the 1904 Welsh revival and the supernatural events associated with it rocked the world. In 1905, the power of the Welsh revival spread to India.[26] In 1907, a massive revival also seized Korea.[27] The 1909 Pentecostal revival in Chile was a harbinger of the religious transformation of Latin America. In fact, Pentecostal revivals erupted throughout the world in the early 1900s. Many were triggered by Methodist missionaries and American Pentecostals who took the revival to other lands.

Of all the Pentecostal revivals that broke out during the formative time of Pentecostalism, none was more significant than the Azusa Street revival in Los Angeles, California.[28] From 1906 through 1909, multitudes of hungry seekers from all over the world came to the warehouse on Azusa Street to be touched by God. In many ways, the revival resembled an old camp meeting with its spontaneity, egalitarian demeanor, exuberance, and abundant demonstrations of the Holy Spirit. Even though church history shows that the Spirit of Pentecost never left the church, it remained largely inaccessible to the larger church until God rekindled it during the Azusa Street revival.

Like the previous reformations, the Pentecostal revival corrected theology and Christian practice by triggering a renewed emphasis on

---

25. For a good review of the Pentecostal revival from the perspective of mission theory, see Tennent, *Invitation to World Mission*, 419–31. The section also discusses Pentecostalism and the rise of the majority world church.

26. Anderson, "Pandita Ramabai," 37–38.

27. According to Young-Hoon Lee, even though the Korean revival was not a Pentecostal revival, it had Pentecostal characteristics that led to the growth of Korean Pentecostalism ("Korean Pentecost").

28. Tommy Welchel shares a compelling oral history of the Azusa Street Revival in Welchel and Griffith, *True Stories*. There is, however, no way to validate that his stories are authentic.

Applying the Missional Hermeneutic to History

eschatology, missions, spiritual gifts, and empowered ministry. Divine healing, prayer, tongues, prophecy, power evangelism, and exorcism loomed large in any assessment of early Pentecostalism. Many Pentecostals believed the end was near and that the church had to use the gift of tongues to preach the gospel to all nations. This belief caused participants to take Pentecostalism all over the world. Since Pentecostalism rewarded those who ministered with an anointing, those who lacked formal training or did not have access to formal training were used by God to push forward his mission throughout the world. These people planted seeds that birthed the great revivals that grew the church in Africa and Latin America starting in the 1960s.

Over time, a deep chasm developed between American Pentecostal churches and mainline Christianity. Simply stated, the traditional Pentecostal churches became so particular and so identified with a specific type of person that the larger population did not relate to them. That began to change in 1960 when leaders in the Protestant and Roman Catholic churches received the baptism of the Holy Spirit. Through the Charismatic movement, the spirit of Pentecost infiltrated all of American Christianity. Soon, the Jesus People began to mainstream it.

The Jesus People movement began on the West Coast in the late 1960s. Evangelist Lonnie Frisbee and Pastor Chuck Smith of Calvary Chapel popularized it. Many other outpourings of the Holy Spirit accompanied the movement. This led to the emergence of Word and Power churches. Others talk about the blossoming of Word, Spirit, and Sacrament churches.

The influence of the Jesus People movement outlived the movement since thousands of its converts moved into leadership positions in American Christianity. Those who did not go into the mainstream churches greatly influenced the growth of the parachurch phenomenon that largely bypassed organized Christianity as it took the mission of God to the world. Its worship style and its music became a global sensation.

The Third Wave movement with John Wimber is widely known in evangelical circles. It gave birth to the Vineyard Church, the New Apostolic Reformation, the Toronto Blessing, and countless local revivals. The movement helped evangelical churches operationalize Jesus' kingdom teaching in ways that aligned evangelicalism with Pentecostalism. The convergence facilitated the founding of independent charismatic evangelical churches all over America and the anglophone world. For example, even though the Bethel Church phenomena originated in the Assemblies of God, it exemplifies the growing merger between the evangelical and Pentecostal traditions. This is a major indicator of the evolving mission of God.

THE RISE OF GLOBAL CHRISTIANITY, THE FOURTH REFORMATION

The rapid rise and global multiplication of Pentecostalism shows the trajectory of God's evolving mission. In 1907, there were one million Pentecostals. Today, there are six hundred million Spirit-filled believers. Based on current trends, the number should swell to eight hundred million by 2025. In terms of percent growth, it is the fastest-growing faith in the world. Significantly, Pentecostal growth is centered in Asia, Africa, and Latin America. In these areas, the Pentecostal/Charismatic renewal movement is transforming Christianity and growing among non-Christian populations.[29]

In speaking of the new face of global Christianity, Phillip Jenkins contends that the "newer churches preach a deep personal faith and communal orthodoxy, mysticism, and puritanism, all founded on clear scriptural authority." To Western ears, their message appears "charismatic, visionary, and apocalyptic." For global Christians, "prophecy is an everyday reality, while faith-healing, exorcism, and dream-visions are all fundamental parts of religious sensibility." For better or worse, if current global church growth patterns continue, the future church will look very Pentecostal. In fact, "Pentecostal expansion across the Southern continents has been so astonishing as to justify the claims of a new Reformation."[30]

Charles Kraft offers a story that illustrates the global appeal of Pentecostal/Charismatic faith. He and his wife went to northern Nigeria as Brethren missionaries. Both were soundly evangelical and academically prepared for their work. Charles Kraft's linguistic training helped him become an expert on the Hausa language.[31] Under his leadership, Nigerians accepted Christ. Yet they continued to consult traditional shamans when they had spiritual problems. Spiritual problems included disease, accidents,

---

29. Center for the Study of Global Christianity, "Christianity in Its Global Context," 10–20, and Jenkins, *Next Christendom*, 1–20.

30. Jenkins, *Next Christendom*, 9–11.

31. From 1963–1974, Charles Kraft wrote the following books on Hausa: *Introduction to Spoken Hausa*, *Workbook in Intermediate and Advance Hausa*, *Hausa Reader*, *Teach Yourself Hausa*, *Introductory Hausa* (with Marguerite Kraft), and *Study of Hausa Syntax* (3 volumes). At that time, he was the world expert on the language.

Applying the Missional Hermeneutic to History

infertility, drought, disruption of relationships, curses, and evil spirits. Based on his Western worldview, Kraft did not address these issues because he did not believe they were spiritual matters. Nonetheless, in Nigeria, the native religions addressed these problems. After a few years, Kraft left the mission field and focused on language training.

Following a protracted immersion in the revival at Fuller Theological Seminary, Kraft returned to Nigeria preaching that the Holy Spirit had empowered the church to do what Jesus did during his earthly ministry. When he did, the demons manifested. This time he was prepared to minister the full gospel. In the aftermath, his preaching attracted the masses and was compatible with the Hausa worldview. When they received the Holy Spirit, the Nigerian Christians no longer needed the help of the shamans because the pastors could minister to the spiritual needs that the Western missionaries had neglected and denied.[32]

Recently, while teaching a class on mission theology in Lagos, Nigeria, I led the students in a lengthy conversation about the contextualization of the gospel in Nigeria. During the discussion, a group of Anglican priests began to describe how they did power ministry. They interpreted dreams, cast out demons, healed the sick, received visions, and freed people from curses. After they presented their stories, I made a very American comment. I said, "I thought you were Anglicans." Without missing a beat, they replied, "Yes, we are African Anglicans."[33] In their minds, the African Christianity that they practiced was a rediscovery of New Testament Christianity. It applied the truth of the Reformation tradition to the African context while adding the power of the Pentecostal experience.

I spent a recent sabbatical preaching, teaching, and researching folk religion in Colombia and Costa Rica. When I ministered, people received Christ, others received healing, and demons occasionally manifested. When the demons manifested, I cast them out. After one dramatic encounter, word got out. The next day, people began to look for me while I was in Santa Ana, Costa Rica. One woman begged me to come to her house because her brother-in-law lived in a black room that was decorated with occult dolls. The spirits would not let him leave the room. Plus, they tormented him. When I arrived at the house, I led the family to accept Jesus before I ministered to the man. It was a good day for the kingdom.

---

32. Kraft, *Christianity with Power*, 3–6.
33. Payne, *Adventures in Spiritual Warfare*, 53.

In an article on folk religion in Latin America, I argue that Latino Pentecostalism and the Roman Catholic Charismatic movement have experienced massive numerical growth since becoming viable options for the masses in the late 1960s because they have become indigenous faith systems that mesh with Hispanic cultures and give folk practitioners functionally equivalent alternatives to the syncretistic practices associated with popular religion and Christian creolism (Christo-paganism). Specifically, as a native religion that engages all aspects of the Latino worldview, Latino Pentecostalism operates at the level of a popular religion without being inherently syncretistic. In this regard, it can be described as "folk Christianity." At another level, it represents a reappropriation of apostolic faith and points to the ongoing mission of God.[34]

FINAL ASSESSMENT

Missional history shows how God works to extend his mission at any given time. It also avers that God is moving history to a climax in which he will culminate his purposes. Missional history is linear, but it is not straight. It has ups and downs. As such, one cannot say if the forward movement of the gospel will continue in the majority world at the same rate that it is currently growing. If that is to happen, it must penetrate the Muslim world and all of Asia. Likewise, one cannot say if the eclipse of apostolic faith in the West will continue. Materialism, rationalism, and humanistic values have waged a winning war against Western Christianity during the last century. As the delegates to the 1910 World Missionary Conference in Edinburgh strategized for the evangelization of the world, few would have imagined that the faith would largely die in Europe by the end of the century.

This chapter has argued that the Protestant Reformation, the great century of evangelical faith missions, the rise of Pentecostalism, and the emergence of the global church represent divinely ordained steps toward an ultimate goal. The Protestant Reformation gave the Bible to the people and corrected theological errors. Later, the truth of the Protestant Reformation was carried forth by circuit-riding preachers and evangelical missionaries who had been spiritually formed by awakenings and revivals. At the right time, God poured out his Spirit on the church and Pentecostalism was born. Soon, Pentecostalism spread to the mainline, Roman Catholic, and evangelical traditions. As of now, that faith has spread to the world.

34. Payne, "Folk Religion," 161–63.

Furthermore, it is the fastest-growing faith in the world. As it penetrates the 10/40 window, multitudes of Muslims, Hindus, atheists, and Buddhists will turn to Christ.

Is the Pentecostal reformation the last reformation before the return of Christ? Some global Christians are reporting visions and prophecies of a coming revival. They claim it will include a spiritual empowerment that the church has never known. It will be a time of great evangelism and great persecution. The descriptions align with the eschatology of the New Testament. That is, the end times will include evangelism, persecution, and wonders.

Normally, eschatological theology is produced by suffering communities who live a liminal existence. It enables them to endure persecution and poverty by imagining how a sovereign God will ultimately rescue those who remain faithful. In the end, they will triumph over their oppressors. For this reason, it makes sense that the global church cares more about the next reformation than the Western church. I have a hunch that the church and the world will be surprised by God in the not-so-distant future. I am imagining the fifth reformation.

Bibliography

Ackerman, Susan. "Asherah/Asherim: Bible." *The Shavi/Hyman Encyclopedia of Jewish Women*, Feb. 27, 2009. https://jwa.org/encyclopedia/article/asherahasherim-bible.
"America's Border Security." *Congressional Record* 170:18 (Jan. 31, 2024) H328–H333. https://www.congress.gov/congressional-record/volume-170/issue-18/house-section/article/H328-3.
Anderson, Allan. "Pandita Ramabai, the Mukti Revival and Global Pentecostalism." *Transformation* 23:1 (Jan. 2006) 38–48.
Arnold, William. "Salvation." In *Evangelical Dictionary of Biblical Theology*, edited by Walter Elwell, 701–3. Grand Rapids: Baker, 1996.
Arthur, Eddie. "Missio Dei and the Mission of the Church." Wycliffe Global Alliance. https://www.wycliffe.net/what-we-do/articles-for-further-reflection/missio-dei-and-the-mission-of-the-church/.
"Asylum Quarterly Engagement, Fiscal Year 2023, Quarter 4, Talking Points." U.S. Citizenship and Immigration Services, Sept. 19, 2023. https://www.uscis.gov/sites/default/files/document/outreach-engagements/AsylumQuarterlyEngagement-FY23Quarter4PresentationTalkingPoints.pdf.
Avnery, Orit. "Pesach Is Literally the Story of a People's Birth." Shalom Hartman Institute, Mar. 18, 2019. https://www.hartman.org.il/pesach-is-literally-the-story-of-a-peoples-birth/.
"Background on the Colonias." The Texas Department of Housing and Community Affairs. https://www.tdhca.state.tx.us/oci/background.htm.
Barram, Michael. "The Bible, Mission, and Social Location: Toward a Missional Hermeneutic." *Interpretation: A Journal of Bible and Theology* 61:1 (Jan. 2007) 42–58.
Barram, Michael, and John R. Franke. *Liberating Scripture: An Invitation to the Missional Hermeneutic*. Eugene, OR: Cascade, 2024.
Beale, G. K. *A New Testament Biblical Theology: The Unfolding of the Old Testament in the New*. Grand Rapids: Baker Academic, 2011.
Beitsch, Rebecca. "Speaker Johnson Backs Abbott's Border 'Invasion' Decree." *The Hill*, Jan. 25, 2024. https://thehill.com/homenews/house/4428993-speaker-johnson-backs-abbotts-border-invasion-decree/.
Bekele, Girma. "The Biblical Narrative of the Missio Dei: Analysis of the Interpretive Framework of David Bosch's Missional Hermeneutic." *International Bulletin of Missionary Research* 35:3 (July 2011) 153–58.
Benko, Stephen. *The Virgin Goddess: Studies in the Pagan and Christian Roots of Mariology*. Boston: Brill, 2004.

Bibliography

Berger, Peter L. *The Sacred Canopy: Elements of a Sociological Theory of Religion.* New York: Anchor, 1969.

Bevans, Steven. *Models of Contextual Theology.* Maryknoll, NY: Orbis, 1992.

Bidegain, Ana María, and Juan Jennis Sánchez Soler. "Religion in Latin America." *Hemisphere* 19:1 (2010) 5.

Blackaby, Henry, and Claude V. King. *Experiencing God.* Nashville: Broadman and Holman, 1994.

Blankley, Bethany. "Illegal Aliens Since 2021 Total More Than Individual Populations of 38 States." *Highland County Press*, June 25, 2023. https://highlandcountypress.com/illegal-aliens-2021-total-more-individual-populations-38-states-illegal-crossings-top-8-million#gsc.tab=0.

———. "Retired FBI Execs to Congress: Invasion at Border 'Perilous' for America." *Washington Examiner*, Jan. 26, 2024. https://www.washingtonexaminer.com/news/2819856/retired-fbi-execs-to-congress-invasion-at-border-perilous-for-america/.

Block, Daniel. *The Gods of the Nations: A Study in Ancient Near Eastern National Theology.* Eugene, OR: Wipf & Stock, 2013.

"Border Sector Chiefs Confirm Operational Impacts of Border Chaos, Increased Gotaways, Closed Checkpoints, and Empowered Cartels." House Committee on Homeland Security, Dec. 20, 2023. https://homeland.house.gov/2023/12/20/border-sector-chiefs-confirm-operational-impacts-of-border-chaos-increased-gotaways-closed-checkpoints-and-empowered-cartels/.

Bosch, David. *Theology of Mission: Missiology and Science of Religion, MSR 201 Study Guide.* Pretoria: University of South Africa, 1980.

———. *Transforming Mission: Paradigm Shifts in Mission Theology.* Maryknoll, NY: Orbis, 1993.

Boyd, Gregory. *God at War: The Bible and Spiritual Conflict.* Downers Grove, IL: InterVarsity, 1997.

Bramer, Stephen. "Kinsman-Redeemer." In *Evangelical Dictionary of Biblical Theology*, edited by Walter Elwell, 456–57. Grand Rapids: Baker, 1996.

Broek, R. van den. "Apollo." In *Dictionary of Deities and Demons in the Bible*, edited by Karel van der Toorn and Pieter Willem van der Horst, 138–43. New York: Brill, 1995.

Brownson, James V. "Speaking the Truth in Love: Elements of a Missional Hermeneutic." In *Church between Gospel and Culture: The Emerging Mission in North America*, edited by George Hunsberger and Craig Van Gelder, 228–59. Grand Rapids: Eerdmans, 1996.

Brunner, Emil. *The Word and the World.* London: World Student Movement, 1931.

Bultmann, Rudolf. *New Testament and Mythology.* Edited and translated by Schubert M. Ogden. Philadelphia: Fortress, 1984.

Cahn, Jonathan. *The Return of the Gods.* Lake Mary, FL: Frontline, 2022.

Cairns, Earle. *Christianity Through the Centuries: A History of the Christian Church.* Rev. ed. Grand Rapids: Zondervan, 1981.

Camarota, Steven A., and Karen Zeigler. "In October 2023, the Foreign-Born Share Was the Highest in History." Center for Immigration Studies, Nov. 30, 2023. https://cis.org/Report/October-2023-ForeignBorn-Share-Was-Highest-History.

Cantrell, Michael A. "Must a Scholar of Religion Be Methodologically Atheistic or Agnostic?" *Journal of the American Academy of Religion* 84:2 (June, 2016) 373–400.

Bibliography

Carriker, C. Timothy. "Missiological Hermeneutic and Pauline Apocalyptic Eschatology." In *The Good News of the Kingdom: Mission Theology for the Third Millennium*, edited by Charles Van Engen et al., 45–55. Eugene, OR: Wipf & Stock, 1993.

Case, Shirley Jackson. "Christianity and the Mystery Religions." *The Biblical World* 43:1 (1914) 3–16.

Castells, Manuel. *The Information Age: Economy, Society, and Culture*. Vol. 2: *The Power of Identity*. Hoboken, NJ: Wiley-Blackwell, 1997.

Center for the Study of Global Christianity. "Christianity in Its Global Context." Gordon Conwell Theological Seminary, June 7, 2013. https://www.gordonconwell.edu/wp-content/uploads/sites/13/2019/04/2ChristianityinitsGlobalContext.pdf.

Ceroke, Christian A. "Principles of Salvation History." *Marian Studies* 16:7 (Feb. 1965) 29–40.

Charles, J. D. "Vice and Virtue Lists." In *Dictionary of New Testament Background: A Compendium of Contemporary Biblical Scholarship*, edited by Stanley E. Porter and Craig A. Evans. Downers Grove, IL: InterVarsity, 2000. https://cranfordville.com/g496cLesso6RIQ2-3Vice-Virtue%20Lists%20in%20NT%20DNTB.pdf.

Childs, Brevard. *Introduction to the Old Testament as Scripture*. Philadelphia: Augsburg Fortress, 2011.

Cohen, Shaye J. D. "Did Ancient Jews Missionize?" *Bible Review* 19:4 (Aug. 2003). https://library.biblicalarchaeology.org/article/did-ancient-jews-missionize/.

D'Angelo, Frank J. D. "The Rhetoric of Intertextuality." *Rhetoric Review* 29:1 (Dec. 31, 2009) 31–47.

Deresiewicz, William. "Why I Left Academia (Since You're Wondering)." *Quillette*, Aug. 17, 2022. https://quillette.com/2022/08/17/why-i-left-academia-since-youre-wondering/.

Derrickson, Scott, dir. *Doctor Strange*. Los Angeles: Marvel Studios, 2016.

Draper, Jonathan A. "Weber, Theissen, and 'Wandering Charismatics' in the Didache." *Journal of Early Christian Studies* 6:4 (Dec. 1998) 541–76.

Edelberg, Wendy, and Tara Watson. "A More Equitable Distribution of the Positive Fiscal Benefits of Immigration." Brookings, Dec. 7, 2022. https://www.brookings.edu/articles/a-more-equitable-distribution-of-the-positive-fiscal-benefits-of-immigration/.

Edward, Rem. "John Wesley's Non-Literal Literalism and Hermeneutic of Love." *Wesleyan Theological Journal* 51:2 (2016) 26–40.

Eliyahu-Oron, Orna, and Barbara C. Johnson. "The Kerala Synagogues: Heritage of the Cochin Jews." In *Growing Up Jewish in India: Synagogues, Customs, and Communities from the Bene Israel to the Art of Siona Benjamin*, edited by Ori Z. Soltes, 115–91. New Delhi: Niyogi, 2021.

Espin, Orlando O. "Mary in Latino/a Catholicism: Four Types of Devotion." *New Theology Review* 23 (Aug. 2010) 16–25.

Eusebius of Caesarea. *Preparation for the Gospel*. 2 vols. Translated by Edwin Hamilton Gifford. Grand Rapids: Baker Book House, 1981.

Fai, Ebenezer, and Olugbenga Samuel Olagunju. "Mystery Religions and Their Influence on the New Testament and Early Christianity." *E-Journal of Religious and Theological Studies* 8:3 (Mar. 2022) 88–97. https://doi.org/10.38159/erats.2022834.

Fant, Clyde E., and Mitchell G. Reddish. "Ephesus." In *A Guide to Biblical Sites in Greece and Turkey*, 178–207. New York: Oxford Academic, 2003.

Bibliography

Faust, Avraham. "The Jubilee Real Estate Law." TheTorah.com. https://thetorah.com/the-jubilee-real-estate-law/.

Fontenrose, Joseph Eddy. *The Delphic Oracle: Its Responses and Operations, with a Catalogue of Responses*. Berkeley: University of California Press, 1978.

Fowler, Kimberley. "Origen, *Against Celsus* II.30." Judaism and Rome, Nov. 29, 2017. https://www.judaism-and-rome.org/origen-against-celsus-ii30.

Fowler, Robert M. "Reader-Response Criticism: Figuring Mark's Reader." In *Mark & Method: New Approaches in Biblical Studies*, edited by Janice Capel Anderson and Stephen D. Moore, 59–94. Minneapolis: Fortress, 2008.

Frazer, James George. *The Golden Bough: A Study in Magic and Religion*. New York, Touchstone, 1996.

Frost, Robert. "The Road Not Taken." In *Mountain Interval*. New York: Henry Holt, 1916. https://www.gutenberg.org/files/29345/29345-h/29345-h.htm.

Gabrielson, Timothy A. "Along the Grain of Salvation History: A Suggestion for Evangelical Hermeneutics." *Trinity Journal* 36:1 (Spring 2015) 71–90.

Galadima, Bulus, and Sam George, eds. *Africans in Diaspora and Diasporas in Africa*. Carlisle, UK: Langham Publishing, 2024.

Garfinkel, Yosef. "The Birth and Death of Biblical Minimalism." Armstrong Institute of Biblical Archeology, Aug. 28, 2023. https://armstronginstitute.org/814-the-birth-and-death-of-biblical-minimalism.

Garver, Rob. "Huge Number of Migrants Highlights Border Crisis." *VOA*, Jan. 3, 2024. https://www.voanews.com/a/huge-number-of-migrants-highlights-border-crisis/7424665.html.

Geisler, Norman L. "Naturalism." In *Baker Encyclopedia of Christian Apologetics*, 521–22. Grand Rapids: Baker, 1999.

Goheen, Michael W. "Continuing Steps Toward a Missional Hermeneutic." *Fideles: A Journal of Redeemer Pacific College* 3 (2008) 49–99.

Gonzalez, Justo L. *A History of Christian Thought*. Vol. 1: *The Cradle of Christianity*. Nashville: Abingdon, 1970.

Green, Michael. *Evangelism in the Early Church*. Grand Rapids: Eerdmans, 2003.

Guy, Laurie. "Naked Baptism in the Early Church: The Rhetoric and the Reality." *The Journal of Religious History* 27:2 (June 2003) 133–42.

Harnack, Adolf. *The Expansion of Christianity in the First Three Centuries*. 2 vols. Translated by James Moffatt. New York: J. P. Putnam's Sons, 1904–1905.

———. *The Mission and Expansion of Christianity in the First Three Centuries*. 2 vols. 2nd ed. Translated by James Moffatt. New York: J. P. Putnam's Sons, 1908.

Hatch, Treven. "Messianism and Jewish Messiahs in the New Testament Period." In *New Testament History, Culture, and Society: A Background to the Texts of the New Testament*, edited by Lincoln Blumell, 51–65. Provo, UT: Religious Studies Center, 2019.

Hawk, Daniel. *Berit Olam: Joshua*. Collegeville, MN: Liturgical, 2000.

———. *Joshua in 3D: A Commentary on Biblical Conquest and Manifest Destiny*. Eugene, OR: Cascade, 2010.

Hedlund, Roger. *The Mission of the Church in the World*. Grand Rapids: Baker, 1985.

Heiser, Michael. "Deuteronomy 32:8 and the Sons of God." *Bibliotheca Sacra* 158:629 (Jan.–Mar. 2001) 52–74.

———. *Supernatural: What the Bible Teaches About the Unseen World—and Why It Matters*. Bellingham, WA: Lexham, 2015.

Bibliography

———. *The Unseen Realm: Recovering the Supernatural Worldview of the Bible*. Bellingham, WA: Lexham, 2015.

Hendriks, H. Jurgens. "Contextualising Theological Education in Africa by Doing Theology in a Missional Hermeneutic." *Koers—Bulletin for Christian Scholarship* 77:2 (2012) 1–8.

Henten, J. W. van. "Dragon." In *Dictionary of Deities and Demons in the Bible*, edited by Karel van der Toorn and Pieter Willem van der Horst, 504–9. New York: Brill, 1995.

———. "Python." In *Dictionary of Deities and Demons in the Bible*, edited by Karel van der Toorn and Pieter Willem van der Horst, 1263–66. New York: Brill, 1995.

———. "Typhon." In *Dictionary of Deities and Demons in the Bible*, edited by Karel van der Toorn and Pieter Willem van der Horst, 1657–62. New York: Brill, 1995.

Hertig, Paul, and Robert Gallagher. "Introduction to Acts." In *Mission in Acts: Ancient Narratives in Contemporary Context*, edited by Robert Gallagher and Paul Hertig, 1–18. Maryknoll, NY: Orbis: 2004.

Hiebert, Paul G. *Anthropological Reflections on Missiological Issues*. Grand Rapids: Baker, 1994.

Hoedemaker, L. A. "The People of God and the Ends of the Earth." In *Missiology: An Ecumenical Introduction*, edited by F. J. Verstraelen et al., 157–71. Grand Rapids: Eerdmans, 1995.

Holland, Glenn. "The Companions of Paul in Acts." In *Alpha: Studies in Early Christianity* (Mar. 18, 2016) 127–32.

Houtman, C. "Queen of Heaven." In *Dictionary of Deities and Demons in the Bible*, edited by Karel van der Toorn and Pieter Willem van der Horst, 1278–83. New York: Brill, 1995.

Howard, George. "Was the Gospel of Matthew Originally Written in Hebrew?" *Bible Review* 2:4 (Winter 1986) 15–25.

Hughes, H. Dale. "Salvation-History as Hermeneutic." *Evangelical Quarterly* 48 (Apr.-June 1976) 79–89.

Hunsberger, George. "Proposals for a Missional Hermeneutic: Mapping the Conversation." Gospel and Our Culture Network, Jan. 2009. https://gocn.org/library/proposals-for-a-missional-hermeneutic-mapping-the-conversation/.

Hunter, George, III. *The Celtic Way of Evangelism*. Nashville: Abingdon, 2000.

"Impeaching Alejandro Nicholas Mayorkas, Secretary of Homeland, for High Crimes and Misdemeanors." H. R. Res. 582, 117th Cong. (2021). https://www.congress.gov/bill/117th-congress/house-resolution/582/titles.

Itzkin, Elissa S. "The Halevy Thesis—a Working Hypothesis? English Revivalism: Antidote for Revolution and Radicalism, 1789–1815." *Church History* 44:1 (Mar. 1975) 47–56.

Jackson, Bill. *The Biblical Metanarrative: One God, One Plan, One Story*. Corona, CA: Radicalmiddlepress, 2014.

Jefferson, Thomas. "An Act for Establishing Religious Freedom, January 16, 1786." Library of Virginia. https://www.virginiamemory.com/docs/ReligiousFree.pdf.

———. *The Jefferson Bible: What Thomas Jefferson Selected as the Life and Morals of Jesus of Nazareth*. Minneapolis: Lakewood, 2011.

Jenkins, Philip. *The Next Christendom: The Coming of Global Christianity*. 3rd ed. New York: Oxford University Press, 2011.

Jensen, Robin M. *Baptismal Imagery in Early Christianity*. Grand Rapids: Baker Academic, 2012.

BIBLIOGRAPHY

Jones, Robert. "The Messiah—in the Old Testament, the Apocrypha, and the Dead Sea Scrolls." SundaySchoolCourses.com, 2002. http://www.sundayschoolcourses.com/messiah/messiah.pdf.

Kadari, Tamar. "Queen of Sheba: Midrash and Aggadah." *The Shalvi/Hyman Encyclopedia of Jewish Women*, Dec. 31, 1999. https://jwa.org/encyclopedia/article/queen-of-sheba-midrash-and-aggadah.

Kahler, Martin. *Schriften zur Christologie und Mission*. Munich: Chr. Kaser, 1971.

The Kebra Nagast (The Glory of Kings). Translated by E. Wallis Budge. Rookhope, UK: Aziloth, 2013.

Keener, Craig. *Acts: An Exegetical Commentary*. 4 vols. Grand Rapids: Baker Academic, 2012.

———. *The Historical Jesus of the Gospels*. Grand Rapids: Eerdmans, 2009.

———. *Miracles: The Credibility of the New Testament*. 2 vols. Grand Rapids: Baker Academic, 2011.

Knoppers, Gary N. *Jews and Samaritans: The Origins and History of Their Early Relations*. New York: Oxford University Press, 2013.

Kraft, Charles. *Christianity with Power: Your Worldview and Your Experience of the Supernatural*. Ann Harbor, MI: Vine, 1989.

———. *A Hausa Reader: Cultural Materials with Helps for Use in Teaching Intermediate and Advanced Hausa*. Oakland: University of California Press, 1973.

———. *Power Encounter in Spiritual Warfare*. Eugene, OR: Wipf & Stock, 2017.

———. *A Study of Hausa Syntax*. 3 Vols. Hartford, CT: Hartford Seminary Foundation, 1963.

———. "Three Encounters in Christian Witness." In *Perspectives on the World Christian Movement: A Reader*, edited by Ralph Winter and Steven Hawthorne, 445–50. Pasadena, CA: William Carey Library, 2009.

———. *A Workbook in Intermediate and Advanced Hausa*. East Lansing, MI: African Studies Center at Michigan State University, 1966

Kraft, Charles, and Marguerite G. Kraft. *Introductory Hausa*. Oakland: University of California Press, 1974.

Latourette, Kenneth Scott. *Christianity Through the Ages*. New York: Harper and Row, 1965.

———. *The Unquenchable Light*. London: Eyre & Spottiswood, 1948.

Lawler, Andrew. "Church Unearthed in Ethiopia Rewrites the History of Christianity in Africa." *Smithsonian Magazine*, Dec. 10, 2019. https://www.smithsonianmag.com/history/church-unearthed-ethiopia-rewrites-history-christianity-africa-180973740/.

Lee, Michael. "Chicago Gangs Clash with Venezuelan Tren de Aragua Members: 'Blacks Against Migrants.'" *Fox News*, Sept. 22, 2024. https://www.foxnews.com/politics/chicago-gangs-clash-venezuelan-tren-de-aragua-members-blacks-against-migrants.

Lee, Young-Hoon. "Korean Pentecost: The Great Revival of 1907." *Asian Journal of Pentecostal Studies* 4:1 (2001) 73–83.

"Lesson One: 'Salvation History.'" Our Lady of the Assumption Parish. https://olaparish.net/learning/basic-catholic-catechism-course/lesson-one-salvation-history.

Lietzmann, Hans. *A History of the Early Church*. Cleveland: Meridian, 1961.

Lloyd, David. "The Rise and Rise of the Queen of Heaven." *Vision* (Summer 2005). https://www.vision.org/rise-and-rise-queen-heaven-731.

Bibliography

Lynch, Joseph. *Early Christianity: A Brief History*. New York: Oxford University Press, 2010.

Martin, Lee Roy. "Hearing the Voice of God: Pentecostal Hermeneutics and the Book of Judges." In *Pentecostal Hermeneutics: A Reader*, edited by Lee Roy Martin, 205–32. Boston: Brill, 2013.

———. "Introduction to Pentecostal Biblical Hermeneutics." In *Pentecostal Hermeneutics: A Reader*, edited by Lee Roy Martin, 1–10. Boston: Brill, 2013.

Matacio, Doug. "Centripetal and 'Centrifugal' Mission: Solomon and Jesus." *Journal of Adventist Mission Studies* 4:1 (2008) 31–42.

Mburu, Elizabeth. *African Hermeneutics*. Plateau State, Nigeria: Hippo, 2019.

McGavran, Donald A. *Understanding Church Growth*. Edited by C. Peter Wagner. 3rd ed. Grand Rapids: Eerdmans, 1990.

McLaren, Brian. *A Generous Orthodoxy: Why I Am a Missional, Evangelical, Post/Protestant, Liberal/Conservative, Mystical/Poetic, Biblical, Charismatic/Contemplative, Fundamentalist/Calvinist, Anabaptist/Anglican, Methodist, Catholic, Green, Incarnational, Depressed-Yet-Hopeful, Emergent, Unfinished Christian*. El Cajon, CA: Youth Specialties, 2004.

McMickle, Marvin. *Living Water for Thirsty Souls: Unleashing the Power of Exegetical Preaching*. King of Prussia, PA: Judson, 2021.

———. "Tuesday Lecture Series || January 10, 2023 || MCBC Akron." Mount Calvary Baptist Church, Jan. 13, 2023. https://www.youtube.com/watch?v=OKGoQOay6I8.

Mellor, Ronald J. "The Goddess Roma." In *Rise and Fall of the Roman World*, edited by Wolfgang Haase and Hildegard Temporini, 950–1030. New York: De Gruyter, 1990.

"Messianic Prophecy." Jews for Jesus (South Africa). https://www.jewsforjesus.co.za/faq/messianic-prophecy.

Mikoski, Gordon S. "Discerning Divine Direction." *Theology Today* 73:4 (2016) 307–11.

Mittelberg, Mark, et al. *Becoming a Contagious Christian: Leader's Guide*. Grand Rapids: Zondervan, 1995.

Mngadi, Thembinkosi Themba Paul. "The Local Church Is a Visible Hermeneutical Community." PhD diss., University of Natal, Pietermaritzburg, South Africa, 1996. https://researchspace.ukzn.ac.za/handle/10413/18408.

Moffett, Samuel Hugh. *A History of Christianity in Asia*. Vol. 1. Maryknoll, NY: Orbis, 1998.

Montgomery, James A. *The Samaritans, the Earliest Jewish Sect: Their History, Theology, and Literature*. Eugene, OR: Wipf & Stock, 1906.

Montiglio, Silvia. "Wandering Philosophers in Classical Greece." *Journal of Hellenic Studies* 120 (2000) 86–105.

Murphy, Nancey, "Phillip Johnson on Trial." *Perspectives on Science and Christian Faith* 45:1 (1993) 33–34.

Mussies, G. "Artemis." In *Dictionary of Deities and Demons in the Bible*, edited by Karel van der Toorn and Pieter Willem van der Horst, 167–80. New York: Brill, 1995.

Newbigin, Leslie. *The Gospel in a Pluralist Society*. Grand Rapids: Eerdmans, 1989.

———. *The Open Secret: An Introduction to the Theology of Mission*. Rev. ed. Grand Rapids: Eerdmans, 1995.

Ng, Kam Weng. "The Scope and Limits of Science: A Response to Scientism—Science and Christianity." Krisis and Praxis, Mar. 4, 2019. https://krisispraxis.com/archives/2019/03/the-scope-and-limits-of-science-a-response-to-scientism-science-christianity-part-36/.

Bibliography

Nida, Eugene A. "The Nature of Dynamic Equivalence in Translation." *Babel: International Journal of Translation* 22:3 (1977) 99–103.

Niebuhr, H. Richard. *Christ and Culture*. New York, Harper Torchlight, 1951.

Niemandt, Nelus. "A Missional Hermeneutic for the Transformation of Theological Education in Africa." *HTS Teologiese Studies/Theological Studies* 75:4 (2019) 1–10.

Noble, Paul. *The Canonical Approach: A Critical Reconstruction of the Hermeneutic of Brevard S. Childs*. Leiden: Brill, 1995.

Norford, Bryan. *Anointed Preaching: The Holy Spirit and the Pulpit*. Lethbridge, Canada: Pebble, 2011.

Nucci, Alessandra. "The Charismatic Renewal and the Catholic Church." *The Catholic World Report* (May 18, 2013). https://www.catholicworldreport.com/2013/05/18/the-charismatic-renewal-and-the-catholic-church/.

Nunez, J. P. "The Story of Our Salvation." Catholic Exchange, Sept. 6, 2017. https://catholicexchange.com/the-story-of-our-salvation/.

Olofinjana, Israel Oluwole. "A Dummies Guide to Reverse Mission." *Evangelical Alliance* (Apr. 26, 2017). https://www.eauk.org/news-and-views/a-dummies-guide-to-reverse-mission.

Omer, Ibrahim. "Sudan Connection: Are Ethiopian Jews Descendants of the Ancient Israelites?" Genetic Literacy Project, Feb., 24, 2023. https://geneticliteracyproject.org/2023/02/24/the-sudan-connection-are-ethiopian-jews-descendants-of-the-ancient-israelites/.

Otis, George. "Community Transformation Through United Prayer." *International Journal of Frontier Missions* 15:4 (Oct.–Dec. 1998) 211–17.

———. *The Twilight Labyrinth: Why Does Spiritual Darkness Linger Where It Does?* Grand Rapids: Chosen, 1997.

Otto, Rudolf. *The Idea of the Holy: An Inquiry into the Non-Rational Factor in the Idea of the Divine*. Translated by John Harvey. Whitefish, MT: Kissinger, 2010.

Partridge, Christopher, ed. *Introduction to World Religions*. Revised by Tim Dowley. Minneapolis: Fortress, 2018.

Pathrapankal, Joseph. "World History and Salvation History." *Svensk Exegetist Årsbok* 68 (2003) 97–117.

Payne, J. D. *Theology of Mission: A Concise Biblical Theology*. Bellingham, WA: Lexham, 2021.

Payne, William. *Adventures in Spiritual Warfare*. Eugene, OR: Resource Publications, 2018.

———. *American Methodism: Past and Future Growth*. Lexington, KY: Emeth, 2013.

———. "Assessing the Student Shift from Conversionist to Inclusivist Theology at Ashland Theological Seminary since 2002." *APM Proceedings* (in publication).

———. "Contextualization: The Movement Between Text and Context." UM & Global, June 29, 2018. http://www.umglobal.org/2018/06/william-payne-contextualization.html.

———. "A Deal with the Devil: Pragmatic Mission and Early American Methodism's Complicity with Slavery." *Asbury Theological Journal* 79:1 (Spring 2024) 9–28. https://place.asburyseminary.edu/asburyjournal/vol79/iss1/3.

———. "Discerning John Wesley's Missional Ecclesiology." *Wesleyan Theological Journal* 49:2 (2014) 24–47.

———. "Folk Religion and the Pentecostal Surge in Latin America." *Asbury Theological Journal* 71:1 (Spring 2016) 145–74. https://place.asburyseminary.edu/asburyjournal/vol71/iss1/12.

———. "How the Missional Hermeneutic Reveals the Missio Dei, Part I." UM & Global, Aug. 10, 2023. http://www.umglobal.org/2023/08/william-p-payne-how-missional.html.

———. "How the Missional Hermeneutic Reveals the Missio Dei, Part II." UM & Global, Aug. 17, 2023. http://www.umglobal.org/2023/08/william-p-payne-how-missional2.html.

———. "Jesus Is Every Race." UM & Global, Dec. 17, 2013. http://www.umglobal.org/2013/12/jesus-is-every-race.html.

———. "Probing Reasons for Mainline Decline." UM & Global, Apr. 28, 2016. http://www.umglobal.org/2016/04/.

———. "Religious Community in a Cuban Refugee Camp: Bringing Order Out of Chaos." *Missiology* 25:2 (1997) 141–54.

———. *Satan Exposed: A Biblical Theology of Spiritual Warfare*. Eugene, OR: Wipf & Stock, 2019.

Peterson, Eugene H. *Eat This Book: A Conversation in the Art of Spiritual Reading*. Grand Rapids: Eerdmans, 2006.

Porter, Stanley E., and Beth M. Stovall, eds. *Biblical Hermeneutics: Five Views*. Downers Grove, IL: IVP Academic, 2012.

Pradhan, Kartikey,. "The Jews of India." *Reflections* 9 (2009). https://www.csueastbay.edu/philosophy/reflections/2009/contents/kart-prad.html.

Pugh, Ben. *Atonement Theories: A Way through the Maze*. Eugene, OR: Cascade, 2014.

Puthiakunnel, Thomas. "Jewish Colonies of India Paved the Way for St. Thomas." *The St. Thomas Christian Encyclopedia of India*, edited by G. Menachery, 2:26–27. Kerala, India: BNK, 1973.

Radner, Karen. "'The Lost Tribes of Israel' in the Context of the Resettlement Programme of the Assyrian Empire." In *The Last Days of the Kingdom of Israel*, edited by Shuichi Hasegawa et al., 101–24. Boston: De Gruyter, 2019. https://doi.org/10.1515/9783110566604-006.

Ramm, Bernard. *Protestant Biblical Interpretation: A Textbook of Hermeneutics*. Grand Rapids: Baker, 1970.

Rappaport, Nolan. "The Massive Burden of Biden's Undocumented Immigrants." *The Hill*, Dec. 1, 2023. https://thehill.com/opinion/immigration/4335598-the-massive-burden-of-bidens-illegal-immigrants/.

Reese, Thomas. "'Freedom to Worship' vs. 'Freedom of Religion.'" *The National Catholic Reporter*, Aug. 19, 2016. https://www.ncronline.org/blogs/faith-and-justice/freedom-worship-vs-freedom-religion.

"Religion in Latin America: Widespread Change in a Historically Catholic Region." Pew Research Center, Nov. 13, 2014. https://www.pewresearch.org/religion/2014/11/13/religion-in-latin-america/.

Richardson, Don. *Peace Child*. Ventura, CA: Regal, 1976.

Ross, Hugh. "The Biblical Truth About ALIENS." Mike Signorelli, Apr. 10, 2023. https://www.youtube.com/watch?v=I_-yODzXVqY&t=46s

———. "Is There Life on Other Planets?" The 700 Club, Aug. 30, 2019. https://www.youtube.com/watch?v=O8X18TxfQUw.

Ross, Hugh, et al. *Lights in the Sky and Little Green Men: A Rational Christian Look at UFOs and Extraterrestrials*. Colorado Springs: NavPress, 2002.

Rukundwa, Lazare S. "Postcolonial Theory as a Hermeneutical Tool for Biblical Reading." *HTS Theological Studies* 64:1 (Mar. 2008) 339–51.

Bibliography

Salinas, Juan, and Pooja Salhotra. "What You Need to Know About the Venezuelan Gang That Texas Is Targeting." *Texas Tribune*, Sept. 18, 2024. https://www.texastribune.org/2024/09/18/texas-venezuelan-gang-tren-de-aragua-abbott-crackdown/.

Samah, Adam M. "Looking Over a Crowd—Do More Interpretive Sources Mean More Discretion?" *New York University Law Review* 92:1 (2016) 554–621.

Sanou, Boubakar. "Missio Dei as the Hermeneutical Key for Scriptural Interpretation." *Andrews University Studies* 56:2 (2018) 301–16.

Sarisky, Darren. "The Meaning of the Missio Dei: Reflections on Newbigin's Proposal that Mission Is the Essence of the Church." *Missiology: An International Review* 42:3 (2014) 257–70.

Schiffman, Lawrence H. "The Concept of the Messiah in Second Temple and Rabbinic Literature." *Review and Expositor* 84:2 (1987) 235–46.

Scobie, Charles H. H. "The Origins and Development of Samaritan Christianity." *New Testament Studies* 19:4 (2009) 390–414.

Shoichet, Catherine E. "'Why Springfield?' How a Small Ohio City Became Home for Thousands of Haitians." *CNN*, Sept. 19, 2024. https://www.cnn.com/2024/09/19/us/springfield-ohio-haitians-immigration-cec/index.html.

Sim, David. "Gentiles, Godfearers, and Proselytes." In *Attitudes to Gentiles in Ancient Judaism and Early Christianity*, edited by David Sim and James McLaren, 9–27. London: T&T Clark, 2014.

Skreslet, Stanley H. *Constructing Mission History: Mission Initiative and the Indigenous Agency in the Making of World Christianity*. Minneapolis: Fortress, 2023.

Smalley, William. "The World Is Too Much with Us." *Practical Anthropology* 5:5 (1958) 234–36. https://doi.org/10.1177/009182965800500508.

Smith, John E. "Time, Times, and the Right Time: Chronos and Kairos." *The Monist* 53:1 (1969) 1–13. http://www.jstor.org/stable/27902109.

Smith, Ralph A. "Paul and the Praetorian Guard." Theopolis Institute, Feb. 2, 2023. https://theopolisinstitute.com/paul-and-the-praetorian-guard/.

Snyder, Howard. *Radical Renewal: The Problem with Wineskins Today*. Eugene, OR: Wipf & Stock, 2005.

Stark, Rodney. *The Rise of Christianity: A Sociologist Reconsiders History*. Princeton: Princeton University, 1996.

Stott, John. "The Biblical Basis for Evangelism." In *Let the Earth Hear His Voice*, edited by J. D. Douglas, 68–78. Minneapolis: World Wide Publications, 1975.

Stovall, John. "The Messianic Prophecies in the Book of Zechariah." Modern Reformation, Dec. 2021. https://modernreformation.org/resource-library/web-exclusive-articles/the-mod-the-messianic-prophecies-in-the-book-of-zechariah/.

Tamawiwy, August C. "A Foundation for a Culture of Justpeace: Church as a Hermeneutic Community to Promote Peace Narratives." *MAHABBAH: Journal of Religion and Education* 2:1 (Jan. 2021) 61–72.

Tennent, Timothy. *Invitation to World Mission: A Trinitarian Missiology for the Twenty-first Century*. Grand Rapids: Kregel, 2010.

Thomas, Norman E. "The Church at Antioch: Crossing Racial, Cultural, and Class Barriers." In *Mission in Acts: Ancient Narratives in Contemporary Context*, edited by Robert Gallagher and Paul Hertig, 144–56. Maryknoll, NY: Orbis: 2004.

Thomas, Robert L. "Dynamic Equivalence: A Method of Translation or a System of Hermeneutics." *The Master's Seminary Journal* 1:2 (1990) 149–76.

Tolkien, J. R. R. *The Fellowship of the Ring*. New York: Ballantine, 1966.

Bibliography

Tong, Sheryl Lee Tian. "Our Land, Our Life: Okinawans Hold Out Against New US Base in Coastal Zone." *Mongabay*, Nov. 25, 2021. https://news.mongabay.com/2021/11/our-land-our-life-okinawans-hold-out-against-new-u-s-base-in-coastal-zone/.

Towns, Elmer. *Evangelism and Church Growth*. Ventura, CA: Regal, 1995.

Wagner, C. Peter. *Territorial Spirits*. Shippensburg, PA: Destiny Image, 2012.

Wallace, Anthony F. C. "Revitilalization Movements." *American Anthropologist* 58:2 (1956) 265–81.

Weigall, Arthur. *The Paganism in our Christianity*. San Diego: Book Tree, 2008.

Weiss, Steward. "The Beta Israel: The Return of a Lost Tribe. *The Jerusalem Post*, Dec. 16, 2021. https://www.jpost.com/diaspora/the-beta-israel-the-return-of-a-lost-tribe-688940.

Welchel, Tommy, and Michelle Griffith. *True Stories of the Miracles of Azusa Street and Beyond*. Shippensburg, PA: Destiny Image, 2013.

Wesley, John. "Of the Church." In *The Works of John Wesley*, edited by Thomas Jackson, 6:392–401. 3rd ed. Grand Rapids: Baker, 1991.

Wildman, Wesley. "Rudolf Bultmann." Boston Collaborative Encyclopedia of Western Theology, 1994. https://people.bu.edu/wwildman/bce/mwt_themes_760_bultmann.htm.

Wimber, John, and Kevin Springer. *Power Evangelism*. New York: Harper Collins, 1992.

Windsor, Rudolph R. *From Babylon to Timbuktu: A History of the Ancient Black Races Including the Black Hebrews*. New York: Exposition, 1969.

Winger, Mell. "Almolonga, the Miracle City." *Renewal Journal* 16 (2012) 9–20. https://renewaljournal.com/2012/05/11/almolonga-the-miracle-city-bymell-winger/.

Wink, Walter. *Engaging the Powers: Discernment and Resistance in a World of Domination*. Minneapolis: Fortress, 1992.

———. *Naming the Powers: The Language of Power in the New Testament*. Philadelphia: Fortress, 1984.

———. *The Powers That Be: Theology for a New Millennium*. New York: Galilee, 1998.

———. *Unmasking the Powers: The Invisible Forces that Determine Human Existence*. Philadelphia: Fortress, 1993.

"Witch Doctor Gets Saved, Healed, Baptized, & Married!" Iris Global Media, July 10, 2015. https://www.youtube.com/watch?v=ubKjWlARF8s

Wright, Christopher. *The Mission of God: Unlocking the Bible's Grand Narrative*. Downers Grove, IL: IVP Academic, 2006.

Wright, N. T. *Paul: In Fresh Perspective*. Minneapolis: Fortress, 2009.

Zegeye, Abebe. "The Construction of the Beta Israel Identity." *Social Identities* 10:5 (Aug. 25, 2010) 589–618.

———. "The Light of Origins: Beta Israel and the Return to Yerusalem." *Religion and Theology* 11:1 (Mar. 2004) 50–70.

Subject Index

Abraham, 35, 36, 37, 90–91, 101
Abraham's seed, 43
"absurdity idea," 1
Acts (book of), 40–98
    filled with villains, 93
    introduction to, 41–43
    as a supernatural story, 98
Adam, 101–2
Adam and Eve, 36
African Americans, Haitians, Black community and, 115n23
African Christianity, New Testament Christianity and, 155
African Hermeneutics (Mburu), 13
Africans, rural feeling connected to the land, 100
Agabus, 85
King Agrippa, 88, 89
King Ahab, 101
Alexander the Great, 70
allegiance encounter, 56
altar to the unknown god, Paul preaching about, 77
America, immigration to, 114–18, 120
Americans, in mainline Protestant churches, 129
Ananias, 59
Anastasia, Greek name meaning resurrection, 76
Androclus, locating Ephesus, 79
angels, in Acts, 94
Anglican Church, not favored in Virginia, 4

Anglican priests, power ministry in Nigeria, 155
animists, 54–55, 83
"anointed one" (*mashiach*), heavenly sign for, 122
"anti-Christian" faith, humanism as, 130
Antioch believers, called themselves Christians (*Christianous*), 63–64
Antioch church, 63–64, 68
anti-Semitism, 148
apocalyptic mission, of Paul, 78n61
Apollo, 70, 71, 79
apostle, meaning to send or dispatch (*apostello*), 67n40
"apostle to the gentiles," Paul as, 42
apostles, 45, 45n8, 51. *See also* disciples
Apostles' Creed, 19
apostolic church, defined by God's mission, xv
appointed time, Daniel referring to, 123n2
Aquila and Priscilla, added to Paul's team, 79
Areopagus, 76, 127, 132
Ark of the Covenant, Menelik and, 57
Arnold, Bill, 142
Artemis, 80, 82–84
Asherah, 103, 103n6, 106n9
Assyria, as God's agent of judgment, 53
Athanasian Creed, 19
atheism, 5, 6, 8
Athens, Paul in, 75–78
Augustine of Hippo, on miracles, 135
Emperor Augustus, 74
Azusa Street revival, 152

Subject Index

Baal Zephon, as a storm god, 93
Baker, Heidi, 55
baptism
    in the Holy Spirit, 47–50
    nude in the Early Church, 48n13
Bar-Jesus, 66
Barnabas, 69, 98
Barnabas and Paul, 63, 66, 67, 69
Barram, Michael, 2, 7
Battle of Milvian Bridge, 136
Beale, G., 31
Bekele, Girma, 7
believers
    Berean sent Paul to Athens, 75
    buried with Christ in baptism, 49
    caring for those in need, 112
    early community of lacking consensus, 19
    gentile, 42, 68
    held everything in common, 47
Berger, Peter, 8
Beta Israel community, 57, 57n25, 59
Bethel Bible School in Topeka, Kansas, 152
Bethel Church phenomena, 153–54
biases, 4, 7–9, 16, 105, 113
Bible
    declaring God's mission, xiv
    generated by God's mission, 32–33
    identifying God's salvific work in history, 142
    illustrating Israel's missional nature, 107
    mansion metaphor for, xiii
    meant to be preached, 21
    missional hermeneutic of, 33
    modeling God's justice, 27
    as not the final authority in canonical criticism, 18
    on ongoing conflict, 24
    postcolonial interpretation of, 17
    reading from a particular vantage point, 7
    salvation history affirming teachings, 144
    showing God working for the good, 36
    showing Israelites understood land, 101
Bible interpretation, 7–8, 11
Bible-reading people, changed Western Christianity, 150
biblical genres, types of, 2n4
biblical interpretation, 2, 11–22, 33
biblical metanarrative, knowing, 23
biblical texts, history of interpretation or "afterlife," 32
bibliolatry, evangelicals accused of, 28
President Biden, influx of unauthorized travelers and, 116–17
biosphere, 34n17
birth of Jesus, came at a ripe moment, 122
black arts, in the ancient world, 72
black magic, 83
Blackaby, Henry, xvi
blinding, biblical examples of, 66–67
Boaz, 109, 110
Book of Acts. *See* Acts (book of)
Bosch, David, xiv, 7
boundary crossing, 98
Boyd, Gregory, 24
Brahmin priest, killed Thomas, 97
Brookings Institute, on immigration, 117
Brownson, James, 28
"bully orthodoxy," correcting, 19
Bultmann, Rudolf, 9, 9n24

Caesar, 88, 135n43
Cahn, Jonathan, 26n7
Canaan, malfeasance of, 101
caretakers of the land, Israelites as, 102
Carey, William, 151
Castells, Manuel, 18n18
Catholic Charismatics, growth in the number of, 118
Celtic mission, rise of, 146
center-set theology, 19
Ceroke, Christian, 141
Charismatics, 21, 153
cherubim, 70
children of God, xv, 66
Chile, Pentecostal revival in, 152
Christ. *See* Jesus Christ
"Christ against culture" approach, 130–31

Subject Index

Christian creolism (Christo-paganism), 156
"Christian impulse," as forward and then receding, 143–44
Christianity
   American courts diminishing, 5
   as the antithesis of Roman religions, 130
   contextualization of, 128
   courts minimizing traditional, 6
   devoid of apostolic character and personal piety, 146
   early wanted Jesus to be the Lord of the Roman Empire, 130
   external factors facilitating the spread of, 136–37
   new face of global, 154
   not conforming to state expectations, 132
   as a quasi-Jewish sect, 126
   rise of global as the fourth Reformation, 154–56
   shared prejudices of Judean Jews, 130
   triumph of, 134–36
Christians, 6–7, 133, 137
   Antioch believers called themselves, 63–64
   early believed Jesus would return quickly, 45
   early embraced the Christus Victor theology, 94
   global reporting visions and prophecies, 157
   new sharing their faith as missionaries, 120
the church
   continuing Christ's salvific mission, 143
   discipling the nations, 140
   as the face of God's mission in the world, xv
   as God's missional agent, xiv
   history focusing on the expansion of, 141
   working with the political system, 27
church and state, separation of, 4

circumcised strangers, to be treated as native born, 109
circumcising, the heart, 49
"circumcision party." *See* Judaizers
civic duty, honoring the gods as, 131
civil religion, of Rome, 132
civilizing, as subjugating and westernizing, 151
clock metaphor, of Deism, 34–35
close relative, right to redeem kin from slavery, 35n18
colonialism, taking the Reformation to the world, 151
commandment to love one's neighbor, 120–21
commandments, Jesus naming the greatest, 112
communistic interpretations of religion, critical theory influencing, 16
conquest narratives, savage imagery of Old Testament, 106
Constantine, 58, 135, 135n42, 136
Constitution of the US, interpreting, 3–7
contagion (sympathetic magic), law of, 83
context, studying, 2
contextual theology, 28
contextualization, 11–13, 77n60, 128, 155
contextualizing community, 29
converts, to Christ wanted to identify as Jews, 126
Corinth, Paul's work in, 78–79
Cornelius the Godfearer, 60–63, 69
corporate sin, personifying, 25
covenant
   allegiance to, 106
   effects of renewing with God, 102, 102n5
   of God with Abraham, 37
   predicated upon Israel keeping God's commandments, 107
creation, grand narrative beginning with, 33
creedal statements, about biblical interpretation, 18
"critical" method of inquiry, exegesis employing, 8

Subject Index

critical theory, connecting with postcolonial approaches, 16
the cross, representing God's predetermined plan, 35–36
crucifixion, as a rite of passage, 48
Cuban Mary statue, 81
Cuban refugee camp, 49, 119
cultural assimilation, in the time of the Maccabees, 38
cultural gap, between Africans and biblical interpretation, 13
cultural influence, 6
cultural sanctification, 131
cultural war, pitting humanism against traditional Christianity, 129
culture, 12n3, 26n8, 131
curse, the law as, 43
Cyprus, Barnabas and Paul preached there, 65–66

Dan, lost tribe of, 58
Daniel's "right time," as the great telos, 122–23
darkness, having no fellowship with light, 72
the "day," of the Lord, 123
Day of Atonement, 34, 44
day of judgment, 123
deacons, 47
"decolonialality," 16n13
deconstruction, 17, 18
defiance, causing the killing of God's Son, 139
Deism, clock metaphor regarding, 34–35
deliverer, needed to lead the people out of Egypt, 39
Delphi, high priestess named Pythia, 70
democracy, spirit of, 133
democratic impulse, of all religions, 78
demonized person, 71
demons, manifestation of, 155
Deresiewicz, William, 17
devil, God destroying the works of, xvi
Diana, 80
Didache, 48, 48n11, 111, 111n13
Diocletian, 71, 135–36, 135n43
disciples, 45, 46, 47, 54. *See also* apostles

discipling, the Roman empire, 129–31
the Divine, sects emphasizing mystical approaches to, 20
"divine hand" approach to history, standard histories rejecting, 143n10
divine inspiration, overemphasis on, 10
divine plan, as the missio Dei, 123
"divine providence," role of, 124
divine serpents, biblical terms for, 70
divine timing, of Jesus' birth, 123
diviner, "spirit of the python" translating as, 71
Doctor Strange cinematic example, 23–24
dragons, referring to winged serpents, 70
dynamic equivalence, 12

earth, as not an accident of chance, 34n17
earthly kingdom, of God, 142
earthquake, sent by God, 73
East India Company, 104
Eastern thought, progress as an illusion, 147n18
Edict of Caracalla, 133
Edict of Milan, 136
Edict of Tolerance, 136, 137
egalitarian church, where all believers were equal, 133
Egyptian magicians, clash between Moses and, 55
Egyptian persecution, of the Hebrews, 41
elders, appointment of, 64, 65
the elect, Paul refers to the called as, 36
Elijah, 30, 55–56
elohim, 31, 37
Emmaus Road encounter, 30
end goal (telos or eschaton), xvii
end times, 157
Engaging the Powers (Wink), 25n6
the English, depersonalized African slaves, 104
Ephesian Jews, rejected Paul and his message, 82
Ephesus, 79–84
  backstory of, 79
  church remained faithful to the gospel and God, 84

Subject Index

Paul preached the kingdom of God boldly in, 81
Esau, 38
eschatological horizon, scripture pointing to, xvii
eschatological theology, 157
eternal punishment, 144
Ethiopian eunuch, encounter with Phillip, 57–59
Ethiopian Jews, 57n25, 58
ethnocentrism, 112
Eusebius, on Christianity as superior, 123–24
evangelical churches, operationalizing Jesus' kingdom, 153
evangelical theology, of immigration today, 99
Evangelical-Pentecostals, number of global, 117–18
evangelicals
    affirming that the Bible is inspired, 21–22, 29
    becoming inclusivists, 78n62
    on the Bible showing God's mission, 99
    emphasizing a high view of Scripture, 28
    employing the missional hermeneutic, 29
    on the established religion of the liberal state, 5
    seeking to align America with Scripture, 129n28
evangelism
    church winning the world through, 130
    defining, 25, 74
    methods of Paul, 73
    minimizing the work of personal, 26
evangelists, 65, 137
evangelizing, 73, 74
evil, as contrary to God's nature, 148
evil sorcerer, in Cyprus, 94
evolution, in the Old Testament, 145
exegesis, 1n1, 2, 9, 10, 15
the exile, served God's purposes, 148–49
Expedition Bible, YouTube channel, 141n2

Ezra, 38

faith, 16–17, 20, 21, 128
the fall, 26, 34, 39
Father, God as a relational, 35
"Father God" theology, 103
Felix, 88
Festus, 88
First Amendment, interpreting, 3
"folk Christianity," Latino Pentecostalism as, 156
folk religion, in Colombia and Costa Rica, 155
Fontenrose, Joseph, 71
foreigners, 103, 108, 109, 110, 114. See also sojourners; strangers
Fowler, Robert, 13
Franke, John, 2, 7
freedom of religion, 5
Frisbee, Lonnie, 153
Frost, Robert, "The Road Not Taken," 14
fulfillment hermeneutic, Beale not discounting, 31
Fuller Theological Seminary, 155
fullness of time, Jesus born in, 123

Gabrielson, Timothy, 11
Galerius, 136
gates of Hades, as Satan's kingdom, 147
gentiles
    as heirs together with Israel, 86
    how they treated the "least of these," 110
    messiah will bring salvation to, 45n7
    as non-Jewish persons, 110n12
    Paul's focus on, 78
ghost (phantasma), Jesus as, 92
giants, genetic contamination from Nephilim, 38
gift from God, land as, 103
gift of tongues, 153
global church, 157
God
    advancing his missional plan, xvi
    always at work, 137, 142
    arranged for Peter to preach to Cornelius, 61

Subject Index

God (continued)
- assigned the promised land to the Jews, 102
- became a Jew, 12n3
- bringing good out of Satan's malice, 147
- brought Jews to Jerusalem before Pentecost, 52
- communicating meaning (theocentric), 21
- covenanting to accomplish his mission, xvi
- cursed the land because of sin, 102
- desired a relationship with humans, 34
- desiring all should be saved, xvi
- destroying powers and principalities, 24–25
- directed Solomon to build a court for the nations in the temple, 108
- directed the church to fulfill his mission, 97
- directed the missionary work of Paul, 69
- drove Canaanite nations from the promised land, 105
- empowered missionaries, 68
- fed the Israelites and taught them his ways, 41
- gave humans rulership as God's representatives, xv
- guiding Paul, 93, 98
- history testifying to his plan, 137–38
- inspiring predictive prophecy, 31
- intervened to enable his mission, 146
- as a just God, 25
- knowing what will happen, 125
- loving humanity, 141
- loving totally, 112
- as a missionary God, xv
- moving history to a climax, 156
- not killing the righteous through his judgment, 91
- as the paragon of justice in the Bible, 27
- permitted spiritual revolt, 147
- planned for Jesus to be the ransom, 36
- pledged that he would redeem wayward people, 35
- prepared Paul, 98
- prepared the Roman Empire, 138
- as primary actor guiding the church, 64
- promised to bless the nations through Abraham, 36
- promised to give the land of Canaan to Abraham and his descendants, 101
- pushing forward his missional objectives, 118
- putting first, 112
- revealing himself through the Bible, 20–21
- saved baby Moses and placed him in Pharaoh's home, 39
- sent Joseph to Egypt, 38
- sent prophets to call Israel back to the covenant, 148
- separating the righteous from the unrighteous, 91
- told Ananias that Paul was his chosen instrument, 60
- told Noah that he could eat any animal with the breath of life, 62
- told Noah to construct an ark, 90
- used persecution to drive the disciples into the world, 52
- utilized a great famine to drive his family to the land of Goshen, 38
- wanted two missionary teams, 69
- wanting all people to be saved, 132
- wanting the church to evangelize the nations, 140
- wanting to partner with humans, 144
- worked through Bible writers in the Old and New Testaments, 31
- worked through both evolution or revolution, 145
- worked through his church to accomplish his mission, xv
- worked through Moses to defeat the gods of Egypt, 39
- worked to accomplish his sovereign plans, 124–25

Subject Index

worked to make Christianity the dominant faith in Europe, 136
working through Israel to bless all the families of the earth, 148
God at War: The Bible and Spiritual Conflict (Boyd), 24
God worshiper, Naaman became, 107
Godfearers, 61, 127
Godfearing man (*phoboumenos ton theon*), Cornelius as, 60
godly people, world needing to be salted with, 91
"God's *Shalom* and the Church's Witness," as the basic evangelism class, 25
Goheen, Michael, xiv, 20
good Samaritan, parable of, 112–13
Goshen, became the womb of Israel, 39
gospel (*euangelion*)
    crossing a major sociopolitical boundary, 56
    divine preparation for, 122–38
    as the good news, 73
    message in Thessalonica, 73–75
    needing to penetrate the Muslim world and all of Asia, 156
    seeding in unreached places, 119
governors and kings, Paul going through to get to Rome, 88
grace through faith, all saved by, 43
Great Commission, 37, 151
"Great is Artemis of the Ephesians!" shout of, 82–83
Great Power of God, sorcerer converted to Jesus, 94
Greco-Roman world, every aspect of life tainted by religion, 131
Greek faith, Paul deconstructed, 78
Greek mystery religions, influence of, 48n12
Green, Michael, 124

Haile Selassie, 57
Haitian immigrants, 115, 115n23
Haitians, 115n21
Halevy, Elie, 26n8

Harnack, Adolf, 61, 124, 126, 127–28, 135, 136–37
Hausa language, 154
hearing, what God says while reading the text, 20
heathen, as a pejorative term, 104
"heavenly realms" (*epouranios*), xivn5
Hebrews, using Egypt as a typology for sin, 48
Heiser, Michael, 24, 92
Hellenism, 76
Hellenistic believers, Paul's instruction to, 86
Hellenistic Jews, as early converts in the New Testament, 125
Hellenistic Judaism, as a template embracing the Roman world, 130
Hellenistic synagogues, Paul's mission took him to, 43
Hellenists, complained that their widows were not being fed properly, 47
helpers, of Paul, 65
hermeneutic, as a means of interpreting a text, 1
hermeneutical community, 29
hermeneutical issues, surrounding the current immigration debate, 99
Hiebert, Paul, 29
hina clause ("so that") indicating a purposeful relationship, 133
Hispanics, starting a ministry with unchurched, 119–20
historical approach, to the study of religion, 2n7
The Historical Jesus of the Gospels and Acts: An Exegetical Commentary (Keener), 9
historical-critical approach, 31
history
    applying the missional hermeneutic to, 139–57
    cyclical movements of, 146n18
    God worked to shape the flow of, 146
    having a telos, 142
    interpreting like Jesus interpreted Jewish history, 140
    producing biased narratives, 141

history (continued)
    as purposeful (not random), 146–47
    selective reading of, 4
holy nation, God chose Israel to be, 106
holy relics, Roman Catholic notion of, 83
Holy Spirit
    abundant demonstrations of, 152
    active at Pentecost, 46
    baptism in, 47–50
    directing and unfolding the missio
        Dei, 145n15
    enabling God's mission, xiv
    exegete not having to affirm all
        Scripture must be spiritually
        discerned, 10
    forbade Paul and his team to enter
        Asia Minor, 69
    as the power behind conversion, 75
    reading the Bible under the guidance
        of, 21
    sent to and empowered church, 27
    as a sign of acceptance, 63
    transforming culture, 131
Holy Writ. *See* Scripture(s)
Honduran immigrant, granted asylum,
    120
hospitality codes, of Israel, 105–8
the "hour," of his coming, 123
House Homeland Security Committee,
    116
Howard, George, 128n24
Hughes, H. Dale, 142
human redemption, creation waiting
    for, 102
humanism
    Christian, 78n62, 129, 144
    establishment of, 5
    grew out of Christianity, 130
    modern universalism reflecting, 78
humanists, 5, 129, 129n28
humanity, needing to be saved, 141
humanization process, through
    liberation theology, 142n6
humans
    needing to be reconciled to God
        through Christ, 26
    as the purpose of creation, 34n17

husbands, on treating Christian wives,
    133–34

Idea of the Holy (Otto), 20
ideology, projecting onto the Scriptures,
    32
idols, as worthless according to Paul, 82
Ignatius, 65n38
immigrant churches, evangelizing
    native-born Americans, 118–19
immigrants, 103, 112, 114, 116, 119
immigration, 115, 117, 121
immigration debate, 99–121
incarnation, as a seminal event, 146
India, Thomas's mission to, 96–97
indigenous church, rise of accompanied
    by a revival, 151
indigenous faith systems, meshing with
    Hispanic cultures, 156
indigenous peoples, 16, 100
indulgences, selling to spiritually anxious
    people, 150
inner-city youth, translating Psalm 23
    for, 12
inspiration, leading to error, 21
institutionalism, hampered God's
    missional plans, 146
intent, of the author, 14
interpretation
    as perspectival and contextual, 7
    of the US Constitution, 3
interpreters, bringing meaning to the
    text, 13
Isis, as the ideal for motherhood, 80
Islamic community (Ummah),
    succession debate in early Islam,
    85–86
Israel
    as a blessing to the nations, 108
    establishment of modern, 147–48
    example of the nation of, 148–49
    God called to be a light unto the
        nations, 106
    God created the nation of, 36
    as God's vineyard, 139
    history of pointed to Jesus, 41

Subject Index

likened to a fig tree to be destroyed, 139
moral obligation to care for strangers and foreigners, 109
national narrative as a birth metaphor, 40–41
not called to evangelize the nations, 107
Israelites, 37, 105–8, 109
It's Supernatural! show, 93

Jackson, Bill, 23
Jacob and his family, surviving as a distinct nation, 37–38
James, the brother of Jesus, 42, 85, 85n75
James and John, Sons of Thunder, 54
Jason the high priest, in Maccabees, 38
Jefferson, Thomas, 4, 8
King Jehu, 53
Jenkins, Philip, 118, 154
King Jeroboam, 53
Jerusalem
  apostles waiting for Jesus in, 44–47
  Paul's work in, 84–87
Jerusalem church, 46–47, 50, 68
Jerusalem Council, 42, 68–69, 85
Jesus Christ
  above all forces of evil, 77–78
  in a boat on the Sea of Galilee, 92
  born during the Pax Romana, 124
  "Christ" as the Greek translation of messiah, 64
  as the culmination of the Jewish metanarrative, 41
  cursed the nation of Israel for rejecting him, 67
  defining neighbor, 112–13
  destroyed the wall separating Jews from gentiles, 43
  embodying the holy remnant of Israel, 36
  evangelized Paul on the road to Damascus, 59
  as the face of God, 27, 82
  fulfilled Old Testament prophecies, 30
  on how Satan was cast from heaven, 91
  incarnating God's mission, xiv
  inviting people to enter the kingdom of God, xvi
  as a Jew, 12n4
  as the Lamb of God, xv, 34
  as the Messiah, 89
  as a moral figure for Jefferson, 8
  as more powerful than the demons, 84
  not claiming the throne of David in Jerusalem, 44
  not trying to overturn the Roman government or the Sanhedrin, 27
  objected when the demon announced him, 72
  as the only true Lord, 78
  Paul described his encounter with, 89
  portraying God as a landowner, 102
  on the purpose of the outer court of the temple, 108
  resurrected, met with the apostles, 45
  satisfied the missional calling of Israel, 149
  as the scapegoat, 35
  as the Son of God at his baptism, 50
  as the Stone that the builders rejected, 139
  subduing all powers aligned against the Father, 144
  teachings of, 30
  timing of the ministry of, 123
  told the church to take the gospel to the world, 51, 149
  told the religious leaders that God will reject them, 140
  treated Samaritans like covenant people, 54
  as the unknown god according to Paul, 77
"Jesus is Lord" declaration, contradicting "Caesar is Lord" (*Kaisar kurios*), 130
Jesus People movement, began on the West Coast, 153
Jew, God entered the world as, 12
Jew Town, a community in Kerala, 96

Subject Index

Jewish believers
    holding to their ethnic privilege as the chosen people, 41–42
    in Jerusalem wanted Paul to separate the Jews from the gentiles, 86
    no reason to separate from gentile believers, 43
    preached the gospel as they dispersed, 51
Jewish Christianity, central role in the rise of Christianity, 126
Jewish community, in the city of Cranganore (present-day Kodungallur), 97n90
Jewish Jesus, becoming any other culture, 12
Jewish members of the new church, not required to keep the law, 43
Jewish mission, 126, 127
Jewish proselytes, converted to Judaism, 61
Jewish thought, Hellenization of, 125
Jews
    attachment to ancestral land, 100
    came to Berea to foment another riot, 75
    as the "chosen people," 104
    commanded to destroy the inhabitants of the promised land, 105
    conflict with Artemis faithful, 82n71
    despised Samaritans, 54
    expected a messiah to deliver them from Roman occupation, 44n6
    leaders not rendering to God what belongs to God, 139
    lived everywhere from Babylon to Spain, 126
    not assimilated in Egypt, 39
    not saved by keeping the law, 42
    persecuting Paul in Corinth, 78
    prepared the world for the church's missionary activity, 149
    rejected Stephen's contention that they murdered the Messiah, 41
    return from Babylonian captivity, 38
    seized Paul and beat him, 87
    traveled as far as India and settled in modern-day Kerala, 96
    tried to kill Paul, 59
Jews for Jesus, 30n8
Jezebel, had Naboth stoned, 101
John Mark, 69
Pope John Paul II, crowned Mary as the Queen of Cuba, 81
John the Baptist, 30, 31, 34, 44, 50
Jonah, story of as a literary device, 9
Joseph, 37, 38–39, 52
Joseph and his family, into the womb of Goshen, 40
jubilee year, 101
Jubilees (book of), 101
Judaism, 125–29, 149n23
Judaizers
    conflict with those who envisioned a global mission, 43
    criticized Peter for socializing with gentiles, 62
    insisted that Jewish believers separate themselves from gentile believers, 42
    opposed by Barnabas and Paul, 68
    Paul's revelation put him in direct conflict with, 86
    wanted gentile believers to become Jewish proselytes, 63
Judean Jews, compared to Hellenistic Jews, 130
justice, as a characteristic of God, 27

kairos moment, disrupting the normal movement of history, 123
Kebra Nagast, Ethiopian legend about the Queen of Sheba and King Solomon, 107n11
Keener, Craig, 9
Khirbet el-Qom inscription, on Asherah's sacred pole, 103n6
kingdom of darkness, Jesus pushed against, 147
kingdom of God, 81–82, 102
kingdom of priests and a holy nation, being, 107
kinsman redeemer, 35, 35n18

Subject Index

Korea, massive revival, 152, 152n27
kosher rules, erecting a social boundary, 62
Kraft, Charles, 56, 154, 154n31

Ladon, serpent-dragon, 70
lame man, healed by Paul, 67
land
    people of, 103–10
    theology of, 100–103
Latin Americans, percentage Evangelical-Pentecostal, 117
Latinized faith, local church receiving and contextualizing, 29
Latino Pentecostalism, massive numerical growth, 156
Latourette, Kenneth Scott, 143, 144
the law, 42, 43, 68–69
laws, obeying like good citizens, 132
the least of these, tending to the needs of, 110–14
Lectio Divina, emphasizing an encounter with God, 20
Lemon Test, 6n13
leprosy, cured by Heidi Baker's ministry, 55
Leventhal, Harold, 4
levirate law, on inheritance of land, 101
liberal ideology, minority faiths aligned with, 6
liberal Protestantism, losing its soul, 129
liberation theology, 15, 25, 142n6
Lietzmann, Hans, 122–23
literal interpretation, 1
literal sense of the Constitution, adherence to, 3
literary interpretation, applying to Robert Frost's poem, 14
"little ones," can be translated least of these, 111
living document, Constitution as, 3
living Word, 20, 21
local spirit or god, fear of, 54–55
"location," interpretation and, 2
Lot and his family, God delivered, 91
love
    enduring all things, 112
    of God, xiv, 35
    of neighbor, 113
    as the primary attribute of God, xvi
Lydia and her family, received Christ and were baptized, 69
Lynch, Joseph, 46, 137

Macedonia, man from appeared to Paul, 69
Maenzanise, Beauty, 100
Magi, witnessed Jesus' natal star, 122
magical scrolls, sorcerers burned, 84
Magisterium, suspicion of, 28
Malta, Paul on the island of, 93–95
manifest destiny
    of the Jews, 38
    justified US Western expansion, 16
Mar Thoma Church, existence of, 97
Martin, Lee Roy, 92n79
Marvel movies, knowing the storyline of, 23–24
Mary. *See* Virgin Mary
Massachusetts, state church of, 4n9
Mburu, Elizabeth, 13
McGavran, Donald A., 26, 26n8
McLaren, Brian, 19
meaning, 13, 15, 103–4
Melchizedek, order of, 45n7
mendicant preachers, wandering philosophers as, 76
Menelik, 57, 107n11
messiah
    Christ as the Greek translation of, 64
    expectations for, 44n7
    as the final judge, 45n7
    historical Jesus as the Jewish, 12n4
    Jesus Christ as, 89
    Jewish expectations about, 44n6
    Stephen on the murder of, 41
metanarrative, 23–27, 37–39
Methodism, meteoric growth of American, 134n38
methodological atheism, 8
methodological biases, 16
methodological naturalism, 9n28
minimalists, on early histories of the Bible, 141n2

Subject Index

miracles
  authenticating the message, 75
  of Paul, 82, 83
  validating Paul's message, 73
missio Dei (God's mission)
  accounting for the work of God, 72
  in action in Peter's response, 69
  affirming central points, xv–xvi
  continuing beyond the eschatological horizon of the Scriptures, 144
  crossing boundaries, 98
  as the divine plan, 123
  extending to the earliest part of creation, 34
  on God as a missionary God, xiv
  on God moving history, 29
  as the grand design of the Bible, xiii
  grand theme of, 24
  inevitable conclusion of, 37
  in the New Testament, xv
  personal examples pointing to, 119–20
  viewing American immigration through, 121
missiologists, 77n60, 145
mission(s)
  centrifugal and centripetal, 51
  as a continuation of Jewish propaganda, 128
  gentile precipitated the Jerusalem Council, 42
  of God, 32, 140
  history of, 145–48
  to the Jews and gentiles, 51n17
  as the mother of theology, xiv
  rise of Protestant as the second Reformation, 151
The Mission of God: Unlocking the Bible's Grand Narrative, 32
missional approach, assumptions capturing, 145
missional assessment, of the Reformation, 149–50
missional hermeneutic
  allowing one to see missio Dei, xiii–xiv
  applying to Acts, 40–98
  applying to history, 139–57
  compatible with Scripture, 29
  described, 32–36
  on God having a plan, 41
  interpreting Scripture with, 28–39
  using, 36–37
missional history, 145, 156
missional purposes, of God, 149
missional reading of Scripture, 99
missionaries
  evangelizing people under the power of a false god, 55
  freeing people from their bondage to the gods, 77
  immigrants as, 118
  as a threat to Satan's hegemony in pagan Europe, 72
  traveling from one side of the Roman empire to the other, 137
missionary apostles, having little social status, 111
missionary God, redemptive purposes of, 35
missionary societies, eighteenth-century rise of, 151
missionary zeal, lack of in the early Reformation, 150
Mngad, Thembinkosi, 29
Moabites, treated Jewish sojourners well, 109
Moffett, Samuel, 97, 97n91
monotheism, taught by Jewish missionaries, 127
Montiglio, Silvia, 76
moon goddess, Artemis as, 81
moral purification, 50
Moses
  as Israel's midwife, 41
  learned pastoral skills, 39
  married an Ethiopian, 58
  more powerful than the sorcerers in Egypt, 66
  signs and wonders of confirmed his calling, 98
  during the time of the Cananites, 38
"Mother Earth" theology, 103
Muhammad, close companions (disciples) versus his biological descendants, 86

Subject Index

Muhammad, Tyrone, 115–16
Murphy, Nancey, 8
Muslims, Christian interactions with, 104
mysterium tremendum et fascinans, examples of, 20
mystery religions, 131

Naaman, 50, 107
Naboth's land, King Ahab wrongly confiscated, 101
names of God, xvi
Naming the Powers (Wink), 25n6
Naomi, 109
nation gods, as the Sons of God who rebelled, 147
nations
    God intended to come to the temple to pray, 108
    Jews changing what they thought about, 126
    Jews mediating Yahweh to, 107
    judgment of, 110
native religions, in Nigeria, 155
natural elements, Jesus proved his mastery over, 92
naturalistic worldview, of Jefferson, 8
neighbors, 112, 113
New Apostolic Reformation, birth of, 153
new heaven and new Earth, Scripture declaring, xvii
New Jerusalem, the church as, 131
New Testament
    authors believed in supernatural intervention, 9
    on God being aware of the fall, 34
    showing later meaning of a prophecy, 31
    on social constructions in the Roman Empire, 133
    teaching believers to care for the poor and needy, 111
New Testament church
    God empowered to continue his mission, 146
    grew best with gentiles familiar with the Septuagint, 125
    as a hermeneutical community, 30
    mythological worldview of, 9n24
    peddled "doctrines of demons" or false techings, 21
    went from Jerusalem to the ends of the earth, 43
New Testament writers, finding Christ in the text, 30
Newbigin, Leslie, xv, xivn8
Ng, Kam Weng, 7–8
Nicene Creed, 19
Nida, Eugene A., 11n2
Niebuhr, H. Richard, 130n29
Niemandt, Nelus, 16n13
Nigeria, contextualization of the gospel in, 155
Nigerians, continued to consult traditional shamans, 154–55
Noah, xvi, 90
non-Jews, terms for in the Hebrew Scriptures, 103
Northeaster (Eurakulon), hurricane wind called a, 91
Nunez, J. P., 142–43

objectivity, requiring a critical analysis of the text, 10
Okinawa, Japan, 100
Old Testament
    foreseeing a time when the nations will come to Jerusalem, 148
    Hellenistic Jews, proselytes, and Godfearers knew, 66
    prophecies in, 30, 31
    reading in light of the Christ event, 35
    showing God working through history, 146
    told the Israelites to care for immigrants, 120
Olympus, Typhon attempted to overthrow, 91
King Omri, made the city of Samaria his capital, 53
oracle at Delphi, on the new location of Ephesus, 79
Origen, 124
originalism, courts followed the doctrine of, 3

Subject Index

Orpah, returned, 109
orthodox faith, affirming, 28
orthodoxy, defining as a wide road, 19
Otis, George, 26n7, 102
Otto, Rudolf, 20
overseer (*episkopon*), 65, 65n38

Palestinians, 100
Pan grotto, at the bottom of Mount Herman, 147n20
Parable of the tenants, assessing the history of Israel, 139–40
parables, of Jesus as not literal, 2
parachurch phenomenon, largely bypassed organized Christianity, 153
the past, interpretive approaches to understanding, 140–45
pastoral oversight, Paul giving to Corinth, 79
pastors, using *Lectio Divina* for their preaching, 21
Pathrapankal, Joseph, 142
Paul. *See also* Saul of Tarsus
    aligning Christianity with Roman culture, 133
    angry with Jewish believers, 42
    in Athens, 75–78
    became like a Jew to win the Jews, 86–87
    calling himself an apostle, 67n40
    cast a spirit out of the slave girl, 72
    championed salvation through faith by grace, 59
    on Christians blessing and not cursing, 67
    cursed the sorcerer in Cyprus, 66
    disputations of, 98
    evangelization by, 73, 87
    everything and everyone trying to kill, 95
    evidence of his encounter with Jesus, 88
    exiled until Barnabas reclaimed him, 60
    on the forces of evil, 147
    on God providing a lamb for a sacrifice, 35
    God wanted him to stay in Corinth, 79
    healing in Malta, 95
    as a high-value target for Satan, 93
    interceding for all people, 132
    on the law as fulfilled in Christ, 68
    loving others as a fruit of the Spirit, 112
    mentioned the kingdom of God five times, 81
    missionary journey with Barnabas, 64–68
    objected when the soothsayer announced him, 72
    pitted the Sadducees against the Pharisees, 87
    preaching, 33, 73n53, 77, 82, 88, 95
    raised as a Roman citizen and a strict Pharisee, 59
    referred to James as an apostle, 85
    returned to the same synagogues on consecutive Sabbaths, 74
    as a Roman citizen, 59, 73
    sent away by the early church, 98
    sent to Rome to stand trial there, 89
    shook a deadly snake into the fire, 95
    speaking to the Jews residing in Rome, 95
    spent twenty-four months preaching in Ephesus, 82
    stoned to death and came back to life, 67
    told crew and passengers of his ship that they would be saved, 90
    trials of, 88–89
    wrote many letters to the Corinthian church, 79
Paul and Silas (Silvanus), 69, 72, 75, 75n57
peace child, among the Sawi people, 77n59
Pentecost sermon, of Peter, 46
Pentecostalism, 152–54, 156
people, of the land, 103–10
persecution
    assuaging Paul's anxiety about ongoing, 79
    of Christianity, 136

Subject Index

created an army of missionaries, 51
God using, 52
Peter
    founded the church in Rome, 95–96
    on God giving the Holy Spirit to Cornelius, 68
    healed the lame man at the Beautiful Gate, 46
    restating that God shows no favoritism, 62
    superseded by James, 85
    thought Jesus would reign in Jerusalem, 44
    vision of unclean animals, 61–62
First Peter, written to a minority community, 133
Peter and John, preaching the gospel in Samaritan villages, 56
Peterson, Eugene, 20
Philip the Evangelist
    connected the kingdom of God to Jesus, 81
    Ethiopian eunuch and, 57–59
    more powerful than the sorcerer in Samaria, 66
    Paul stayed with in Caesarea, 85
    went to Samaria, 53
philosophers, 76, 137
Pietists, world missions and, 150
pilgrims, to the temple of Artemis, 82
place of prayer, in Philippi, 69
plain meaning rule, interpreting the Bible literally, 1
Plan of Redemption, xivn6
Plato, relationship with Augustine of Hippo and, 137
poem, meaning of on many levels, 15
politicians, 115
politicking, distinguishing from preaching, 27
Polycarp, 65n38
polytheism, 132
postcolonial approach, to literature, 17
postcolonial biblical criticism, 16
power encounters, 54, 56, 66
power evangelism, 46

powers, in the Greco-Roman world, 91n78
The Powers That Be (Wink), 25n6
Praetorian Guard, Paul evangelized, 96
prayer of illumination, before reading the Bible, 21
preaching
    as an evangelism verb in Acts, 46
    in folk religion, 155
    of Paul, 33, 73n53, 77, 82, 88, 95
    sacrament of, 21
predictive prophecy, authenticating Yahweh, 31
prevenient grace, 124n6
priesthood, Samaritan compromised by Jeroboam, 53
priesthood of all believers, Luther's idea of, 150
priestly authority, of the messiah through the order of Melchizedek, 45n7
priests, having special access to God, 107
proconsul in Cyprus, hearing the gospel, 66
profane history, 141, 143
pro-immigration laws, in the Old Testament, 120
prophecy, xiv, 85, 154
prophets and teachers, headed the Antioch church, 64
prophets of Baal, 54–55, 83n72
proselytes, as the first to accept Christ, 127
Protestant and Roman Catholic churches, received the baptism of the Holy Spirit, 153
Protestant missions, rise of as the second Reformation, 151
Protestant Reformation, 156
Protestants, continued the marriage of church and state, 150
purgatory, not getting stuck in, 150
purification vow, taken by Paul, 87
purifying, of the heart, 49
Pythia, 70, 70n42, 71
python spirit (*pneuma puthona*), girl with, 70–72
Pythonos, 70, 70n42, 91

Subject Index

Queen of Heaven
    Artemis as, 80
    both Artemis and Mary as, 81
Queen of Sheba, 57, 107

Rabban, Joseph, leader of a Jewish trade guild, 97n90
ransom, Jesus as, 35
reader-response approach, 13–15
rebellion, God foresaw, 34
reception criticism, of biblical text, 32
reconstituted kingdom, described in Psalm 17, 42n5
redemptive analogy, 77
Reformation, 149–50, 151
reformers, functioning like prophets of the Old Testament, 149
rejection of Jesus, as the rejection of God, 139–40
relational ethos and faith, 19n21
religion
    alleviating individual and corporate anxiety, 131
    as a basic right, 4
    establishment of, 3
    feeding the inner soul, 132
    minimizing the public influence of, 6
    political parties not agreeing on the definition of, 5
    supporting those in power, 16
religious (*deisidaimonesterous*), Athens leaders as, 77
religious boundary, Paul's conversion not crossing, 59
religious clause in the First Amendment, 4
religious elite in Athens, Paul evangelized, 77
religious freedom, Obama administration attempted to redefine, 5
religious freedom bill, Thomas Jefferson's, 3–4, 3n8
religious knowledge, as not neutral or innocent, 16
religious leaders, not giving God's prophets what God required, 139
religious minorities, 5, 6

renewalist churches, 118
resurrected Christ, met with the apostles, 45
"Resurrection," as Jesus' consort goddess, 76
resurrection of Jesus, not accepted by Bultmann, 9
revelation, appeal to as subjective, 21
Revelation (book of), calling Satan the great dragon, 70
"Revitalization Movement" (Wallace), 26n8
revivals, paralleling times of stress and anxiety, 131
revolution, 145, 146
right practice, disagreement swirling around, 19–20
ripe moments, examples of in American history, 122
rite of passage, baptism symbolizing, 48
ritual purity laws, 106
rituals, enabling return to God, 20
"The Road Not Taken" (Frost), 14
Roman army official, renouncing his status, 60
Roman Catholic Charismatic movement, 156
Roman Catholic Church, renewed by Spirit-filled Charismatics, 118
Roman Catholicism, followed explorers to exotic places, 151
Roman citizen, Paul as, 59, 73
Roman Empire
    religion in, 131–34
    special status of Hellenistic Jews, 125–26
    triumph of Christianity in, 134–36
Roman law, as fair, 133
Roman leadership, heard the gospel from Paul, 88
Roman soldiers, 87, 96
Roman way of life, affirming, 131
Romans, destroyed the Second Temple, 140
Rome
    as the last barrier Paul had to cross, 87
    needed stability, 135

Subject Index

Paul in, 95–96
as religiously tolerant, 76, 132
Ross, Hugh, 34
Roth, Sid, 93
royal herald, proclaiming good news called an evangelist, 74
Ruth, 109, 110
Ruth (book of), 109

sacerdotal duties, versus the care of a hurt neighbor, 113
sacred history, 33, 141, 142
sacrificial system, pointing to God's redemptive plan, xv, 35
sailors, prayer of, 91
salvation
  as being freed from one's sinful nature, xvii
  flowing through Jesus, 141
  of humanity, 144
  included the gentiles, 89
  as people are freed from social oppression, 25
  as a relational concept, 142
salvation history
  beginning in the garden of Eden, 141–42
  Bible as the story of, 143
  Catholic understanding of, 142–43
  describing how God works, xivn6
  not moving beyond the biblical text, 144
Samaria, mission to, 52–56
Samaritan traveler, provided first aid, 113
Samaritan woman at the well, evangelization of, 54
Samaritans, 53, 54, 56, 113
Sanou, Boubakar, 33
sapient life, zero evidence of on any other planet, 34
Sargon II, 53
Satan
  agitated unbelievers to stone Barnabas and Paul, 67
  called the great dragon in Revelation, 91
  disrupting God's purposes, 147

enabling his followers to divine and do miracles, 72
impeding the work of God in Thessalonica and Berea, 75
interplay with God, 98
as the serpent guarding the Tree of Knowledge, 70
targeted Paul via a terrible storm, 92–93
wanted to neutralize Paul, 95
worked through anti-Semitic tyrants and evil governments, 148
Satan Exposed: A Biblical Theology of Spiritual Warfare (Payne), 24
Saul of Tarsus. *See also* Paul
  conversion of, 59–60
Sawi people, killing and eating their enemies, 77n59
scandal of election, 36, 37
scapegoat, 35
scattering, of the Jerusalem church, 50–52
scholars, doing exegesis, 7
scholarship, assured results of, 10
scientific method, 10
scientifically informed mindset, 8
Scobie, Charles, 53
Scripture(s)
  assuming a chronological progress, 147n18
  disobeying as sin, 99
  Reformation's emphasis on, 150
  revealing God's missional heart, xvi
  revealing Satan's work, 147
  spiritual warfare underlying, 24
  submission to as submission to God, 17
  treating as cultural artifacts from a bygone era, 15
second coming of Christ, Jerusalem church preparing for, 45
second coming (parousia), delayed, 47
Second Great Awakening, 26, 134n38, 146
Second Temple literature, not included in the Hebrew Scriptures, 44n6

Subject Index

sectarian controversies, Acts and Galatians chronicling, 128
secular humanism, de-Christianizing influence of, 118
secularism, 5
Seed of the Woman, crushed the head of the Serpent, 36
self-focus, as the opposite of love, 112
self-identification categories, 100
seminary, propagating Western approaches to theology, 12
Sennacherib, 53
Septuagint, Greek-speaking masses reading Jewish Scriptures, 125
serpents, in many ancient myths, 70
Shalom, tied to a political theology, 25
Shia, on leader of Islam, 86
signs and wonders, through the disciples, 46
Silas (Silvanus), 69, 72, 75, 75n57
Simon the Magician, 54
sin(s), 49, 106
sinners, turning into victims, 26
Skreslet, Stanley, 143, 145n14
slave girl with the python spirit, 71
slave masters and slaves, Christian, 134
Smith, Chuck, 153
snake bite, Paul using to evangelize in Malta, 94
social construct, profane history as, 141
social justice, as a grand narrative, 25–27
social theory, utilization of, 16n15
society, assigning identity to people, 18n18
sociopolitical goals, realizing carrying risk, 18
sojourners, 105n8. *See also* foreigners; strangers
Solomon, 96, 107–8, 148
sons of God, 36, 77, 90
sons of Sceva, 83–84
sophists, philosophers as, 76
sorcerers, local turned to Christ, 84
Spanish, as the dominant language, 117
spies, said that giants lived in Canaan, 38
spiral process, as what hermeneutics should be, 11

Spirit, giving of as a supernatural sign, 56
Spirit of Pentecost, rekindled during the Azusa Street revival, 152
spiritual attachment, to land, 100
spiritual discipline, using to get a word from God, 21
spiritual forces, 93
spiritual gift, Paul taught that prophecy was a, 85
spiritual leaders, divine mandate to manage God's vineyard, 139
spiritual link, connecting people in contact with each other, 83
spiritual revolution, from translating the Bible in Europe, 150
spiritual warfare
    Acts as, 94
    attached to God's salvific mission, xvi
    to defeat Satan and advance God's kingdom, 66
    as a metanarrative, 24–25
    pattern of, 95
    with Satan, 72
spiritual warfare hermeneutic, 98, 147
"spoiling the Egyptians," process of borrowing from philosophers called, 137
Springfield, Ohio, Haitian influx, 115
Stark, Rodney, 125–26
state church (Anglicanism), in Virginia, 3
state cult, not satisfying the spiritual needs of the individual, 132
statue story, about Artemis in Ephesus paralleling the Virgin Mary statue in Cuba, 81
Stephen, 33, 41
storm gods, as the strongest gods, 93
storm spirit, Jesus confronted, 92
Stott, John, 74n55
strangers, 104, 109. *See also* foreigners; sojourners
substitutionary atonement, taking away the sin of the world, 34
Suffering Servant, Jesus as, 34
supernatural spirits, manipulating natural elements, 92
supernatural worldview, 94, 98

Subject Index

suspicion, hermeneutic of, 16
synagogues, early missionaries preached in, 65, 125

Tamawiwy, August, 29–30
temple, Solomon's dedicatory prayer for, 108
temple tax, Jews did not pay to Artemis, 82n71
temple to Artemis, in Ephesus, 80
tenants, parable of, 102–3
Tennent, Timothy, 37, 145n15
testimony, 88–89
Texas National Guard, deployed by Abbott, 117
theological education, in the Global South, 12
theological universalism, 78
theology, 28, 43, 100–103
third heaven, Paul's out-of-body experience in, 67–68
Third Wave movement, with John Wimber, 153
Thomas (disciple), mission to India, 96–97
Thomas, Robert, 12n2
throne of Jesus, 94
time (kairoi) of the gentiles, ending of, 123
timetable, God's determined, 124
Timothy, 65
Timothy and Silas, 75
tithe, sharing with the foreigner, 109
Torah, 53, 104
Toronto Blessing, birth of, 153
Towns, Elmer, 74
translation, missiologists favoring dynamic equivalent, 11
Tren de Aragua armed gang from Venezuela, 115
true believers, worshipping God in Spirit and truth, 54
truth encounter, 56
the twelve, called apostles in Matthew, 67n40
Typhon (god), 91, 93
typhoon, Paul battling, 89–93
Tyrannus Hall, Paul relocated to, 82

unclean thing, results of touching, 113n14
undocumented immigrants, American evangelicals caring for, 110
unified message, unlocking the Bible's, xiii–xiv
United States Citizenship and Immigration Services, 116
universality, of Jewish faith, 126–27
universe, expansion rate of accelerating, 147n18
Unmasking the Powers (Wink), 25n6

vices, transformed into virtues, 26n8
vineyard, God taking, 102–3
Vineyard Church, birth of, 153
Virgin Mary, 80–81, 80n68
Virgin of Charity, in Cuba, 81
virgins, parable of the ten, 2

Wagner, C. Peter, 26n7
Wallace, Anthony, 26n8
washing tradition, symbolizing purification, 50
wave theory of history, of Latourette, 143
Weiss, Steward, 57
Welsh revival, spread to India, 152
Wesley, John, 1, 1n3, 65n38, 104, 124n6
the West, as a mission field, 118
Western Christianity, winning war against, 156
"what does it mean" question, answering, 23
"white" experience, American nationalism normalizing, 105
Wimber, John, 153
Wink, Walter, 25–26
witch doctor, encounter with Heidi Baker, 55
Word and Power churches, emergence of, 153
working relationships, as another category, 113–14
Wright, Christopher, 32

xenophobia, 104, 105

Subject Index

Yahweh, 103

Zechariah, "Jesus" prophecies of, 30

Zegeye, Abebe, 58
Zen Buddhism, 49
Zeus, 93

Scripture Index

OLD TESTAMENT

Genesis

	90
2:7	xv
2:16	xv
3	70
3:17–19	102
3:21	35
6:1–4	38
6:7–8	90
6:11–21	xvi
6:22	xvi
9:2–4	62
11:10–27	101
12	xvi, 101
12:1–3	101
12:2–3 NIV	108
12:3	36, 148
18:24	90
19:11	66
22:8	35
50:20	39, 52
50:24–25	39

Exodus

	50
3	xvi
3:1–17	20
7:8–13	66
7–12	55
10:21–23	66
12:40	101
19:3–6	36, 106
19:4–6 RSV	107
19:5	102
19:5–6	148
30:17–21	50

Leviticus

	105
7:21 RSV	113n14
16	xv, 34, 44
17:8	104
18:24–25	102
18:24–26	38
18:24–30	38
25:4–5	102
25:13	101
25:18	105
25:23	102
25:44–45 KJV	103
25:44–45 NIV	105n8
25:45	104

Numbers

	105

Deuteronomy

	36, 105
7:1	105
7:1–6	62
7:1–6 NIV	106n9

Scripture Index

Deuteronomy (continued)
25:5–10	101
32:8	24n5
32:8 RSV	77
32:8–9	37, 147
32:8–9 RSV	36
32:9	146, 148

Joshua
	105
14:2–5	101
14:6–15	38

Ruth
	109

1 Samuel
17	xvi

1 Kings
8:41–43	148
8:41–43 NIV	108
10:1–13	57
12:31	53
15:13	103n6
16:23–24	53
18	55
18:26–29	83n72
21	101
21:3	101

2 Kings
5	107
6:18–23	67
7:14 LXX	50
12–17	53
13:21	83
18:4	103n6
21:7	103n6
23:6	103n6

2 Chronicles
	103n6
9	107

Ezra
	106
4:10	53
9:10–12 RSV	38n26
10	106
10:1–3	38
10:3	104

Nehemiah
	106
4:2	53
9:2	106
10:28–31	106

Job
41	70n44

Psalms
	108, 126
2	44
8:5–6	xv
9:11 NIV	127
15:4	61
17	42n5, 68n41
18:49 NIV	127
23	12
24:1	102
25:12	61
33:11	41
57:9 NIV	127
67	108
82	147
82:1–4	37
87:4	57
91:11–12	30
96:1–2	149
96:1–10 NIV	127
96:10a	149
105:1 NIV	127
108:3 NIV	127
110:1	30
112:1	61
115:13	61
118:4	61
118:22	139

Scripture Index

Song of Solomon
    1

Isaiah
    32
2:10–22   44
6:1–3   20
7:13–16   31
10:11–21   53
11:11   57
11:11–12   46
11:12   44
41:23   31
42:9 NIV   31
48:3 NIV   31
49:6   106, 148
53   32, 34, 57
53:7–8   58
56:7   108
60:3   148
61   30

Jeremiah
8:3   46
28:3–8   46
30:10   46
31:8   46
32:37   46

Ezekiel
13:5–23   44
22:29   109
30:3–26   44
37:19–28   44
47:22   104

Daniel
    123n2
1–6   148
7:13–14   44
9:24–27   122
9:25   122
11:35   123

Hosea
13:16   53

Jonah
1:5   91

Micah
1:6–7   53
5:2   44

Zechariah
8:20–23   148
9:9   44
12:10   44

Malachi
3:1   30
3:23   30

DEUTEROCANONICAL BOOKS

1 Enoch
46:1–4   44
48:2–7   44
69:26–29   44

2 Esdras
7:28–29   44
12:31–34   44
13:32   44

Jubilees
    101
10:27–34   101
10:32   101

1 Maccabees
    76

2 Maccabees

	76
4:7–22	38

NEW TESTAMENT

Matthew

	81, 128n24
2:2	122
3:6	50
3:13–17	50
4:1–11	123
4:6	30
5–7	17
5:13	131
5:14	1
6:10	147
8:29	123
10	111
10:2	67n40
10:9–11	111
10:9–13	111
10:18–20 NIV	89
10:40–43 RSV	111
11:2–6	44
11:14	30
16:18	147
16:22	44
17:1–8	20
19:16–26	xvi
19:28	45
21:11	44
21:18–19	67
21:33–45	103
21:41	140
22:11–13	50
22:35	112
23:15	127
24:36	123
25	110, 111
25:1–13	2
25:41–46 RSV	110
25:46	111
28:18–20	140
28:19	37, 77, 140, 146
28:19–20	45

Mark

	81
1:1–3	31
1:7	31
1:15	123, 123n4
1:21–27	71
1:24	71
3:17	54
4:35–41	92
4:41	92
7:1–5	49
7:4	49, 50
7:14–15	49
10:37	44
10:39	48
10:45	35
11:8–9	139
11:12–14	139
11:27–28	139
12:1–12	139
12:9	140
12:10	139
12:17	139
12:36	30
14:22–23	92
16:15	140

Luke

	81
3:14–18	60
4:21	30
7	61
7:5	61
7:6–7	61
7:8	61
7:9	61
9:50–55	54
10	112
10:1	67n40
10:25–37	112
10:28	112
10:29	112
13:10–16	71
18:10	91
21:24–26	123
24:13–35	45

Scripture Index

24:25–27 RSV	30	2:20	123
24:26–27	58	2:37–40	56
24:47	140	2:42	33
		2:42–44	46
John		2:42–47	51
	30, 140n1	2:44–46	47
1:12–13	xv, 66	3:9	46
1:29	xv, 34	3:15	41
1:36	xv	4:1	46
3:16	xvi, 144	4:1–22	46
3:18	xvi	4:30–31	46
3:34	50	4:34–35	47
4:1–42	54	5:12–16	46
4:23	54	5:14	46
5:17	124	5:17–20	46
5:39	30	5:19	73
6:15	44	5:40	46
8:44	66	5:42	46
11:48 RSV	140n1	6:1–7	47
12:16	30	6:6	64
12:34	44	6:8–15	46
20:21	xv	7	33
		7:9–36	41
Acts		7:17	41
	41, 42, 43, 46, 51n17,	7:52	41
	52, 53, 54, 56, 57, 59,	7:58—8:1	59
	60, 64, 68, 71, 74, 81,	8	55, 58, 66, 69, 94, 96,
	87, 89, 91, 93, 94, 95,		146
	97, 98, 128	8:1	42, 50
1	45	8:1–4	50–52
1:1—7:60	44–47	8:5–25	52–56
1:3	81	8:10	54
1:4–8	47	8:12	81
1:6	45, 81	8:14–17	56
1–7	45	8:18	64
1:8	41, 45, 51n17, 52, 97,	8:26	53, 64
	140	8:26–40	57–59
1:21	45	8:36	47
1:21–22	65	8:39	64
2	46, 47–50, 146, 152	9	64
2:1–3	56	9:1—10:18	60–63
2:5–11	46	9:1–31	59–60
2–6	46, 51	9:2	64
2—8:1	52	9:8	67
2:14–36	56	9:17	64
2:17	45n8	9:20	66
		9:22	66

Acts (continued)

Reference	Page
9:22 NIV	59
9:23	95
9:27	63
9:29	95
9:30	75
10	64
10:28	61, 62
10:30	61
10:34–35	62
10:47	56
11:3	61
11:19	51
11:19–21	63
11:19–26	63?
11:25	60
11:30	64
12:5–7	73
12:17	85
13:1—14:28	64–68
13:5	65
13:13	69
13:13–41	33
13:14	65
13:16	61
13:16–41	66
13:26	61
13:32–33 RSV	33
13:33	41
14:1	65
14:3	67
14:4	67
14:5	95
14:5–6	95
14:14	67
14:19	95
14:20	67
14:22	81
14:23	64
14:26–28	64
15	42, 64
15:1	68
15:1–35	68–69
15:5	59, 63, 68
15:6–11	69
15:11	42
15:13–21	85
15:29	42
15:36–41	69
16:6–7	69
16:10	69
16:14–15	69
16:16–18	70
16:16–40	69–73
16:23	95
17	88
17:1–5	43
17:1–15	73–75
17:2	65
17:2–4 NIV	73
17:5	95
17:10	65
17:14	65
17:16–34	75–78
17:18–21	132
17:22	61, 77
17:22–34	127
17:23	76, 77
17:26	77
18:4	65
18:9–10 NIV	79
18:19	65, 78–79
18:28	79
19	79–84
19:1–6	47
19:8	66, 73, 81
19:8–10	82
19:11	73
19:11–12	83
19:11–17	71
19:13–16 NIV	84
19:17	84
19:19–20	72
19:20	83
19:20–21	84
19:27 NIV	82
19:28	82
19:29	95
19:34	82
19:35–36	80
20:17	64
20:17–38	84
20:22	85
20:25	81, 85

20:38	85	7:1–6	43
21:4	85	7:25	43
21:10–11	85	8:1–4	43
21:18	64, 85	8:9	47
21:20	86	8:9–12	102
21:20–21 RSV	43	8:22	143
21:21	42	8:28	36
21–23	84–87	8:33	36
21:24–26	87	10:4	43
21:25	86	10:17	21
21:28	87	11:17	43
21:31	95	12:14	67
22:1–21	87	13:1	132
22:3	59	16	96
22:4	64		
23:11 NIV	87		
23:12	95		

1 Corinthians

24:3	95		79, 86
24:14	64	2:13–14	10
24–26	88–89	3:16	47
25:11	88	6:19	47
25:23	88	9:5	85
25:27	88	9:19–22 NIV	87
26:7	41	10:1–2	48
26:9–11	89	11–14	85
26:12–18	89	12:3	21
26:23	89	12:10	22
26:28	89	12:28	85
26:29	89	13:4	112
26:32	89	13:4–7 RSV	112
27	89–93	14:5	85
27:14	91, 95	15	45
27:22–23	91	15:4–8	67n40
28:1–10	93–95	15:7	85, 85n75
28:3	95	15:24	144
28:9	95		
28:11–31	95–96		

2 Corinthians

28:23	81		79
28:31	81	4:1	15n12
		5:17	48
		5:19	xv

Romans

		6:14	72
1:8–12	95	11:23–26 NIV	95
2:25–29	49	12:2–4 NIV	68
3:23	26		
5:10	35		
6:4	49		

Galatians

	86, 128
1	67n40
1:6–9	42
1:19	85
2:7–10	42
2:9	85
2:11–18	63
2:12	42, 85
2:15	43
3:13	43
3:26–27	49
3:27–28	133
3:28–29	43
4:4	123, 123n4
5:1	43
5:12	42

Ephesians

1:3	xivn5
1:4	34
1:19–20	xiv
1:20	xivn5
1:23	77–78
2:6	xivn5
2:8–9	43, 59
2:11–16	43
2:14	62
2:22	47
3:6 NIV	86
3:10	xivn5
4:22–24	49
5:8–9	2
5:18	47
6:12	78
6:20	xivn5

Philippians

1:12–13	96
2:7	50
2:10–11	xiv

Colossians

1:13	66
1:20	xvi

2:12	49
2:15	25
3:11	43

1 Thessalonians

2:13	73n53
2:18	75
3:1–3	75n57
3:5	75
3:11	75
4:13	45
5:4–8	47
5:5–11	2
5:12	65

2 Thessalonians

3:10–13	47

1 Timothy

2:1–4	132
2:1–4 NIV	132
2:4	144
2:5–6	35
3:1–7 NIV	65
4:1	21
4:14	64

2 Timothy

3:16–17	10

Titus

2:13	xvii
3:1	132

Hebrews

2:16–18	35n18
3:14—4:11	48
4:14–16	35n18
7:25	144
8:6–12	37
9:7	35
9:13—10:18	35
9:28	144
12:1–2	xvii

Scripture Index

13:12 — 35

James

2:14–17 — 112

1 Peter

1:18–19 — 133
1:19–20 — 35
2:12 — 34
2:13 — 132
2:13–17 — 132
2:18–24 — 134
3:1–7 — 134
3:15–16 NIV — 134
3:22 — 134, 25

2 Peter

3:9 — xvi

1 John

3:2–3 — xv
3:7–12 — 66
3:9 — xvi
4:4 — 72
4:16 — xvi
4:19–21 — 112

Revelation

2–3 — 24, 133
5:9 — 35
12:7–12 — 91
12:9 — 70
12:13 — 70
12:15 — 93
13:8 — 34
20:10 — 24
20:14 — 24
21 — xvii

APOCRYPHA (NEW TESTAMENT)

Acts of Thomas

6 — 97n91, 97

EARLY CHRISTIAN WRITINGS

Augustine of Hippo — 135, 137

Didache — 48, 48n11, 76n38, 111n13

1:1–7 — 111

Eusebius of Caesarea

Preparation for the Gospel — 123n5

Origen — 124

GREEK AND ROMAN LITERATURE

Aristotle — 137

Plato — 137

www.ingramcontent.com/pod-product-compliance
Lightning Source LLC
Chambersburg PA
CBHW062027220426
43662CB00010B/1505

"For the last forty years, as a pastor, seminary president, denominational leader and now as a bishop, I've taught the bible to the people I've been called to lead. My intent wasn't simply to tell those under may care what the bible says, but how to read God's word in a way that helps them encounter the author. Helping people understand the larger missional narrative of the scripture helps them understand there's not a page in the bible absent of God's divine mission to redeem and save his people. This important work by Dr. William Payne provides the theological framework for what I've intuitively known for forty years—a missional hermeneutic. He adeptly helps the reader to see and understand that God is always at work fulfilling his perfect will and plan to redeem and save his people. This is true even when we can't see it—whether afflicted by famine or trapped in bondage of some sort. God doesn't waste a thing in our lives, but rather often uses the situations of our lives to draw or drive us to him. As a result, God really does turn all things together for the good of those who love him . . . "

—JEFFREY E. GREENWAY, bishop, The Global Methodist Church

"Bill Payne is one of the best teachers of evangelization in the English-speaking world and is a man of serious original insight. I expect this project will become a game-changer for many church leaders."

—GEORGE G. HUNTER III, distinguished professor emeritus, Asbury Seminary

"'God is a missionary God,' so asserts Dr. Payne. He has sent his Son and the Holy Spirit into the world to reach us with his saving love. The *missio Dei* is the metanarrative in which the church is called to participate and offer salvation to a lost and dying world. How can we understand God's mission, specifically as it is revealed in the Bible? Dr. Payne prescribes a missional hermeneutic as the way in which the church can apprehend God's mission and interpret holy scripture. William Payne offers the reader a comprehensive primer on the dynamics of a missional hermeneutic that will equip the reader to navigate through the Bible, follow God's divine footprints, and serve his mission."

—PETER J. BELLINI, professor of church renewal and evangelization in the Heisel Chair, United Theological Seminary, Dayton, Ohio

"For years, I have encouraged churches to pray, 'Holy Spirit, where are you working in our community, and how can we be a part of it?' In his book, *Divine Footprints*, Dr. Bill Payne masterfully traces God's footprints through the Bible and invites us to find them in our world today so we can be a part of his mission. Any church seeking to engage its community would do well to read this book."

—JAY THERRELL, conference superintendent, Florida Conference of the Global Methodist Church

"In this succinct and systematic treatment, Bill hits the ground running by asserting that 'God is a missionary God.' This communicates both that we are the target of God's affections and partners in the cosmic scope of reconciling all things to himself. In this highly recommended book, Bill makes the case that the metanarrative of the *missio Dei* allows one to see God at work in seemingly disparate events, making all history salvation history."

—DAVID ANTHONY BASHAM, assistant professor of New Testament, Ashland Theological Seminary